# The Tennessee

## VOLUME ONE

**Southern Classics Series**

**M. E. Bradford, Editor**

# Southern Classics Series

## M. E. Bradford, Series Editor

---

# The Tennessee

## VOLUME ONE

---

## The Old River: Frontier to Secession

### DONALD DAVIDSON

Illustrated by
Theresa Sherrer Davidson

with an introduction by
Thomas Daniel Young

J. S. Sanders & Company

NASHVILLE

*Library of Congress Catalog Card Number:*
91-62454

ISBN: 1-879941-01-5

Published in the United States by
J. S. Sanders & Company
P. O. Box 50331
Nashville, Tennessee 37205

Distributed to the trade by
National Book Network
4720-A Boston Way
Lanham, Maryland 20706

1991 printing
Manufactured in the United States of America

Dedicated to
Samuel Cole Williams
of Tennessee
Historian and Jurist in
Admiration and Esteem

# Contents

# Introduction

As a writer of expository prose, Donald Davidson had few peers, even among the distinguished members of the significant literary groups of which he was an important member. Characterized by its stylistic grace, persuasive logic, cogent reasoning, and demonstrated authority, his prose, as Gerald Johnson once noted, is "not merely correct, it ... [is] lucid, smooth, supple." Few Americans of his generation, Johnson continues, have employed "a more carefully chiseled style, agreeable to the eye and ear without trumpery ornamentation, clear to the understanding without falling into puerility."[1]

Davidson's mastery of English prose allowed him to achieve a broad range of emotional effects and to indicate with great precision specific intellectual attitudes. He displayed that mastery in both volumes of *The Tennessee*, published initially in the Rivers of America series. The theme of volume one, which covers the river's history up to the Civil War, is succinctly stated: "One of the chief peculiarities of the old Tennessee is that, of all the great rivers east of the Mississippi, it has been least friendly to civilization." In fact, Davidson would accept Carlyle's statement that history is the biography of great men, if he were allowed to employ the river itself as a character in the dramatic tale he is relating. For the story he tells is one of man's attempts to harness nature, to use its power and resources for his own benefit.

1. Gerald W. Johnson, New York *Herald Tribune Weekly Book Review*, January 25, 1948, p. 1.

Like many modern ecologists, Davidson is deeply concerned about the senseless destruction of our wilderness. Behind almost every conclusion drawn in *The Tennessee* is the deeply felt conviction expressed in the Introduction to *I'll Take My Stand*: "Religion is our submission to the general intention of a nature that is fairly inscrutable; it is the sense of our role as creatures within it. But nature industrialized, transformed into cities and artificial habitations, manufactured into commodities, is no longer nature but a highly simplified picture of nature."[2] Davidson is careful to point out time and again that the Tennessee absolutely refused to cooperate in man's attempts to convert the natural environment around it into an artificial and "highly simplified picture of nature." It fought with great resourcefulness until it was completely subdued by the TVA engineers intent upon converting its natural power into forms that would benefit all of the inhabitants of the region. The history of the Tennessee "begins with legend," Davidson says, and "ends with statistics."

The Tennessee was a formidable opponent for those who would tame it, convert it into an economic tool for their own use. Almost nothing the Tennessee does is predictable. Although its length and size would suggest that it must flow into an ocean or sea somewhere, it does nothing of the sort. The river flows for five hundred miles, but in the process "it doubles back on its course . . . , goes to much trouble to arrive nowhere in particular, and finally runs into another river." Not only does the Tennessee follow a strange and unexpected course, but before the 1930s it contained so many natural obstacles, especially in the upper river above Florence, Alabama, that it could hardly be navigated. Such phenomena as Muscle Shoals, the Narrows, the Boiling Pot, and the Suck made travel up and down the river almost impossible. To navigate this portion of the river, the pioneer claimed and Davidson agrees, "one needed not only to combine the virtues of the horse and alligator, but to add something of the frog, snapping turtle, raccoon, buffalo, and shikepoke." Even the lower end of the

2. "Introduction," *I'll Take My Stand: The South and the Agrarian Tradition* by Twelve Southerners (Baton Rouge, 1977), p. xlii.

river—from Florence, Alabama, to Paducah, Kentucky, where the Tennessee flows into the Ohio—although relatively safe and sane, does not act as a river should because it flows north; therefore it confounded the bargeman's natural expectations of how he could use this waterway to move freight from one point to another. He could not depend upon loaded barges moving with the current from north to south as he could on most North American rivers.

In this volume Davidson covers the history of this cantankerous river from early frontier days, while suggesting something of its pre-historic origin, to secession. His discussion of the people who lived along its banks and largely controlled the river leads him into an informative and evocative presentation of the habits and customs of the natives who occupied the Tennessee Valley before the white man came. The Cherokees, for most of the time the white man's friend, found it much easier to accept new customs and beliefs because their culture did not include many deeply imbedded myths and taboos. The Creeks, on the other hand, were much reluctant to give up their old traditions and adopt the strange new ones of the white men who moved through their land. The Cherokees had "no real cycle of cosmic myths and only a slight trace of a migration legend. They had no official priesthood." One white man who lived among them in the latter part of the eighteenth century found them "accustomed to look forward to new things rather than to dwell upon the past." Their rather unstable culture made the Cherokees a much less forbidding obstacle to the advancement of the white man than the more firmly organized tribes of the north and west. The Cherokees were the quickest of the Indian peoples to assimilate the white man's culture, and their generally friendly and cooperative attitude was of tremendous assistance to the early frontiersmen who were trying to settle the beautiful and fertile Tennessee Valley and to conquer the natural obstacles that made navigation of the upper river an experience as hazardous as it was uncertain.

Davidson's account is not confined, of course, to the efforts of the river to prohibit man's use of it. He includes, too, the exploits of some well-known figures, as well as some of the almost nameless men and women, who never ceased in their efforts to force the Tennessee to aid the inevitable westward movement of civilization. The familiar adventures of Andrew Jackson,[3] John Sevier, James Robertson, and John Donelson are well rehearsed, but so are others, of almost equal importance in the settlement of the region: those of Abraham Wood, Gabriel Arthur, Jean Couture, Thomas Nairne, Price Hughes, James Adair, Sir Alexander Cuming, and many others.

Davidson's necessarily selective treatment of the Tennessee's past includes many significant historical events and developments. These include struggles of the French, English, and Spanish for control of the Tennessee Valley; the rise and fall of Fort Loudoun;[4] the establishment of friendly relations with the Indians (some of them) and the infamous means by which the Indians were driven from their lands and resettled in the west. Davidson's attitude toward this last-named maneuver is unmistakable:

> In the Creek country, serious disorders occurred. Under the treaty of 1832, provision was made for the orderly purchase of the lands of those who would voluntarily remove according to the government's plan. Protection was promised. Unlawful intruders upon Creek lands were to be expelled. An appropriation of $100,000 was promised to liquidate tribal debts. But the solemn words were empty of meaning. Not only did the government fail to fulfill the treaty specifications, but in cynical negligence it permitted the very outrages that the treaty was designed to avoid. Swarms of white intruders multiplied into hordes.... Since most of the Indians did not know the value of their lands ... or even the English language, it was easy for swindlers to cheat them.   (259)

3. Davidson's view of Jackson, following that of his good friend Harriet Owsley, stresses Old Hickory's position as a nationalist. He underplays Jackson's usual role as that of Indian hater.

4. Davidson's statement that "all the officers were killed," along with "twenty-three privates and three women" in the massacre at Fort Loudoun, is contested by some modern authorities (see pp. 112–24). Director Duane King of the Museum of the Cherokee Indian claims that only about two dozen soldiers were killed on August 10, 1760.

The actual removal was even more scandalous. In the early 1830s when the transfer began, the Cherokees, who on the whole had been friendly to the white man and had adopted many aspects of his culture, numbered about seventeen thousand persons. Back in 1820 they had adopted a republican form of government and one member of the tribe, Sequoyah, had devised a Cherokee syllabary or alphabet. After a native had learned the eighty-five characters of Sequoyah's syllabary, he could read anything written in Cherokee. Even a bilingual newspaper, the *Cherokee Phoenix*, was established in 1828. The Cherokees had long since ceased to be members of the Stone Age. They were agriculturalists and cattle raisers: they grew corn, wheat, potatoes, and other garden vegetables, as well as cows and hogs, just as their white neighbors did. The Cherokees were even beginning to establish mercantile and manufacturing facilities. They thought of themselves as American citizens and even aspired to advancing their nation to statehood.[5]

In spite of the Indians' desires, as well as their just claims, laws were passed annexing the Cherokee lands and declaring tribal laws and customs null and void. It was decreed that the Indian was not a competent witness in a court case involving a white man. Although the Cherokees tried to establish their rights through the courts and even to protect their lands through guerilla warfare, they were overcome by superior force in both instances. Consequently fifteen thousand Cherokees were marched under military guard to stockades, where they were forced to remain until river transportation could be provided. Only a very small portion of the tribe was ever transported down the river; the main body moved by land, crossed the Tennessee at Tucker's Ferry, and marched through Nashville and across Kentucky to the Ohio River. By the time the huge columns had reached the area around Cape Girardeau, Missouri, the winter rains were setting in and the roads fast

5. Historian Ronald Satz contends that "the Cherokees really didn't want American citizenship; they wanted to be Cherokee citizens and to retain their land" (letter to Louis Iglehart, April 10, 1978).

became almost impassable. Davidson's account of the forced march is most evocative:

> The advancing winter found the greater part of the Cherokee nation still on the road, with their sufferings increasing. In bitter privation and hardship, they crossed the Mississippi at Cape Girardeau, the river filled with ice, hundreds of the sick and dying penned in wagons or stretched upon the ground. . . . About four thousand of the Cherokees never reached the western lands. In other words, nearly one fourth of the nation died along the way, or in the stockades before the march began, were killed by soldiers, or else escaped.  (277)

History records few instances in which a civilized nation has shown less compassion for a friendly people who had a legitimate claim to property that the first nation wanted. Only the color of the Tennessee Indian's skin precluded him from going west along with the white man a good many years later, when the tide of civilization was moving in that direction. He was sacrificed in the name of a good cause, or he was the victim of the white man's lust for material possessions.

Even with the Indians gone, one enemy of civilization remained: a treacherous river, one badly needed as a means of moving products to and from the market but one that could not be navigated with a reasonable degree of safety or even with an acceptable expectation of success. Although attacks on the Muscle Shoals, the Suck, and the Narrows continued with increasing frequency in the period just before the Civil War, navigation of the upper river, from Florence to Knoxville, was so hazardous that steamboat traffic on that part of the waterway was never dependable. A few brave and resourceful steamboat captains, including George Washington Harris, author of the Sut Lovingood yarns, were able to move up and down that portion of the river with a fair degree of success, but history records a far greater number of failures. One passenger on a steamboat traveling from Knoxville to Chattanooga in the 1850s found the " 'scenery on the river . . . bold and pleasing without ever rising to sublimity,' " but, then, "of course he never tried Muscle Shoals."

The golden years on the river were soon over, Davidson states in the conclusion of this first volume of the history of the Tennessee, because "in pillared mansion and log cabin, all innocent and peaceful hopes were to be hurled into ruin." The Civil War came and the main thrust of the Federal attack was straight up the line of the Tennessee River.

Although Davidson acknowledges that his story of the Tennessee "begins with legend," contemporary scholars may feel that he has on occasion stressed legend to the detriment of historical fact and at other times has confused the two.[6] In describing the people who might have inhabited the Tennessee Valley before the white man's coming, as recorded in the writings of Hernando De Soto, Davidson relates the legend of the "Welsh Indians," a story now largely discounted that made its way around wilderness campfires. It was often rumored that some white race had preceded the American pioneers on this continent. They were Welshmen, the story went, who settled in America before Columbus discovered the continent.

Interwoven with this tale are speculations about who built the elaborate mounds and earthworks found at many points along the Tennessee and its tributaries. The pioneers thought it unlikely that these structures could have been built by the Indians they knew. The Indians themselves denied any responsibility for them, so, Davidson concludes, "surely they must have been built by the legendary Welshmen." Then, to compound the effect of his tongue-in-cheek attitude, Davidson quotes Oconostota, a Cherokee chief, telling John Sevier that these mounds and fortifications "had been made by the white people who had formerly inhabited the country." Yet finally, after presenting this and additional evidence supporting the existence of the mythical "Welsh Indians," Davidson correctly dismisses them as legendary. He offers additional explanations for the ancient fortifica-

6. Many modern anthropologists and historians disagree with some of Davidson's "facts." Many argue, for example, that it is highly unlikely that Needham and Arthur ever reached the Little Tennessee River. Others believe, however, that they did reach Chota (see pp. 64–66).

tions and mounds, including those "of a curiously antiquarian and romantic tendency," without citing any of the findings of modern archaeology and anthropology. Much of this scientific information must have been known to him because his good friend Jesse Wills had since the early 1930s been making regular reports on the findings of Cyrus Thomas, Gates P. Thruston, Henry Clyde Shetrone, Joseph Jones, W. E. Meyer, and others to the Old Oak and Coffee House clubs,[7] of which both Davidson and Wills were members. Davidson dismisses the whole question with a simple statement. "Modern archaeology and anthropology cannot wholly dispel the mystery," he insists, although he admits that the scientists say the mounds "were built by the prehistoric Indian tribes who, so far as we know, were the first human inhabitants of the Tennessee."

Davidson is ready to move on to another subject, the early Indian inhabitants of the Tennessee. The first of these primitive peoples mentioned is a tribe who were "content to live chiefly upon the abundant mussels of the river." Living as they did among mounds of mussel shells, Davidson asserts, "they must have been surrounded by a bad smell of unholy proportions, but they were primitives and did not mind bad smells." Before we interpret Davidson's attempt at humor as the expression of an anti-Indian attitude, we should examine his treatment of the courage, daring, and honesty of the Cherokee and other tribes. Davidson's attitude toward the Indian was far in advance of his time.

Even as archaeologists and anthropologists cannot dispel the mystery of the identity of the state's first inhabitants, Davidson cautions, neither can they make completely intelligible the activities and accomplishments of prehistoric Indians.[8] Davidson after

7. Two well-established Nashville literary clubs.
8. The specialists referred to will insist that there is nothing "mysterious" about the identity of the first inhabitants. They were Indians, known to have lived in Tennessee for at least 10,000 years before Europeans settled the land. Anthropologist Charles Faulkner observes that we not only know who these people were but also basically how their culture changed and developed during the thousands of years of their occupation.

all was neither a scientist nor a social scientist but a humanist; therefore—like many of his colleagues, including his good friend, John Crowe Ransom—he believed in the validity of myth. He was interested in more than facts, those phenomena which have been registered by one or more of the five senses of an honest and reliable narrator. He could accept a myth that was frankly fable because often that myth helped him to comprehend phenomena in their entirety by concerning itself with other than the phenomena's natural dimensions. Legend and myth can help man perceive a world of a magnitude that goes beyond its own natural history.

Thus, after Davidson has carefully surveyed many of the early attempts of the United States Corps of Engineers to make the upper Tennessee navigable and has meticulously detailed the reasons for its lack of success, he offers another explanation for its failure, for the existence of the Suck, the Narrows, and other impediments to navigation on the upper river. Just before the forceful removal of the Indians from their native lands, the story goes, the people living in the Hiwassee Valley heard strange voices:

> Hearkening, they understood these voices to be warning them and urging them to gather in their townhouses and fast in religious silence for seven days in order that they might be transported to the home of their old supernatural visitants, the Nunnehi, with whom they could dwell forever. One townhouse, where the people obeyed the voices and religiously fasted, was carried off bodily by the Nunnehi, and it can be seen today, changed into a great rock, on a certain mountaintop.... The Nunnehi transported the people of another town to a place underneath the waters of the Hiwassee, where they lived forever. It is a place where fishers' nets always hang, as if caught on rocks. But it is not rocks, it is the hands of the people of the lost Cherokee town that clutch the nets and remind the fishermen that they are still there in the deep underwater home of the immortals. (278–79)

We can understand, therefore, Davidson's fascination with the old river. Why man's scientific knowledge could not conquer the upper Tennessee until the 1930s when he built a new river is also clear. Like Davidson, we may find this new river, "the product of engineering operations of such calculated daring that the imagination is daunted to find precedent for them," less interesting. The present waterway supplants the historic Tennessee; it is really a chain of lakes, the river of the TVA.

THOMAS DANIEL YOUNG

# The
# Tennessee

VOLUME ONE

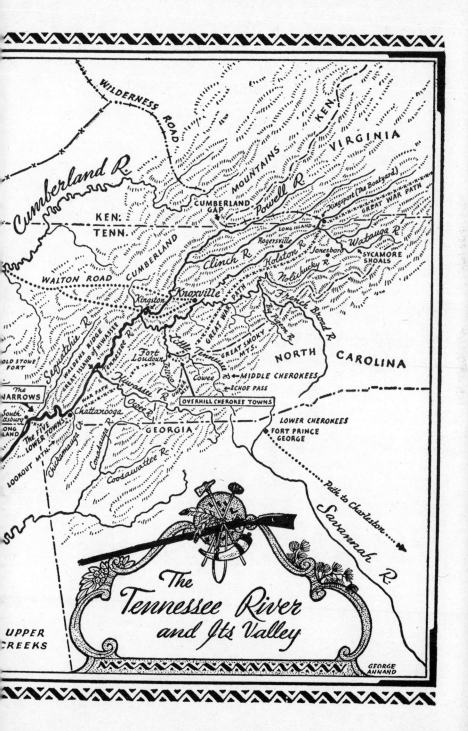

The Tennessee River and Its Valley

GEORGE ANNAND

CHAPTER I

# Two Rivers in One

Down the valley of the Tennessee two rivers flow —two rivers blended indistinguishably where for centuries there was only one. They slant southwest, then west, then north, in the wide curve that marks the course of the Tennessee. One of these, uppermost and immensely obvious, is the new Tennessee, a man-made river, the product of engineering operations of such calculated daring that the imagination is daunted to find precedent for them. A unique modern contrivance, designed and finished in a little over a decade, it is less a river than a chain of lakes, formed by the impounding of river waters behind great dams that stand athwart the valley in Egyptian impassivity. It is one of the best-advertised rivers in the world, and has been visited and studied by the emissaries of many foreign governments as well as by ever-increasing throngs of American tourists. With reason, it is an object of supreme interest to all who want to learn how to control the waters of a river valley and how to convert their force into electrical energy, while achieving at the same time material benefits which are thought not to be readily attainable by other means. This shining, modern thing, so new that its concrete structures have not had time to weather, is the river of the TVA.

Beneath the giant stairs of great lakes, merged with them and all but lost in them, flows another river—the old Ten-

5

nessee, the river of the Cherokee Indians and of their Creek and Chickasaw neighbors. To one of its small upper branches came the pioneers who made the first permanent settlement west of the Appalachians. Its actually recorded history covers about four centuries, from the visit of Hernando De Soto, in 1541, to the beginning of the presidency of Franklin D. Roosevelt, in 1933. Many times in those four centuries it has been at the center of the conflicts and decisions that have shaped the American republic. But it has not been well advertised, and therefore is not well known to the modern generation. Historians have neglected it. Even the natives of its valley have somehow lost acquaintance with it.

There is good cause for this inattention. One of the chief peculiarities of the old Tennessee is that, of all the great rivers east of the Mississippi, it has been least friendly to civilization. Until the advent of the Tennessee Valley Authority it defied every human attempt at conquest. It could be used, but only at great hazard and on terms forbidding to commerce and industry. So it remained a wild river, cherishing its wildness while civilization rushed across it or away from it. It mocked the schemes of improvers. It wore out the patience of legislators. Tawny and unsubdued, an Indian among rivers, the old Tennessee threw back man's improvements in his face and went its own way, which was not the way of the white man. The white man therefore withheld his praise. So today there are no fine romantic songs about the Tennessee. Poets, novelists, makers of ballads and folk tales, all have passed it by. This volume is the story of the old Tennessee, a river now utterly gone. To tell its story would seem worth while, if only for the reason that one who does not know the lost river cannot possibly understand its offspring and conqueror, the TVA. The story of the new river created by TVA will be the subject of a second volume. But the history of the old Tennessee would be remarkable even if the TVA had never been invented.

None of the rivers west of the Appalachians is an orthodox river, by European or Atlantic standards, but even among these unorthodox rivers the Tennessee is distinct and peculiar. It is long enough and big enough to flow into some ocean or other, but instead it doubles back on its course over a long distance, goes to much trouble to arrive nowhere in particular, and finally runs into another river, the Ohio—which in turn runs into a greater river—the Mississippi—that carries all the waters of the interior to the Gulf.

The early Virginians, well acquainted with tidewater, could not imagine a phenomenon like this. They had heard of rivers rising west of the Blue Ridge, but being as ill acquainted with the interior of North America as were the mapmakers of that day, they assumed that such rivers would run into "the great sea." Governor Berkeley in 1649 resolved to go, with fifty horse and fifty foot, and "discover this thing himself in person." But Berkeley never got around to discovery, nor did Virginians in general for another century. A new breed of men had to be developed before the inland rivers could be fully known—men who very properly boasted that they were half horse, half alligator.

People who write learnedly about American humor seem to take this boast as a wild frontier joke, born of high spirits and drunken exaggeration. But the humor is of the kind that cloaks utter peril and hardship with rough pleasantry. To get up and down the Tennessee one needed not only to combine the virtues of the horse and alligator, but to add something of the frog, snapping turtle, raccoon, buffalo, and shikepoke.

The ordinary difficulties of navigating a western river were disastrously increased on the Tennessee by the presence of great obstacles at Muscle Shoals and the Suck. These famous obstacles had a determining influence upon the history of the river. But their historic importance cannot be understood completely until one visualizes the extraordinary course of the Tennessee and the ramifications of its upper tributaries.

At its lower end, the Tennessee looks simple. It is the river that flows into the Ohio at Paducah, Kentucky. Here it invites no questions, but one would do well to remember that the Tennessee, although a tributary of the Ohio, is in many ways quite as much a river as the Ohio itself.

At its upper end—or rather in its upper reaches— nothing is simple. The Tennessee has no clearly identifiable upper end. In the highlands and valleys of its eastern parts, the Tennessee is a far-reaching system of rivers which run together in such an unaccountable way that argument has waxed great as to which is the main stream and which are the tributaries. No man can say what is *the* source of the Tennessee. It draws its waters from all points of the compass within an area extending over the southwestern end of the Valley of Virginia and the lofty, impenetrable mountains of East Tennessee, western North Carolina, and northern Georgia.

Most remote from its mouth are the headwaters of the Holston, which rises in southwest Virginia at a distance of 916 miles from Paducah. If the Holston can be identified with the Tennessee, as it often used to be, then 916 miles would be the length of the main river. In 1889 the legislature of Tennessee supported this view to the extent of declaring Kingsport, in Sullivan County, to be the upper limit of the Tennessee. But in 1890 a federal statute recognized the junction of the French Broad and the Holston, a few miles above Knoxville, as the point where the Tennessee ought properly to begin. This legislation cut the official length of the Tennessee to 652 miles—from which a few miles may now be subtracted for channel shortenings achieved by the TVA.

On its north side, the Upper Tennessee has only one large tributary, the Clinch, which, like other parts of the Tennessee system, seems more like a main branch than a tributary. Running southwestward along one of the great valleys of the Cumberland plateau, the Clinch parallels the course of the Holston and the Tennessee for a long distance before it joins the main river at Kingston. The Powell, running down another long valley, keeps up a similar parallelism until it joins the Clinch. Farther west, Duck River, meandering across Middle Tennessee, parallels the main river until it approaches and enters the Lower Tennessee. The Cumberland River, which is a tributary of the Ohio, imitates in a flattened arc the more wide-flung crescent of the Tennessee and, at last closely approaching, narrowly misses becoming a tributary of its sister river. For about a hundred miles the Tennessee and the Cumberland run side by side with a narrow strip of land between them; then the Cumberland enters the Ohio at Smithland, only twelve miles above the mouth of the Tennessee. The proximity of the Tennessee and the Cumberland is one of the most astonishing features of the geography of the region.

But there is no end to astonishment when one looks at the conformation of the Tennessee and its tributaries. From its left, or southern, bank, the Upper Tennessee receives the waters of three great rivers: the French Broad, the Little Tennessee, and the Hiwassee. All three of these tributaries seem perversely to flout nature's law, since they take what looks like an uphill route to join the main stream. They rise far away to the east on the western slopes of the Blue Ridge, and then they flow, not south or southwest as one would expect, but northwest *across* the tremendous barrier of the Great Smoky Mountains. Along their pathways are mountains that tower well above six thousand feet—the loftiest mountains in the eastern part of the United States; their long ridges, which take a general northeast-southwest line, come squarely athwart the paths of the rivers over a very wide region. Nevertheless, the rivers cut through the mountains and obstinately seek an outlet to the northwest. They have carved out deep gorges, above whose precipitous rocky walls tower thick, almost primeval forests of spruce and balsam resembling, in their upper zones, the great woods of New England and Canada, yet interspersed, too, with grassy "balds" and with the tangles of rhododendron and laurel characteristic of the southern mountains.

In their upper reaches, the three rivers are clear, brawling, boulder-strewn mountain streams, always full of water and subject to sudden freshets because they drain a region that has the heaviest rainfall in the eastern United States. But in their lower reaches, where the mountains thin out, they are navigable rivers coursing amiably through pleasant, fertile valleys where cornfield and pasture land invade the hardwood forests characteristic of the lower mountain slopes and valley land.

No valleys in America are more beautiful or more inviting to American eyes than the valleys of the French Broad, the Little Tennessee, and the Hiwassee, especially in the region where they flow out of their mountain fastnesses to approach the Tennessee. Because they have been thus inviting, since the time when hunters and traders first looked upon them, their history is intertwined with the history of the Tennessee. And so, too, for the same reason, is the history of the Watauga, which runs into the Holston, and the Nolichucky, which runs into the French Broad.

The Little Tennessee has special importance, for several reasons. The Overhill Cherokees built their principal towns along its west bank. Here was Chota, their "old beloved town," the sacred capital of the Cherokee nation. Close by Chota was the town called "Tanase" or "Tenese"—with many variations of spelling—from which the Little Tennesseee, the Big Tennessee, and the sixteenth state of the Union all derive their names. Indeed, the name "Tennessee" was applied to the Little Tennessee long before it was familiarly given to the main stream. This usage persisted throughout early pioneer times and has confused many a reader of old letters and documents.

When the main river finally gathers its upper branches and becomes one river, it flows in a wide parabola with the vertex curving irregularly westward across North Alabama, its eastern side lying across East Tennessee and its western side across West Tennessee and West Kentucky. Thus it twice crosses the state of Tennessee and approximately encloses, on all sides but the north, the region known as Middle Tennessee. Yet despite the fact that it crosses the entire width of West Tennessee and West Kentucky, the river becomes for one brief stretch the boundary between the two states. It forms the "jog" in the boundary line, a jog caused by errors in early surveys and the interstate quarrels and adjustments that ensued.

The vertex of the parabola, where eccentric changes of direction take place that finally cause the river to double back on its course, is known as the Great Bend of the Tennessee. Historians have been tempted to follow the vague tradition which holds that the Indian word "Tennessee" meant "the great bend" or "the bends." There is no authority for any such meaning; the original meaning of "Tennessee" has been lost. Yet the bending course of the Tennessee is one of the marks of its uniqueness among American rivers. No other great American river, after pointing its course for 350 miles in one general direction, changes its mind, veers around, and flows for 200 miles in the opposite direction. No other great river of the continent, except the distant Mackenzie, flows north for as great a distance as does the Tennessee.

No less remarkable are the three minor bends, or changes of course, within the Great Bend.

Just below Lookout Mountain, instead of continuing the southwestward line it has followed from Knoxville to Chattanooga, the river turns abruptly northwest and cuts a deeply entrenched, S-shaped gorge across the high barrier of Walden's Ridge. It issues into another valley—the Sequatchie Valley—parallel to the one abandoned and very much like it. Then the river pursues its course in exactly the same direction as before.

In wantonly choosing a tortuous path through Walden's Ridge the Tennessee creates—or did create before it was tamed—a series of fearsome perils to navigators. To these the early boatmen gave names that ring with humorous eloquence: the Suck, the Boiling Pot, the Skillet, the Frying Pan. These phenomena were caused by the sudden narrowing of the channel and the resulting constriction of the mighty waters of the Upper Tennessee. In old times this thirty-mile stretch was known as the Narrows. Later, the name of the first obstacle, the Suck, was often applied to the whole series. At the head of the dangerous passage, overlooking both the city of Chattanooga and the deep river valley, stands the bold promontory of Lookout Mountain; and directly opposite the mountain is Moccasin Bend, where the winding river outlines a shape which, seen from above, has the appearance of an Indian's moccasin-shod foot. Even the advent of modern highways and river improvements has not disturbed very much the wild beauty of the panorama that unrolls here.

After crossing into Sequatchie Valley and resuming its southwest course, the Tennessee flows on for about a hundred miles to Guntersville, Alabama. At Guntersville, it seemingly ought to continue southwest, in such a course as is taken by the Black Warrior River, whose two forks rise near Guntersville. Instead, the contrary Tennessee again abandons its open valley—which continues to the southwest—and turns northwest across Alabama. In so doing it creates—or, again, once did create—the famous river hazard, Muscle Shoals. The great shoals begin near the mouth of Elk River and continue all the way to Florence. In this historic stretch the Tennessee falls more than three and a half feet to the mile over a distance of nearly forty miles. A tortured, irregular formation of hard, nonerodable rocks overlies and mingles with the softer rock of the river bed. The resulting extensive rapids, dotted with islands and segmented by reefs and bars, made Muscle Shoals for centuries the greatest single barrier to navigation of the Tennessee.

Somewhere between Florence and the northwest corner of Mississippi, the Tennessee may once have emptied into the Gulf, or into what was the Gulf in a former geological age. If so, then why does it not now continue in that path and join the Father of Waters somewhere below Memphis? The Tennessee does not take that seemingly convenient route. It turns away to the north and runs 200 miles to its junction with the Ohio.

Despite much theorizing, geologists have achieved no really provable explanation for the eccentric course of the Tennessee. The theory now in good standing is rather complex, but it makes sense.

The most ancient parts of the Tennessee system, geologists say, are the French Broad, the Little Tennessee, the Hiwassee. These flowed in their present channels at a time when the land now west of the mountains was occupied by a great inland sea. They drained the old continent, or portion of a continent, which lay to the east. In time, the floor of this sea, already filled and shallowed by deposits from these rivers, was uplifted, and at the same time a folding process began which forced up the mountains into their present striking parallel ridges. During this period of convulsion and change, the three rivers were turned southward and were gathered into one river, the theoretical "Appalachian River" which may have been the direct ancestor of the eastern part of the Tennessee. This river flowed into the Cretaceous Sea of those times, which, though it no longer invaded the North American continent as deeply as before, still had an extension, called the Mississippi Embayment, which reached northward as far as the present mouth of the Ohio.

The turns of the Tennessee—which form the Great Bend —are thought to have been produced by shiftings of the mouth of the ancient "Appalachian River" as the land under the sea was upheaved and warped, and as sea and embayment retreated. In one stage, the mouth of the Tennessee may have been near Chattanooga, or somewhere south of that point. The river was turned west when the land rose across its old path and forced it to seek a more westward course. It shifted from one valley to the next and found entrance to the sea at another point. This point was, say, Guntersville. Again the uplifting and warping process began and the Tennessee had to turn northwestward into the Mississippi Embayment. Now all was quiet for a long period and to north and south of the old river mouth there was formed a long bar, and behind it a lagoon, not unlike the bars and lagoons found on the Texas coast today. When the last great rising of the land occurred, and the Mississippi Embayment shrunk up and became the Mississippi River, the Tennessee turned northward along the old lagoon. There it runs today.

In its different parts, then, the Tennessee recapitulates the geological changes through which the whole region has passed during many thousands of years. It is a "young" trunk on an "old" head, and the different parts of its anatomy are of different ages. Its southeastern tributaries, which rise among the very old crystalline rocks of the Blue Ridge, are among the oldest of our rivers. The more northern branches, the Holston and the Clinch, cut through the younger sedimentary rocks and alluvial deposits of the Appalachian Valley. From Florence to Paducah, the Tennessee runs through the youngest region of all—as any casual motorist can see when he dashes through the deep cuts in the rolling land between Nashville and Memphis and notices at the roadside the raw clay and gravel banks, the soil not yet mellow, the uncheerful forests of scrub oak and underbrush in which roving Indians and the land pirates of the Natchez Trace used to lurk.

Thus did the terrestrial accidents of the remote past wrench the Tennessee into an oddly circuitous path and to a large extent predetermine its strange destiny as a river provokingly beautiful and powerful, yet stubbornly unwilling to bear man's yoke and carry his burdens.

In one respect, and perhaps only one, has it been regular and predictable. Its banks are stable, because they are cut from stone. Therefore, once its course was established, it has kept that course. The Tennessee makes no oxbow lakes, it does not suddenly leave its main channel to make a new one, it does not undermine its own banks and swallow up houses, farms, and towns.

In other respects it is as irregular, as various, as rebellious as the huge valley region that it drains. That valley contains over forty thousand square miles of southern land, an area as large as England and Scotland combined. In it is all the rich variety of man and nature which gives the South endless diversity within its fervently cherished pattern of unity. In the east, the Tennessee belongs to the Upland South, and to the very distinct upland region that is East Tennessee. The Great Bend touches the Deep South on one side and Middle Tennesseee on the other and is the central artery of a region that combines two southern traditions. In its lower reaches the Tennessee issues from the land of cotton and pine to pass through a borderland, which was debatable country even in Indian times. It looks at last toward the edge of the northern prairies and makes friends with Cincinnati, Cairo, St. Louis.

To all these varied regions, the old Tennessee brought as much anxiety and frustration as benefit. In addition to the common sort of navigation troubles, the Tennessee had Muscle Shoals, which cut the river in half and made the Upper and Lower Tennessee seem, for purposes of navigation, like two separate rivers. The Narrows, though less formidable than Muscle Shoals, divided the upper river almost as conclusively. Even when river conditions permitted navigation, the Tennessee ran the wrong way for boatmen who desired to reach New Orleans.

Furthermore, the flow of the Tennessee was extremely variable. The normal width of its channel varied at different points in unexpected and inconsistent ways, and at those different points that normal width was subject to seasonal changes. At Muscle Shoals, under normal conditions, the river might be as wide as at Paducah, but in a flood season it spread over the flatlands and became ten times as wide. The depth of the channel underwent similar variations, from very shallow to very deep, according to the amount of rainfall in the different parts of the great valley. At Knoxville, a flow of nearly a hundred times the normal low-water flow has been recorded.

Throughout colonial times and all of pioneer history, the Indian held the banks of the Tennessee at strategic points and grimly blockaded the river. The imperial rivalries of Great Britain, France, and Spain made the Tennessee Valley a center of international and tribal intrigue, the scene of wars and ambushes, the goal of land speculators and utopian dreamers. For half a century the Indian wars reddened its banks and filled its forests with the smoke of burning towns. The States came into being. The Tennessee gave its name to the state that it divided—and then helped, in other than geographic ways, to keep that state divided. Time went on. Flatboat and keelboat succeeded the pirogues of the French coureur de bois. The steamboat came to compete on hazardous terms with flatboat and keelboat. Then, as the stubborn wildness of the Tennessee began to be deplored more systematically, the army engineers began their patient surveys. The problem of Muscle Shoals was argued and reargued, and remained unsolved. The Civil War broke out. The Tennessee became a route of inva-

sion for the Federal armies. Gunboats and transports crowded
its waters, and because the Tennessee ran the wrong way for
the South, the invasion succeeded, and the war went badly for
the Confederate armies of the west. Another half century
went by, with new attempts at taming the river. These also
failed. Civilization could get over the Tennessee, by ferry,
bridge, or airplane, but it was still what it had always been—
an obstacle to be crossed rather than a path to be followed.
The railroads, so prone to lay tracks along river valleys, or
even to hug the banks of the more docile rivers, did not follow the Tennessee for any great distance. They connected
with it, they bridged it, but they took care to lay their main-
line tracks at a respectful distance. In comparison with other
rivers of its kind and size, the Tennessee turned few mill
wheels and carried few boats. For all its great length and
beauty, its banks were sparsely inhabited. Towns and cities
did not flourish in great number along its stream. It disappointed the hopes of Knoxville and Chattanooga. It flouted
the recurrent speculative dreams of the Alabama "Tri-cities"
—Florence, Tuscumbia, and Sheffield. Those dreams arose
again with the advent of World War I and the building of
Wilson Dam. But still the problem was less than half solved,
and the circling, tumbling, contrary river was unsubdued.

Now, at long last, the old wild river is submerged, is lost
in its great progeny, the river of the TVA. Destiny, or whim,
or some man's bold wish, or some Platonic dream, has decided that this untamed river creature should become, of all
the rivers of the world, the one most deftly chained, the one
most thoroughly subdued to man's designing will. The Tennessee is now a civil and obliging stream. One flick of a switch
by the tenderest human finger, and the Tennessee is any man's
obedient slave, though he be a thousand miles away. Tourists stare at it in immaculate safety from observation booths
placed on points where long ago, it was as much as a man's

life was worth to be seen. The Indians are gone, and the Indian river wears the manacles and dress of civilization. How all this came about is a long story and a strange one. It begins with legend. It ends with statistics.

## CHAPTER II

# First Comers

A STRANGE fancy haunted the pioneers of Tennessee and Kentucky. As they followed the buffalo and Indian paths into the new country, they were sometimes plagued with an eerie sense of elusive presence about them. They felt that they were walking in the footsteps of men of an older time, not red men but white men, who had journeyed through the wilderness before them. The feeling took shape, and became legend. Around the wilderness campfires went the tale of some white race that preceded the American pioneers on this continent, a bearded people, blond and blue-eyed. They were Welshmen, the tale said, who settled in the interior before Columbus discovered America and who, merging with the Indians, finally became "Welsh Indians." Sometimes the legend became highly circumstantial. A Welshman, one tale said, was captured by a strange tribe of Indians. He overheard them debating whether to burn him at the stake or just enslave him. Suddenly he realized that they were speaking his own tongue, Welsh. He reproached them in vivid Welsh, and was then released and welcomed as a brother.

In the Tennessee Valley this widespread legend became attached to the ancient mounds and elaborate earthworks found at many points along the river and its tributaries. The pioneers thought it unlikely that these mysterious structures could have been raised by the Indians whom they knew. Indeed, the Indians themselves disclaimed all responsibility. Then surely they must have been built by the legendary Welshmen.

John Sevier, the first governor of Tennessee, on one occasion took the trouble to question Oconostota, the great war chief of the Overhill Cherokees, about this intriguing question. Who built the "ancient tho' regular fortifications" on the banks of the Hiwassee, he asked the old chief. Oconostota replied that "it was handed down by the Forefathers that the works had been made by the white people who had formerly inhabited the country." This was at a time when the Cherokees lived much farther south, in what is now South Carolina. Moving north into the mountains, the Cherokees encountered the white men and warred with them. Finding them embarking in large boats to descend the Tennessee, the Cherokees intercepted them at Muscle Shoals and there waged battle for several days. "At length," said Oconostota, "the whites proposed to the Indians that if they would exchange prisoners and cease hostilities, they would leave the Country and never more return, which was acceded to." Oconostota understood that these people were Welsh, who had long before landed near Mobile and had been driven inland by hostile natives. After their truce with the Cherokees, they were supposed to have descended the Tennessee to the Ohio, and finally to have settled in the upper Missouri country.

If there is any truth in the Cherokee tradition, then these shadowy Welshmen were the people who left among the Indian tribes certain "old books," much rumored about but never seen, and who dropped the Roman coins dug up by amazed pioneers at one or two places in the Tennessee Valley. Surprisingly enough, there are on the European side some shreds of evidence which may be taken to support the legend of the Welsh. The Welsh bards had tales of Madoc, son of Gwynneth, who in the twelfth century sailed westward with ten ships and many companions, and at last reached an un-

known country, presumably America. Hakluyt, the Elizabethan chronicler, tells the story of Madoc in his *Principall
Navigations*, treats it as accepted tradition, and uses it to
justify England's claim to American lands. Centuries later,
George Catlin, while traveling among the western Indians
and drawing his remarkable pictures of them in their native
condition, found among the Mandan Sioux, a small tribe of
the upper Missouri, Indians with fair complexions and blue
and gray eyes. He told himself that they must be a remnant
of the ancient Welsh colony, and argued as much with warm
conviction in his book, *North American Indians*.

But more likely the Welsh legend, for all its persistence,
is only an example of a curiously antiquarian and romantic
tendency among the pioneers. Judge Haywood, the first historian of Tennessee, was a member of an antiquarian society
that flourished happily while the Tennessee settlements were
barely emerging from the buckskin and log cabin stage. Lying
on a bull's hide spread beneath a large tree, the portly judge
composed his history with his books and documents heaped
around him in the shade; and he embodied in his work, with
a strong preference for the most antique explanation possible,
many legends of former races and many speculations about
the origin of the ancient cairns, mounds, and earthworks.
James Adair, who lived for forty years as a trader among
the southern Indians, was firmly convinced that the historic
Indians known to him were the relics of the Ten Lost Tribes
of Israel, and he devoted a large part of his *History of the
American Indians* to proving, by systematic comparisons of
language and customs, that the Chickasaws, Creeks, and
Cherokees were close kin to the ancient Hebrews.

Modern archaeology and anthropology cannot wholly
dispel the mystery, but they can do much to answer the question of who built the "ancient tho' regular fortifications" and
other earthen structures that still may be traced out beneath
the forest cover or that rise up, in unaccountable knolls,

along the bottom lands, amid corn rows flourishing, often enough, on the very spot where the Indians planted their corn. The mounds and fortifications, the archaeologist says, were built by the prehistoric Indian tribes who, so far as we know, were the first human inhabitants of the Tennessee Valley.

By far the most lowly and primitive of these were certain obscure, hardly identifiable· groups of Indians who were content to live chiefly upon the abundant mussels of the river. Where this simple, oysterlike food could easily be gathered, they apparently lived for long intervals, retreating temporarily when floodwater drove them from their homesites near the stream, and returning when the flood receded to resume their perpetual banquet of shellfish. They also hunted and fished in the manner normal to men of the Stone Age, but they are distinguished from other Indians by their slothful craving for mussels—and, for that matter, snails, which they gathered in the shallows along with other mollusks. As they ate, they tossed aside the empty shells, and therefore lived in the midst of, or even on top of, the vast middens, or heaps of shell refuse accumulated by their insatiable appetites. They must have been surrounded by a bad smell of unholy proportions, but they were primitives and did not mind bad smells. They had no pottery; they did not know how to make it. They could cook only in rude clambake style, with hot stones placed in a pit. They finally gave way to more enterprising Indians, of a much superior stage of culture, but the great shell mounds, being relatively imperishable, remained to mark their abodes. One such abode is the station called Shellmound, on the N.C. and St.L. Railroad, near Nickajack Cave, about thirty miles west of Chattanooga.

Except for their extraordinarily permanent shell mounds, the mussel-eating Indians left no impression upon the Valley, and they seem hardly worth remembering. Yet between these utterly humble creatures and our proud modernity there is one undeniable link. They were drawn to the great river by its profuse beds of mussels; and that is one of the prime reasons why civilized man has sought it. From the most ancient Indian times to the present day, the gathering of mussels has been a continuous occupation along the Tennessee River. Unlike the primitive Indian, the mussel fishermen of the Tennessee River throw away the meat and keep the shells, for mussel shells are worth so much a ton when sold to the button-making industry. Nevertheless, they do gather mussels, where the Indians gathered the remote ancestors of the same shellfish. And, like the Indians, they look for fresh-water pearls, since our women, though not our warriors, value pearls for ornament. We may well imagine, too, that the name Muscle Shoals (often spelled "Mussel" Shoals) may have an antiquity greater than we ascribe to it. The great Shoals, with its numerous rocks and shallows and ever-moving currents, must always have been a habitat especially agreeable to mussels. It may always have been known, even in lost Indian tongues, as the place where the mussels grew. Later on, one may suspect that the boatmen who rode the dangerous stream, dragging their craft over reefs and wrestling with pole or paddle against the current, may have made a sardonic pun on the word "muscle." But Muscle Shoals was always, surely, first of all the place of mussels.

The numerous earthen mounds and ramparts left by the more advanced Indian tribes tell quite a different story, which archaeologist and anthropologist can now make reasonably intelligible. Again, legend enters to argue that the "mound builders" were a mysterious race, greater and more ingenious than the well-known historic tribes who succeeded them; possibly they were survivors of sunken Atlantis or wanderers from the Lost Continent of Mu. And again the historic Indians, as reported by the early historians, catered to our love of mystery when they talked about the mounds. In the sonor-

ous language of Ramsey, the Indians are made to speak like
this: "They considered [the mounds] as the vestiges of an
ancient and more numerous population, further advanced in
the arts of civilized life than their own people. For these
relics they seemed to entertain some peculiar veneration, and
never appropriated them to any secular purpose or use."

The tribes composing this "ancient and more numerous
population"—the so-called "mound builders"—were not some
completely unknown people, the modern scientist says. They
were offshoots of the great Mayan stock which developed
its culture in Mexico and Central America and pushed out
wandering groups that came north in a long series of migrations. To the Tennessee Valley, as elsewhere, they brought
the maize culture—the native corn and all that goes with
it—and their rather advanced arts and crafts.

The first stage of migration out of the old Mayan home
produced the Pueblo culture of the Southwest. The mounds
and earthworks of the Tennessee Valley belong, it is thought,
to a second stage, in which the migrants entered the wood-
land area of the Southwest. The shapes of the mounds, which
are conical or pyramidal, and their flat tops, are structural
echoes of the stone pyramids of Mexico. The pottery, stone
vessels, engraved shells, tobacco pipes, copper ear ornaments,
and breastplates excavated from the mounds often repeat the
plumed serpent motif and other art patterns of the Mayans.
Both the conventionalized decorative designs and the bird
and animal effigies incorporated in pottery and tobacco pipes
exhibit a skill of craft and a beauty that are often of a very
high order.

Between the historic Indians and the mound builders
there are cultural links which tend to persuade us that the
mound-building culture merged imperceptibly into the culture of the Indians we know. There was much shifting of the
aboriginal population back and forth along the curving valley of the Tennessee, but there was probably no catastrophic

change, no sudden destruction of a superior race by some barbaric newcomer, although there may have been local wars of extermination. The Green Corn Dance of the southern Indians would alone be enough, almost, to link them with the maize culture of the Mayans. The well-developed migration legend of the Creeks is another link; in racial memory they knew that they had come, long before, from the west. The arts of the later Indians, though simpler, echoed the arts of the mound builders. The modern archaeologist, indeed, often distinguishes the artifacts of the mound builders from those of the historic Indians only by the presence of modern trade articles mixed with the pottery which, but for that telltale evidence, might be deemed to belong to an earlier people. The townhouses, or tribal assembly halls, of the Cherokees, to judge from the historic descriptions of them, did not differ very much from the townhouses of the people who antedated them, and whom they dispossessed or absorbed. The floor plan of the Cherokee townhouses was round in shape; and that is almost the only feature that distinguishes them from the presumably much older townhouses recently excavated in the valleys of the Clinch and Powell rivers, where no Cherokees lived in historic times. Excavations sponsored by the TVA disclose that the Clinch and Powell townhouses had a rectangular pattern; the "post hole pattern," very ingeniously unearthed by the archaeologists, proves that. But, like the Cherokee townhouses, they were built of logs, set upright, and the structure, roof and all, was covered with earth. There. was but one narrow door. A fire was built in a clay basin in the center of the one large room. There might be a high seat, shaped out of clay, for the chief or priest. And all around were seats for the assembly, covered with mats of split cane. Periodically, it would seem, the townhouse structure was burned and leveled, fresh earth was spread over all, and a new structure was raised on the site of the old one. Thus the mound grew larger through the years.

The large mounds of the Tennessee Valley region were nearly always, it would seem, the sites of townhouses. The smaller mounds seem to have been dwelling sites, or sometimes were burial mounds. Large burial mounds, like those found at Hopewell, Ohio, are lacking in the Tennessee country; and there are no examples at all of the great effigy mounds, built in the shape of snakes or birds, which are found farther north.

The most recent excavations disclose a greater variety of village patterns and a more complex mixture, or succession, of Indian cultures than earlier archaeologists had uncovered. The Indians of the "Mouse Creeks" culture, who lived in the Hiwassee Valley and had a settlement also on the Tennessee River, excavated the floors of their townhouses below the ground level, and grouped their habitations close by, within a stockade, an arrangement quite in contrast with the usual straggling village plan. The modern anthropologist is inclined to identify these Indians with the Yuchi, a small tribe about whom little is known. On the main Tennessee, the Indians of the "Dallas" culture also had a stockaded village, but built their townhouses upon an elevated foundation, and in one instance constructed an extremely elaborate townhouse with two vestibuled entrances. These were probably Indians of the Muskhogean, or Creek, group, who entered the Tennessee Valley from the Deep South. They may have been among the Creek tribes against whom the Cherokees warred, according to their own tradition, when they entered the Tennessee country and established their homes along the Little Tennessee.

Of much greater interest, however, to the average valley dweller are the great enclosures, evidently fortified works, situated in excellent strategic positions on bluffs and in the forks of streams. Anybody can see that these were made by the mighty men of old, and they are the more mysterious because they have never been thoroughly studied. One of the most remarkable of these enclosures is situated a little west of the Tennessee River, not far from the battlefield of Shiloh. The outer defenses of this, the Cisco mound group, consist of embankments, which were probably once topped by palisades, and which have a total circumference of six miles. Within the outer defenses there are inner citadels, and thirty-five mounds of various sizes are scattered through the enclosure. The largest mound—a massive work 73 feet high and 300 by 370 feet at its base—commands a view of the surrounding country. Across the river at Savannah, Tennessee, is a similar but less ambitious fortified enclosure.

The "Old Stone Fort" near Manchester, Tennessee, is one of the rare instances of a primitive work built in the remote uplands. It has no mounds within its large enclosure. It was evidently designed to withstand long siege. It is built in the forks of Duck River, on the brow of a deep ravine, and it could hardly have been better placed by a military engineer. The name is a misnomer, for the walls are made of earth, like other primitive ramparts; but at some points the core of the earthen fortification is a stony rubble. It has one entrance, an intricate gateway cleverly designed to be hard to attack and easy to defend. Some have been inclined to think that the Old Stone Fort was erected by a band of Spaniards who strayed far inland. This is very unlikely. It is in the region, however, to which De Soto sent two scouts from his camping place at Chiaha, and may therefore possibly have been the Chisca of the Spanish narratives. But all that anybody can say of it conclusively now is this: it is an old haunted place in the oak barrens of the plateau; no Indians dwelled there in the times we know about; and few people go there now.

The age of the mounds cannot be determined with any real accuracy. They are centuries old, and their history is largely conjectural. With the coming of De Soto we reach

the beginning of the recorded history of the Tennessee—
the sixteenth century.

The legend of the early Welsh invaders is, after all, little
more curious and little more improbable than the actual
story, recorded in four Spanish narratives, of the great De
Soto expedition. It was a thoroughly ambitious affair, half
medieval crusade, half Renaissance junket, and it came to
the banks of the wilderness river with lance and armor,
arquebus and crossbow, bearing side by side the pennon of
a noble house, the banner of a great Catholic monarch, and
the crucifix. This was before Elizabeth reigned in England,
before the birth of Shakespeare, before either Anglican or
Puritan made settlements in America.

Hernando De Soto, leader of the expedition, had been
made governor, captain general, and adelantado of Florida
by Charles V of Spain. He was authorized to explore and
colonize the southern part of the continent, to conquer the
inhabitants, if there were any, and to convert them to the
Catholic faith. Incidentally, too, he expected to get rich
from gold and plunder and to heighten his prestige at the
Spanish court. The noble Spaniard had with him both cavalry
and foot soldiers—a carefully picked body of troops, chiefly
Spanish and Portuguese, experienced in the wars of a nation
which at that time was the most military-minded in all
Europe. Among his officers were several skilled campaigners,
already famous for their exploits in Peru or Mexico. De Soto
himself had made a distinguished record in Pizarro's campaigns in South America and had all the qualities that marked
the great Spanish conquistadores. With the various secretaries,
civil officers, and attendant priests, the expedition numbered
six or seven hundred Europeans. Along with them, generally
impressed into the Spanish service, went always a large body
of Indian carriers, varying in number according to the degree
of persuasion that the adelantado could exercise upon the
Indian towns he visited. The Spaniards had a good supply of

excellent horses, and they drove with them, for extra provision, a great herd of hogs. Strangely enough, the hogs multiplied en route, despite the appetites of the soldiers—and also despite, we may imagine, the appetites of the bears, who through De Soto got their first memorable taste of hog meat. Tradition says, with some show of truth, that the razorback hog of the southern backwoods is a lineal descendant of De Soto's porkers, either those who escaped to the woods or those occasionally given to the Indians. But tradition is wrong in asserting that the wild horses of the American plains are descended from De Soto's cavalry mounts, for hardly any of the De Soto horses survived when the remnant of his expedition, under Moscoso, finally reached Mexico, after four years' wandering.

There seems to have been one Englishman among De Soto's soldiers. He was an archer, and with the stubbornness of his race he refused the Spanish crossbow and carried his own cherished weapon—an English longbow. It would have been better for De Soto if there had been more English longbowmen, to shoot quick and true against the quick-shooting Indians. Crossbow and arquebus were poor weapons for forest combat. If this lone English archer survived to reach the banks of the Tennessee, then he was probably the first Englishman to look upon the river. It is pleasant to imagine this man, a descendant of the longbowmen of Crécy and Agincourt, as sending one clothyard shaft across the waters where the long rifles were later to speak.

De Soto's expedition landed at Tampa Bay, in late May, 1539, and after lengthy hesitations wandered uneasily north and northeastward. His exact route of march is not easy to determine and has often been debated. If we accept the findings of the most recent study, which are set forth in the "Final Report of the United States De Soto Expedition Commission," we would visualize the Spaniards as moving up the Flint River, in Georgia, and reaching the

Indian town of Cofitachequi, later known as Silver Bluff, on the Savannah River, in the spring of 1540. There De Soto made captive and took with him the Indian "queen" known as the Lady of Cofitachequi—she was really the niece of the chieftainess. From Cofitachequi he went north to Chalaque, through a poor country, with little maize—a "tobacco road" country, even that far back. The soldiers became slightly mutinous. The weather turned bad. A terrifying hailstorm rattled down upon the steel casques. The Spaniards began to learn about the southern climate.

The expedition entered the southern highlands, probably by the Keowee trail, which ran along the divide between the Savannah and Saluda rivers and which later became a main route of communication between Charles Town and the Overhill Cherokee country.

At Xuala, among the mountains near the northwestern tip of North Carolina, De Soto turned westward, climbed the mountains of the neighborhood, probably by a precipitous path called the Winding Stair, and marched in the vicinity of Highlands, North Carolina. Near Franklin, North Carolina, he crossed the headwaters of the Little Tennessee, and came to the Hiwassee near Conasauga Creek, which still bears, in an only slightly different form, the name recorded in the Spanish narratives—Canasoga. Whether he marched on to the north and visited the Great Island at the mouth of the Hiwassee or bore westward on the old war path now followed by Federal Highway 11 is a matter still open to some question. At any rate, De Soto reached the Tennessee River somewhere in the region of Chattanooga.

In this country the Indians were very amiable. The Spaniards feasted upon "mulberries" (probably the mountain serviceberries), which were brought to them in baskets. They rested in a pleasant camp in a pine woods. Then appeared, says the Spanish historian, Ranjel, "peaceful Indians from Chiaha and brought corn. The next day, Saturday, in the

morning, the Spaniards crossed one arm of the river, which
is very broad, and went into Chiaha, which is on an island
in the same river."

The De Soto Commission locates Chiaha on Burns Island,
in the Tennessee River just north of the Tennessee-Alabama
line, but it may have been farther east, on Hiwassee Island.
Anyhow, at Chiaha, De Soto and his men took a long rest,
and for the time being life went pleasantly for them. It was a
disappointment, of course, that the Indian queen had de-
camped. She escaped at a confused moment when they were
crossing a stream and took with her a treasure of pearls which
De Soto had greedily admired. Two soldiers and some slaves
had deserted. The troops were starved and exhausted from
their mountainous journey. It was a good thing the Indians
were friendly. From them the Spaniards got maize in plenty,
oil extracted from nuts, bear fat put up in gourds, and, a
rare thing, a pot of bee's honey to sweeten their palates. They
went swimming with the Indians, for it was early summer
and the water was right.

The chief of the Chiaha Indians showed De Soto how
they obtained pearls from the river mussels. Since life was
going so pleasantly, De Soto dispatched two scouts to investigate a place called Chisca, in the mountains to the north.
Later on, at Coste, the scouts returned. Their tale was that
they had had a difficult trip through mountains where there
was little maize and only one poor village—and no great city
at all, such as De Soto had been led to expect. They brought
with them no gold or jewels, but only a "cow-skin"—probably a buffalo hide—"as soft as the skin of a kid, with hair
like that of the soft wool of sheep between that of the common and that of the merino."

The expedition loafed at Chiaha for two weeks and more,
and then left because of the prospect of trouble with their
hosts. Suddenly and mysteriously, the Indians ran away,
wrote Ranjel, "for something that the Governor asked of

them; and, in short, it was because he asked for women."
Through cajolery or force, De Soto persuaded the Indians to
return, and got from them carriers, but no women.

From Chiaha, the expedition moved down the Tennessee through several unnamed villages. After spending the
night in a pine grove, the Spaniards crossed the river.
"There," wrote Ranjel, "they had much labour in crossing a
river which flowed with a strong current, and they made
a bridge or support of the horses in the following manner,
so that the foot soldiers should not be endangered, and it was
this way: They put the horses in the river in line, head
and tail, and they were as steady as they could be, and on
each one his master, and they received the force of the stream,
and on the lower side, where the water was not so violent,
the foot soldiers forded, holding on to the tails and stirrups,
breast-pieces and manes, one after the other. And in this
way the whole army got across very well."

This crossing may have been somewhere among the
swift currents of the Narrows, or it may have been farther
down river. The Spanish narratives are vague and confused
for this stage of De Soto's journey. Apparently, traveling
southwest along the Tennessee, the expedition crossed and
recrossed the river, or arms of the river, two or three times
before they reached Coste. The supplies of maize that the
army needed were in the Indian villages or their adjacent
fields, and the villages were on the numerous large islands so
characteristic of the river in this part of its course. Evidently
the Spaniards returned from island to mainland only to find
that they must seek the islands again when they needed food
and rest.

Coste, the next important stop, is located by the De Soto
Commission as on the upper end of Pine Island. It was inhabited at that time by the Koasati Indians, a tribe which later
moved southward and joined the Creek confederation.

At Coste there was Indian trouble. The chief complained

that his uninvited guests were robbing his corncribs, and he demanded that the outrage be stopped. De Soto settled the business by a trick in which he was already well practiced; it was, in fact, his consistent policy with Indian chiefs. Feigning a conciliatory manner, he awaited his opportunity, then seized the chief and carried him along as a hostage. During the week's stay at Coste, the scouts returned from Chisca, and the sick and wounded who had been left at Chiaha were brought down the river in canoes.

The next stage of the journey brought the Spaniards farther downriver to the island village of Tali, which was probably on McKee Island near the bend of the river at Guntersville. There was some show of active hostility at Tali. Perhaps the word had gone out that the Spaniards must be watched. Anyway, men and women began to "take to the woods" as if to be out of the way of a battle. De Soto managed to intercept them, possibly because he could command the river with his crossbows and arquebuses, but he remained only one day at Tali, and then turned toward the south, away from the river. It was his last sight of the Tennessee. He marched south, through the uplands of North Alabama, to reach the town of Coosa, of which he had heard great report. Ahead of him was the disastrous battle with Tuscaloosa, the Black Warrior, and his hosts of determined Mobilian Indians, and after that, the turn northwest again, the fatal battle with the Chickasaws, the wanderings across the Mississippi and back, and at last death and defeat in the wilderness he had aimed to conquer.

In his long zigzag march De Soto encountered the ancestors of the "Five Civilized Tribes," famous in later history, and fragments of other tribes less well known. In the Tennessee Valley he crossed the territory of the Cherokees (who may or may not have reached their historic homes by that time), the Creeks, and the Chickasaws. He saw their towns, some of which were stockaded, some not, and sat in their townhouses, pitched upon mounds. Sparse though it is, the account of Indian life given in the narratives of Ranjel, the Gentleman of Elvas, Biedma, and Garcilaso, is the first authentic eyewitness information we have concerning these Indians and their country, at the time when they were emerging from vague prehistory into actual history. The four narratives of the De Soto expedition fill out and sustain to some extent the conjectural reconstruction which archaeologist and anthropologist can draw, in outline, from their studies.

Seen in perspective, too, the Spanish narratives reveal Indians essentially like those the English and French later encountered in the Tennessee country. They were courteous and dignified in intercourse with the white men, and were not one whit abashed in the presence of civilization. They were generous—more generous than the Spaniards—as long as they had reason to think the strangers were friends who might be treated as honored guests. But they were valorous and skillful in combat, when they discovered that the honored guests were no better than freebooters.

In the southern Indians, indeed, the great conquistador and his picked force of trained European soldiers met their match. They narrowly escaped extermination. It was a hard lesson. The European invader of a later time, although he came with much superior weapons, had to learn it over and over again.

De Soto, though he deemed himself experienced in Indian warfare, did not after all understand what he was up against. We have no record of his thoughts, but he must have assumed that he would find in "Florida" great capital cities, like those in Mexico and Peru, where his armored and disciplined soldiers could overcome the ill-armed masses of a Montezuma, or else by stratagem deceive and enslave them. He did not realize that civilization was already overrefined and decadent in Montezuma's cities; that it was rotten-ripe, not crudely barbaric, and for that reason was ready to fall. In the "Florida" to which De Soto came for conquest and glory there were no such cities, and there was no such decadence. The tribes of the Southeast had escaped all that by their migration into a new country. Some of their old religious and cultural practices they had retained—the mounds like pyramids, the forms of worship, the Stone Age weapons, the elaborate featherwork and kindred arts. In the arts, indeed, the sixteenth century Indians of the Spanish narratives seem to have been more skillful and advanced than their successors of the seventeenth and eighteenth centuries. And certainly they had a greater abundance of boats, and used the river more freely.

In other respects they were about what they were later —a people of small, scattered settlements, loosely confederated at best, leading a life that was a combination of agriculture, hunting, and war. The wilderness, which was the Spaniard's enemy, was their friend. They forced the Spaniard into battles where he was at a disadvantage. His powerful blows accomplished little, for there was nothing importantly central for him to capture or destroy. These Indians, indeed, could not be conquered and destroyed by a mere expedition. On the contrary, they could easily have destroyed De Soto at any time if they had realized the nature of his designs.

In 1566 and 1567 small expeditions, led by Juan Pardo, were sent into the interior from the Spanish settlements on the southern coast. These reached some parts of the Tennessee region earlier visited by De Soto, but they accomplished nothing. After Pardo, occasional parties of Spaniards went into the Indian country to work mines or to trade. Relics of Spanish mines have been found in the mountains, and there are stories of Spanish initials carved on rocks.

But when De Soto and Pardo vanished into the great pine and oak forests, the Spaniard as an effective presence was gone forever from the Tennessee country. The influence of Spain would be felt now and then in politics or trade, but thus early, in the sixteenth century, it was decided that the Tennessee would not become a Spanish river.

# CHAPTER III

# The River of the Cherokees

To THE Indian tribes of the Tennessee Valley, the visit of the Spaniard was an odd, isolated occurrence that hardly stayed in the race memory long enough to make a legend or a tale. The Spaniard came, the Spaniard went, and for nearly two centuries afterward the Indians were left in comparatively undisturbed possession of their inland paradise. They built new towns upon old townsites, heaped grave upon grave, and planted choice river bottoms in maize, beans, and squash. They fought their traditional enemies from time to time, and smoked ceremonial tobacco with their traditional friends. Occasionally they won new ground by conquest, or yielded it to a stronger tribe. Sometimes they migrated, as primitive folk will, to get better hunting and fishing. Or when their small fields no longer yielded good crops, they moved on and made new clearings by the simple process of girdling the trees, for it was hard to cut down big trees with flint axes. The fields that they abandoned became the "Indian old fields" known later to the white settlers and frequently occupied by them. But in all this process nothing changed fundamentally. Gradually they began to know the white man, but they felt no real pressure as yet from the settlements far away on the seaboard.

It is true that traders and explorers came with increasing frequency. The goods of the trader were welcome, especially

37

his clever new implements, the hunting knife, the hatchet and adz, the musket, and finally the rifle. After a while they began slowly to take the modern path. They learned to think of these luxuries as necessities and by imperceptible stages became dependent upon their relationship with the distant world of the white man. Yet it was a good bargain, from the Indian standpoint, to swap a few deerskins for a knife. The deer were numberless, but steel knives were a rarity, and vastly superior to flint knives. Along with steel knives, of course, they were trading for other articles less clearly valuable: glass beads to replace the old ones of shell; ready-made shirts and coats; liquor, diseases, subversive ideas. But as yet the trade articles did not mean a great change of life. The fish still thronged to the weirs, the deer was in the thicket, there were always scalps to be taken somewhere. The Tennessee was an Indian river, the river of the tribes who dwelt in its valley and claimed the lands it drained, and much more land besides.

The early names of the river reflect this long Indian occupancy and suggest phases of river history that are all but lost to us. The early cartographers caught up names learned from the Indians by the first explorers and put them down on the vacant places in their curiously distorted maps. Generally these were names of tribes that were said to live on the unknown inland river. Thus, in the seventeenth century, the French used the name "Casquinampo" or, in its shortened form, "Kasqui," after the Casquinampo Indians who are indicated in French maps of 1681 and 1688 as living on an island below Chattanooga. The name "Cussate" appears in 1708 on a map made by Thomas Nairne of South Carolina, and is used by other Carolinians of that time. This name is evidently another spelling of the "Coste" of De Soto's time, and refers to the Koasati Indians. In Popple's map of 1733 there are three different names for three different parts of the stream: "Hogohegee" for the lower part,

"Callamaco" for the middle, "Acanseapi" for the upper. The historian Ramsey, echoing the early usages, insists on "Kalla-muchee" for the main stream; "Cootcla" for the portion from the mouth of the Little Tennessee to the French Broad; and "Hogohegee" for the Holston. Dr. John Mitchell's map of 1755 shows the Tennessee as "River of the Cherakees or Hogohege or Callamaco"; the Little Tennessee as the "Tenassee or Satico (Settico)"; the Hiwassee as the "Euphasee"; the Clinch as the "Pelisipi." Christopher Gist called it simply the Cherokee River, or sometimes the "Cuttawa," after the name "Kituhwah" which the Cherokees applied to themselves. The name "Tennessee" in its present spelling first appears in 1754, in the usage of Governor Glenn of South Carolina; but then it referred to the present Little Tennessee, and was derived, as has been earlier stated, from the old Cherokee town, "Tanasi," on that river.

The Indians themselves always called the river "Hogo-hegee"—meaning "the Big River." They never called it "Tennessee." But the name of the river has always been some Indian word and never anything out of English, French, or Spanish.

For many reasons, the happiest and most descriptive of the early names is "River of the Cherokees," which was used by both English and French in the eighteenth century. From the first beginnings of the white man's encroachments west of the mountains until the Cherokee Removal of 1838, the Tennessee was in very fact the "River of the Cherokees." Although it was also in some measure the river of the Chick-asaws and the Creeks, the Cherokees made their homes upon its banks and controlled the largest portion of its waters. Of all the tribes whose history is connected with the Tennessee, they resisted most sternly and consistently the white man's invasion of their homeland.

The mountainous eastern part of the Tennessee Valley, where the Cherokees lived, was in fact the inner citadel of the Indian race in the country east of the Mississsippi. The oncoming white population could, and did, flow around it in all directions, but did not finally enter and possess it until the sixty-second year of the independence of the United States.

From the east and southeast, this citadel was guarded from access by the bulwark of the Appalachians, "a world of mountains piled upon mountains," in William Bartram's phrase, which send long ridges far south into the upcountry of South Carolina and Georgia. To the north was the "good savannah land" of Middle Tennessee and Kentucky, bordered on its eastern flank by the wild interminable plateaus and ridges of the Cumberland highlands. In colonial times, all the country between the Tennessee and the Ohio was a "hunting ground," unoccupied except by some small fragments of the Shawnee tribe, who lived precariously at the "French Lick" (Nashville). The white invader finally reached this country from the east, by way of the Valley of Virginia and Cumberland Gap, but any white invader who came from the north had first to break through the stubborn Iroquois and then dare the Shawnees of the Ohio Valley. Nobody attempted that route in the early days. On the southwest, guarding the approaches up the Mississippi Valley, were the Chickasaws, who blocked every approach made by the Spanish and French. To the south, the great confederation of the Creeks occupied the prairies and broken lands between the Tennessee River and the Gulf, on whose coastal plains lived the Choctaws and the Seminoles. The Cherokee country, in short, was difficult to approach and still more difficult to penetrate. To this day, despite the railroads and highways that cross it or thread its valleys, it remains rather inaccessible, and the thin population of mountainfolk who inhabit it cherish their isolation and independence as did their Cherokee predecessors.

At the time when the tribes of the Valley first became

well known to the English and French—that is, the late
seventeenth century—the domain of the Cherokees covered
the upper part of the Tennessee Valley and stretched southeast into the uplands of Georgia and South Carolina. Seemingly, they had no towns on the north side of the Tennessee
River at this time, and the Hiwassee Valley was the western
limit of their actual habitations. Their territorial claims, however, though always a little vague, included all of East and
Middle Kentucky, all of Tennessee up to the line of the Tennessee River on the west, and even extended south into Alabama and northeast into a part of Virginia and North Carolina. With the Chickasaws they acted as traditional guardians
of the "hunting ground" between the Ohio and the Tennessee, and in 1715 they combined with the Chickasaws to
drive out the Shawnees from the French Lick, on the Cumberland. The Chickasaws claimed all the land between the
Tennessee and the Mississippi, as far north as the Ohio, but
they had no towns on the Tennessee during historic times.
Their home was the headwaters of the Yazoo River in northern Mississippi. They were a small tribe, but their martial
spirit and courage made them important out of all proportion to their numbers. James Adair, who lived among them
for many years, loved them best of all the southern tribes,
and always referred to them as "gallant" or "brave" or
"cheerful brave Chikkasah." South of the Great Bend of the
Tennessee was the land of the Muskhogee tribes, more commonly known as the Creek Indians. At some early time there
must have been Creek towns on the Upper Tennessee, from
which they were driven by the Cherokees. There was traditional enmity between the Cherokees and the Creeks, and the
two nations were frequently at war. As a result of certain
victories over the Creeks, the Cherokees avowed a claim to
the land immediately south of the Great Bend, as far west
as Bear Creek, but this claim was never very stoutly maintained. The famous Creek Path intersected the Tennessee near

Guntersville, Alabama, and this intersection was long familiarly known as Creek Crossing Place. From the Creek Crossing Place the Indian traveler could go north into Tennessee,
or he could bear southeast to the Carolina frontier. Although
the home of the Creeks was far to the south of the river,
they used the Tennessee regularly in their forays to the north,
and their shadow fell menacingly upon the stream until Andrew Jackson broke their power at the Battle of Horseshoe
Bend.

The true seat of the Cherokee Nation, as distinguished
from the territory they claimed and used, extended from
the south bank of the Tennessee, in its eastern part, to the
headwaters of the Savannah. There were three divisions of
the nation. The Upper, or Overhill, Cherokee towns began
at the mouth of the Little Tennessee and were scattered south-
eastward along its valley and the valley of the Hiwassee—
those north of the Hiwassee being sometimes referred to as
"Valley" towns. The Middle Cherokee towns were farther
south, in the upland region near the source of the Little Tennessee and the head of the Savannah. The Lower Cherokee
towns were still farther south and east, along the Keowee and
its branches. There were small differences of dialect among
these three divisions, but all were one nation, and all looked
upon Chota, on the Little Tennessee, as their sacred town and
capital. It was a city of refuge, not unlike the Biblical cities
of refuge, in that it furnished sanctuary for a manslayer or
prisoner of war. No blood could be shed within its bounds.
It was their "old beloved town," the place where they met to
negotiate and to make treaties.

The word "Cherokee" has no meaning in the Cherokee
language. They referred to themselves as "Tsalagi" or "Tsar-
agi," or, better still, as "Ani-Yunwiya"—"the real people" or
"the principal people." For ceremonial usage they called
themselves "Ani-Kituhwagi," or "people of Kituhwa." They
were, as their language shows, a people of Iroquoian stock,

and at some distant time may have seceded from the Iroquois nation and wandered south in a series of migrations which brought them to their mountain home. Possibly they did not reach the Tennessee country until the seventeenth century.

Like other eastern tribes, the Cherokees called the Delawares "Grandfather" and showed them ceremonial deference. Thus Cherokee usage helps to authenticate the legend of the Walam Olum, or Indian "Edda," which credits the Delawares with being first progenitors. During their wanderings, which the historic Cherokees could but dimly recall, they lived at one time in the country of the upper Ohio. Other fragmentary memories connected them with the region near Charlottesville, Virginia, the Peaks of Otter, in Virginia, and Watauga Old Fields, on the upper Holston.

Among the Indians of the South the Cherokees were a somewhat peculiar and separate people. Whether because their long wandering cut them loose from their traditions or because their temperament naturally inclined them toward new things, they had a definitely progressive turn. They forgot their own traditions and history with a facility that seems amazing in a primitive people. Although not fundamentally unlike other Indians in customs and beliefs, they dropped off and simplified where others, through sheer accretion, got involved in accumulations of myth and taboo. The Creeks, for example, had more than forty "clans" on which to base their complicated rules for marriage; but the Cherokees, in contrast, had only seven: Wolf People, Deer People, Bird People, Paint People, Blue People, Kituwah People, and Long Hair People. They had no real cycle of cosmic myths and only a slight trace of a migration legend. They had no official priesthood. The story is that once they had a priesthood, a hereditary caste called the Nicotani, as elevated and strict as existed among the Natchez Indians. These Indian ecclesiastics became insolent and overbearing, and abused their personal privileges

to an intolerable degree. By a kind of droit de seigneur, they
even went so far as to appropriate the wives of young warriors who were away on the warpath. A young warrior, thus
injured, formed a conspiracy against the priesthood. The
offending Nicotani were massacred to the last man, and from
that time such religious wisdom as remained was preserved
by individual shamans who passed along the tradition as best
they could.

The progressiveness of the Cherokees makes them a little
annoying to anthropologists, who naturally want primitive
peoples to exhibit a rigid conservatism. James Adair, the
trader, who preferred the Chickasaws to the Cherokees, spoke
of the latter as "a nest of apostate hornets" who paid "little
attention to grey hairs and have fast been degenerating from
their primitive religious principles." James Mooney, who investigated the Cherokees during the eighteen-nineties, with
special attention to the most primitive fragment of the tribe,
the people of the Qualla Reservation in North Carolina,
found them "accustomed to look forward to new things
rather than to dwell upon the past."

Their unstable culture may have rendered the Cherokees
a somewhat less forbidding obstacle to the advance of the
white man than the more firmly organized Iroquois of the
north. Their tribal government, if the term may be used,
did not bind them closely. They were always falling apart
into factions, which followed rival chiefs. They had no Long
House like the Iroquois, and no federal compact, only an
extremely loose confederacy of widely scattered towns.

Yet these same tendencies made them very adaptable,
and they were the quickest of all the Indian peoples to assimilate the white man's civilization. Whether or not this was a
virtue depends on the point of view. At any rate, shortly
after they came into close contact with the English settlers,
they began to take over the white man's agricultural economy
and his political institutions. During the post-Revolutionary

period Sequoyah, a Cherokee who could not speak or write English, invented the Cherokee alphabet, or syllabary. Under his tutelage the Cherokees rapidly achieved literacy in their own language, without waiting to be prompted by white schoolteachers and missionaries. No other Indians on the continent displayed exactly this kind of genius.

Although rightly called the mountaineers of the Indian race, the Cherokees lived among the mountains rather than upon them, choosing for their homes the fertile valleys along rivers and creeks, the sheltered coves, the low bluffs between river and mountain, the wooded islands in the river itself. No visitor to the old Cherokee country can today fail to be impressed with its surpassing beauty. Of all the southern lands inhabited by Indian peoples, the Cherokee country is most like that famous country of upper New York State in which Fenimore Cooper's imagination placed Uncas and Chingachgook. Even more seductively than the northern country it invites the traveler to think, as he looks at its greens merging hazily into blues, with no sharp outline anywhere, that here, surely, was the true home of the "Noble Savage," as that ideal being was conceived by Chateaubriand and Rousseau. There is no point in all this country which does not have on its horizon the enormous mass of blue mountains, range piled on range; swift-running rivers and creeks always close at hand; alluvial fields good for corn and pasture; and limitless forests full of wild game and wild fruit. To the American pioneer who had lately left the sand and pine belt of Virginia and the Carolinas, the Cherokee country seemed desirable beyond compare. He looked at it with admiring and possessive eyes, and even while Cherokee bullets were whistling about his ears, made a mental note that hither he would return, here he would live.

In 1777 the American botanist, William Bartram, to whose *Travels* Wordsworth and Coleridge and other great European romanticists owe a considerable debt, visited Cowee

and other Middle Cherokee towns in western North Carolina and turned back from his projected trip just across the
mountains to the Overhill towns only because trouble was
rife between the Cherokees and the white settlers in Tennessee. His descriptions of the Cherokees and their habitat,
though overluxuriant for the modern taste, are full of a
charming conviction both of the beauty of the natural
scenery and of the nobility of the Cherokee inhabitants. In
the neighborhood of Cowee, on the headwaters of the Little
Tennessee, he encountered a band of Cherokee girls, engaged
in gathering the wild strawberries with which the valleys
abounded, and thus recorded his experience:

Proceeding on our return to town, continued through part
of this high forest skirting on the meadows; began to ascend the
hills of a ridge which we were under the necessity of crossing; and
having gained its summit, enjoyed a most enchanting view; a vast
expanse of green meadows and strawberry fields; a meandering
river gliding through, saluting in its various turnings the swelling,
green, turfy knolls, embellished with parterres of flowers and fruit-
ful strawberry beds; flocks of turkies strolling about them; herds
of deer prancing in the meads or bounding over the hills; companies of young, innocent Cherokee virgins, some busy gathering
the rich fragrant fruit, others having already filled their baskets,
lay reclined in the shade of floriferous and fragrant native bowers
of Magnolia, Azalea, Philadelphus, perfumed Calycanthus, sweet
Yellow Jessamine and cerulean Glycine frutescens, disclosing their
beauties to the fluttering breeze, and bathing their limbs in the
cool, fleeting streams; whilst other parties, more gay and libertine,
were yet collecting strawberries, or wantonly chasing their companions, tantalising them, staining their lips and cheeks with the
rich fruit.

The sylvan scene of primitive innocence was enchanting, and
perhaps too enticing for hearty young men long to continue idle
spectators.

In fine, nature prevailing over reason, we wished at least to
have a more active part in their delicious sports. Thus precipitately

resolving, we cautiously made our approaches, yet undiscovered, almost to the joyous scene of action. Now, although we meant no other than an innocent frolic with this gay assembly of hama-dryades, we shall leave it to the person of feeling and sensibility to form an idea to what lengths our passions might have hurried us, had it not been for the vigilance and care of some envious matrons who lay in ambush, and espying us, gave the alarm, time enough for the nymphs to rally and assemble together. We however pursued and gained ground on a group of them, who had incautiously strolled to a greater distance from their guardians, and finding their retreat now like to be cut off, took shelter under cover of a little grove; but on perceiving themselves to be discovered by us, kept their station, peeping through the bushes; when observing our approaches, they confidently discovered themselves, and decently advanced to meet us, half unveiling their blooming faces, incar-nated with the modest maiden blush, and with native innocence and cheerfulness, presented their little baskets, merrily telling us their fruit was ripe and sound.

We accepted a basket, sat down and regaled ourselves on the delicious fruit, encircled by the whole assembly of the inno-cent jocose sylvan nymphs; by this time the several parties, under the conduct of the elder matrons, had disposed themselves in companies on the green turfy banks.

My young companion, the trader, by concessions and suitable apologies for the bold intrusion, having compromised the matter with them, engaged them to bring their collections to his house at a stipulated price; we parted friendly.

Meetings of white man and Indian in the Cherokee country were not always so idyllic, of course. Yet there were elements of the idyllic in Cherokee life, and the myth of the Noble Savage, to which Bartram obviously subscribed, was not pure fiction.

With a shrewd eye for convenience and for the pieties of life, the Cherokee lived where he had mountains at his back and a river in his front. The invading enemy could be met in a narrow mountain pass, far away from his retreat, or at some ford overhung with trees and cane, and there ambushed and quelled at a safe distance. But if the enemy pushed near, in a surprise attack, the Cherokee slipped into the mountain forests with his women and children, and left his simple dwellings to be ravaged. They could easily be rebuilt. The dwelling mounds and townhouse mounds got a fresh layer of earth above the debris and ashes, and thus grew a step higher. Destruction of the crops in the fields near by was a more serious matter; but the crops did not often suffer destruction until such men as Nolichucky Jack Sevier began their swift raids, in the bad times when every new treaty begot a new war.

Bathing in the river was for the Cherokee as much a sacred duty as a pleasure and a sanitary necessity. The Cherokee was likely to reverse the white man's practice, and decline to go bathing in very hot weather; that was bad for the health. At other times, especially in the coldest weather, bathing was in order, and it was compulsory when the Cherokee warrior wished to purify himself, body and soul, for a hunting expedition, for a religious festival, or for a battle. Before bathing, the warrior steamed himself in a small "hothouse" or "sweathouse" until all impurities were distilled away. To aid the sweating, he took copious draughts of the sacred "black drink," or *Cusseena,* brewed from a holly-like shrub called "cassine." Then, to use the words of Adair: "In the coldest weather, and when the ground is covered with snow, against their bodily ease and pleasure, men and children turn out of their warm houses or stoves, reeking with sweat, singing their usual sacred notes, *Yo, Yo,* &c. at the dawn of day, adoring Yo He Wah, at the gladsome sight of the morn; and thus they skip along, echoing praises, till they get to the river, when they instantaneously plunge into it. If the water is frozen, they break the ice with a religious impatience: After bathing, they return home, rejoicing as they run for having so well performed their religious duty, and thus purged away the impurities of the preceding day by ablution."

For failure to bathe, the Cherokees raked the arms and legs of the sinner with snake's teeth. The women, for modesty, were not required to take part in the mass bathing but purified themselves separately, and as their discretion directed them. The sweating and bathing process was supposed to be a cure of disease, and was regularly practiced for that purpose. But when the smallpox first hit the Cherokees, and became epidemic among them, the old remedy produced terrible fatalities; for in a high fever, with the pustules upon them, the warriors drank and sweated and plunged into the icy river, and forthwith died.

The river was also a roadway connecting the Cherokees with neighbors and with distant nations. In a dry season, when the water was low, the Cherokee might prefer one of the well-known overland paths. But often enough he chose the river. Going north up the Holston, he might hide his canoe and then walk on through the Shenandoah Valley. Or he might go down the Little Tennessee to the Big Tennessee and so finally into the Ohio or Illinois country. According to Ramsey, a voyage from the headwaters of the Holston to the mouth of the Wabash required, in Indian parlance, "two paddles, two warriors, three moons." The Cherokees made little use of the bark canoe favored by the northern Indians, but preferred the "dugout canoe," which was hollowed and shaped by fire from a pine or poplar log. Since it took long to burn a canoe into the proper size and shape, they were glad to adopt the white man's ax and adz as soon as they learned about these tools. The canoes might be thirty to forty feet long, and two or three feet wide at the center. These would carry fifteen or twenty men. Still larger canoes, as much as sixty feet in length, were also used; in the early times these were called "pirogues." The Cherokees managed their craft skillfully, with paddles for ordinary navigation, with poles for a heavy pull upstream. For stream-crossing and short bits of navigation they sometimes used the "bullboat"— a round-shaped coracle made of buffalo hides calked with pine pitch and fitted on a frame of light wood.

# CHAPTER IV

# Myths and Games of the Cherokees

**M**OUNTAINS and rivers of the Cherokee country were the scene of legends and myths, some of which have been preserved for us by James Mooney in his great study, *Myths of the Cherokee*. The mountains, said the Cherokees, were made by the Great Buzzard who flew over the world shortly after the waters receded from the island that is the earth. "When he reached the Cherokee country," the story goes, "he was very tired, and his wings began to flap and strike the ground, and wherever they struck the earth there was a valley, and where they turned up again there was a mountain. When the animals saw this, they were afraid the whole world would become mountains, so they called him back, but the Cherokee country remains full of mountains to this day."

The eagle was the great sacred bird of the Cherokees, and they used its feathers in their Eagle Dance, as well as for other ceremonial purposes. These feathers could be procured only by a professional eagle-killer, preferably a man of another village or tribe, who was chosen because of his exact knowledge of the ritual for killing an eagle and the means of averting the vengeance of the eagles from the tribe who caused an eagle to be killed. The killing could be done only in the late fall or early winter, after frost had fallen and the snakes had hibernated. Otherwise the snakes, hearing the songs used for the Eagle Dance, would become greatly offended and would vent their anger upon the people.

The eagle-killer had to go alone into the mountains and fast and pray for four days or more. Then he killed a deer and placed its carcass on a high cliff, while he hid near by and sang in a very low voice the magical songs that call eagles down from the sky. Inevitably an eagle would come and alight on the carcass of the deer, and the eagle-killer would shoot it.

And then, did he go triumphantly back to the village? Nothing of the kind. He stood over the eagle's body, solemnly explained the situation, and begged its spirit not to seek vengeance—because, he cunningly declared, it was a Spaniard, not a beloved Cherokee, who had done the foul deed. Whereupon he went off, leaving the body on the rocks. There it must lie until the parasites had had time to crawl away. On his return to the village he said, in a casual way (so that the snakes would continue to be fooled and the eagles along with them): *A little snowbird has been killed*. After further elaborate ceremonies and precautions, hunters were appointed to secure the feathers. The Eagle Dance was then held.

The Cherokees feared and reverenced snakes and took care not to kill them. This feeling applied especially to the rattlesnake, which was considered chief of the snake tribe and was the focus of much sacred lore. The Cherokees also had stories of the Uktena, a mythical snake descended from a monster of early times. The Uktena haunted river pools and lonely places in the high mountains, and it was dangerous to meet one, or even to see one. The creature was as large as a tree trunk, and had a glittering crest in which was a diamond of great magical power. The Uktena could be killed, but only by a shot shrewdly aimed at one of the spots along his neck—the seventh spot from his head. The daring man who could hit this spot would become the owner of the gleaming precious stone, and thereby would be endowed with great powers as a wizard, provided he knew precisely how to tend and watch the stone.

The Tlanuwa, or great hawk, was another monstrous and exceedingly dangerous creature. In old times a pair of these great hawks had a nest in Blount County, Tennessee, on a high cliff that overhangs the Little Tennessee River, near the mouth of Citico Creek. They carried off dogs and even children and were a constant menace to the Cherokee towns along the river. A valiant medicine man let himself down over the cliff by a rope made of linn-tree bark at a time when the two old birds were absent from the nest. With great difficulty he twisted and swung past the overhanging cliff and with a crooked stick pulled himself into the cave where the nest was. There were four young Tlanuwa in it. He tossed the young hawks into the river far below. A great Uktena serpent rose from the deep pool and swallowed them. At that very moment the two old hawks returned. The medicine man hastily scrambled up the cliff and ran away. The old hawks did not notice him, for they saw the Uktena's head and know it had devoured their young. One of them swooped and seized the great snake and flew upward with it. The other tore at it with his beak and rent it into little pieces. The pieces, falling, made holes in the top of the cliff. These may still be seen. And below the cave where the nest of the Tlanuwa used to be are white streaks, caused by the droppings from the nest in those old times.

In the Little Tennessee, just above the mouth of Tellico River, there once lived a great fish called the Dakwa. The Dakwa upset a canoe full of warriors and swallowed one of them whole. Groping around in the darkness of the fish's belly, he found a mussel shell, and with its sharp edge cut his way out again. But he was baldheaded after that because the juices of the Dakwa's stomach scalded the hair off his pate.

An elaborate mythical story about Untsaiyi, the great

gambler, was localized in the Narrows of the Tennessee, just below the Suck, where the eddying currents produced the phenomenon known to the Cherokees as Untiguhi ("Pot in the Water") and to frontiersmen as the Boiling Pot. In this Cherokee story, a boy, the son of Thunder, journeyed west to look for his father, since he had sores all over his body that Thunder could cure. On his way he came to Untiguhi, which was the home of the great gambler, Untsaiyi. Untsaiyi, whose name means "Brass," was insatiably fond of gambling; in fact, he invented the "wheel and stick," or "chungke," game played by the Indians. Invariably he challenged every passer-by to a game with him. So when the son of Thunder came to the great flat rock beside the river which was Untsaiyi's home and asked him to tell where Thunder lived, the great gambler tried to lure him into playing. " 'Well,' said Untsaiyi, 'he lives in the next house; you can hear him grumbling there all the time . . . so we may as well have a game or two before you go on.' The boy said he had nothing to bet. 'That's all right,' said the gambler, 'we'll play for your pretty spots (the sores).' "

The boy refused and went on to the house of Thunder. There, after proper identification, Thunder acknowledged him as son and ordered his wife to boil a pot of water. He put some roots into the pot, boiled his son with the roots for a long while, then told his wife to hurl both boy and pot into the river. The boiling pot sank deep in the water and caused the great whirl known as Untiguhi. The steam from the pot scalded the trunks of the service tree and the calico bush which grew on the bank, and so they have blotches on their bark to this day. But the son of Thunder emerged with a clean, healthy skin.

There were sundry other tests and ordeals, from which the boy issued triumphant (because, of course, the son of Thunder is Lightning). Finally he was properly clothed by his father in buckskin suit and headdress, with a rattlesnake for a necklace, copperhead snakes for bracelets and anklets, and was equipped with a war club. Then the boy told his father how Untsaiyi had challenged him to a chungke game. "I will see that you win," said Thunder. And around the boy's wrist he tied a small gourd, from a hole in which protruded a string of beads. There was no end to the string inside, but Untsaiyi would not know that; he would want to play for the beads. " 'Now,' said his father, 'go back the way you came, and as soon as he sees you he will want to play for the beads. He is very hard to beat, but this time he will lose every game. When he cries out for a drink, you will know that he is getting discouraged, and then strike the rock with your war-club and water will come, so that you can play on without stopping. At last he will bet his life, and lose. Then send at once for your brothers to kill him, or he will get away, he is so tricky.' "

Sure enough, all happened as Thunder had said. Again and again the boy staked a string of beads long enough to reach around the playground. Each time Untsaiyi lost, but they played on, for the string of beads was endless. Untsaiyi wanted to stop for a drink, but the boy struck the rock, and water came. So they played on until Untsaiyi staked his wife, then his life, and lost.

" 'Let me go and tell my wife,' said Untsaiyi, 'so that she will receive her new husband, and then you may kill me.' " But the house had two doors. Untsaiyi slipped out the back and vanished. They boy summoned his brothers, and with their dog, the Horned Green Beetle, they began the chase. After a while they met an old woman who tried to deceive them by saying that Untsaiyi had not come that way. But the Beetle darted against her forehead, and it clanged like brass, making the sound *Untsaiyi-i-i-i!* So they knew the old woman was the gambler. The chase began once more, and went on to the edge of the world. There they caught Untsaiyi at last and pinned him down with a stake in the great water. There he lies forever, with two crows guarding the top of the stake.

Some of the brass from Untsaiyi's forehead rubbed off on the Beetle, and marks it today. The pot continues to boil in the waters below the Suck. And on the great flat stone where Untsaiyi played there can still be seen the grooves made by the rolling of Untsaiyi's wheel. Or they could be seen until the white man changed the river.

Another Cherokee legend of the Boiling Pot tells how canoes navigating the Narrows used to hug the bank and wait for the moment when the intermittent whirls of the Pot slackened and so permitted safe passage. Once two warriors going downriver checked their canoe to watch the motion of the Pot, but instead of slackening, the whirls widened and sucked in the canoe. The two warriors were thrown out of their boat and into the vortex. One man was seized by a great fish and disappeared instantly. "The other was taken round and round down to the very lowest center of the whirlpool, when another circle caught him and bore him outward and upward until he was finally thrown up again to the surface and floated out into the shallow water, whence he made his escape to shore. He told afterwards that when he reached the narrowest circle of the maelstrom the water seemed to open below him and he could look down as through the roof beams of a house, and there on the bottom of the river he had seen a great company of people, who looked up and beckoned to him to join them, but as they put up their hands to seize him the swift current caught him and took him out of their reach."

Undoubtedly the people who beckoned from the house at the bottom of the whirlpool were the Nunnehi, a race of supernatural beings who had townhouses deep in the river or on lonely balds, where few men ever climbed. It is hardly likely that the TVA, for all its wonder-working changes, has been able to eliminate the Nunnehi; they are not sub-

ject to mortal authority. Do the scientists of the TVA's floating laboratories or the pilots of towboats pushing barges
along the nine-foot navigation channel ever hear strange
drumming sounds in the water beneath them? Do surveyors
and foresters ever hear similar sounds on the slopes of the
remoter mountains? If they do, let them beware, for those
are the drums of the Nunnehi.

Like the Irish *sidhe*, the Nunnehi are of the shape and
appearance of mortals, and like to inveigle mortal men into
dwelling with them. The Cherokees had many tales of the
Nunnehi, in which sometimes the mortal visitor to their
habitations returns, and sometimes does not. Once a Cherokee
boy who was making a fishtrap in the river was approached
by one of the Nunnehi. The boy took him to be some person
of the neighborhood whom he could not exactly identify.
Upon invitation, this boy went with the Nunnehi to a village
near by that he had never seen before, feasted with the
people there, and had a pleasant overnight visit. Next morning his hosts put him on the road to home, but when he
had gone a step or so he looked back, only to discover that
his hosts and their houses, fields, and orchards had all suddenly vanished, and there was only wild empty country
everywhere around him. Wandering on, he was finally met
by his greatly distressed family, who had been searching for
him for a long time. When he told them his story, they
knew at once that he had dined with the Nunnehi, because
there was no other Cherokee town near by.

The story of this boy is unusual, in that he was permitted to return and lead a mortal life after eating the food
of the immortals. In stories about the Nunnehi—as in English and Celtic tales of the same kind—the visitor is in the
power of the immortals if he partakes of their food. Yahula
the trader, in one Cherokee story, ate with the Nunnehi, and
never thereafter consorted regularly with mortal folk. But
his songs, the crack of his whip, and the jingle of his ponies'

bells could long after be heard of nights in the mountains of North Georgia—and perhaps may still sometimes be heard, even today.

Most imperishable of all Cherokee myths are the animal stories which, in the delightful rendering given them by Joel Chandler Harris, have gone out over the world and are known as the tales of that wise and amiable darkey, Uncle Remus. Although nothing is more arguable than the source of an ancient folk tale, there is much probability that the Uncle Remus stories are at least partially of Indian origin, and there would be good reason to think that the Cherokees contributed heavily to Uncle Remus's stock of tales, along with other southern tribes. Contact between the Indian and the Negro began in the seventeenth century, when Indian war captives were enslaved and worked the low-country plantations along with the Negroes. It is supposed—though there were other types of contact—that the animal tales were carried by the captive Indians to the Negro slaves with whom they worked. The Indians, as Mooney points out, would have been less likely to accept and transmit the tale of the Negro than the Negro would be likely to absorb the tales told by the Indians.

At any rate the Rabbit, a wily, schemy character, is the center of many Cherokee tales, and is remarkably like the Br'er Rabbit of Uncle Remus. The Cherokees had the tale of Br'er Rabbit and the Tar Baby, but in their version it is the Rabbit and the Tar Wolf. In this story, a great drouth prevails, and all the animals, lean and thirsty, note that the Rabbit stays sleek and fine. They suspect that the rabbit is stealing their hoard of water and decide to catch him. They make a wolf out of pine gum and tar and put it near the well. The Rabbit comes up and sees the black image. " 'Who's there,' he said, 'but the tar wolf said nothing. He came nearer, but the wolf never moved, so he grew braver and said, 'Get out of my way or I'll strike you.' Still the wolf never moved and the Rabbit came up and struck it with his paw, but the gum held his foot and it stuck fast. Now he was angry and said, 'Let me go or I'll kick you.' Still the wolf said nothing. Then the Rabbit struck again with his hind foot, so hard that it was caught in the gum and he could not move, and there he stuck until the animals came for water in the morning."

There are many other Cherokee tales of the Uncle Remus type: "How the Terrapin Beat the Rabbit," "Why the Possum's Tail Is Bare," "Why the Deer's Teeth Are Blunt," and so on. In all of them the animals have human characteristics and dance, sing, and eat like Indians. The tribe of the Bears was viewed by the Cherokees as a clan of their own nation which had lapsed into a completely wild state. The Bears were therefore "brothers" of the Cherokees in a special sense. But in a more general sense all the animals were "brothers," and the appellation "br'er" used in the Uncle Remus tales may be taken as one indication of an Indian origin. Although all the tribes of the South had animal tales and must therefore have shared in the process of transmitting them to Negro and thence to white folklore, it is interesting to reflect that the Cherokees, who were so negligent about preserving their own traditions, may have had a considerable share in passing along what is now a definite part of American tradition.

Like other tribes of the South, the Cherokees were great sportsmen, and played with gusto the games known to all. The famous ball game was the most spectacular of these. The ball was handled by means of a racquet, or a pair of racquets; it might be better to say, sticks, with a simple form of cup or bowl at one end. Any number of players could take part, and each side strove to throw the ball between the goals, a pair of upright poles set at each end of the ball ground. It was a game of vehement and disorderly roughness, in which players were at liberty to interfere with their opponents in any way that occurred to them; they could strike, kick, or wrestle at pleasure. When a ball play was scheduled, weapons were always left at home, lest the two sides and their supporters be tempted to engage in actual battle. Before entering the game, the players were ceremoniously scratched on the naked skin with a sharp seven-toothed comb of turkey bone. The scratches had to draw blood from head to foot before they were deemed sufficient. In order to hit with the force of lightning, ball sticks were often made out of wood from a lightning-struck tree. "To play ball with" somebody meant, in Cherokee slang, the opposite of what it means with us. If the Cherokees said they had "played a ball game" with the Creeks, they might mean that they had met the Creeks in battle. An invitation to "play ball," when bad feeling was rife between two tribes, was a challenge to mortal combat.

The wheel and stick, or chungke, game said to have been invented by the gambler Untsaiyi required a carefully leveled yard or green of considerable dimensions. The "wheel" was a polished stone disk, "two fingers broad at the edge and two spans around." The sticks were javelinlike poles, eight feet long, tapering to a flat point. The game could be played by one or two on a side. The method of playing is well described by Adair:

They set off abreast of each other at 6 yards from the end of the playground; then one of them hurls the stone on its edge, in as direct a line as he can, a considerable distance toward the middle of the other end of the square. When they have ran a few yards each darts his pole, anointed with bear's oil, with a proper force, as near as he can guess in proportion to the motion of the stone, that the end may lie close to the stone. When this is the case, the person counts two of the game, and in proportion to the nearness of the poles to the mark, one is counted, unless by measuring both are found to be at an equal distance from the stone. In this manner the players will keep running most part of the day at half speed, under the violent heat of the sun, staking their silver ornaments, their nose, finger, and ear rings: their breast, arm, and wrist plates, and even all their wearing apparel except that which barely covers their middle. . . . The hurling stones which they use at present were time immemorial rubbed smooth on the rocks, and with prodigious labor. They are kept with strictest religious care from one generation to another, and are exempted from being buried with the dead. They belong to the town where they are used, and are carefully preserved.

When a war dance was not in progress and no prisoner was being tortured at the stake for a victory celebration, a Cherokee town like Chota, Toqua, Tomotley, or Great Tellico must have seemed a pleasant place, especially during the green months. It might even have had a touch of the idyllic about it, such as Bartram found at Cowee. For, to begin with, every Cherokee town was built upon a naturally beautiful site. Back of it, always, was some thickly wooded hillside or mountain slope, beyond which mountain ridge overlapped mountain ridge far into the blue and hazy distance. And in front of it, always, was some river or creek, its winding course marked by sycamores and willows, with canebrakes densely crowding its islands and its marshy edges. The town itself lay in the flat green valley between the high ground and the river. It blended unobtrusively into its surroundings; it made no great display of its presence.

In the center of the town, not far from the friendly river, rose the townhouse, pitched on its lofty mound, its one narrow door reached by steps cut in the earth or by a slanting path. It gave the general effect of a tower or rotunda, since it occupied most of the space on the top of the mound and was made of logs set upright in a circle, then plastered, roof and all, with earth. It was the "community center." Within its firelit interior warriors met in council, religious feasts were celebrated, and communal dances were held.

In front of the townhouse stretched the level chungke yard, which on good days always had its quota of eager athletic players. While they played and gambled, the old men sat in the shade and commented, women went to and fro on their tasks or sat near their cabin doorways at their basket weaving or skin dressing, children and dogs kept up a lively tumult, and a canoe passed now and then on the river or a young man came in from his fishtrap or his morning hunt.

The dwelling houses straggled along the river according to no particular plan. There were no streets; there were only paths. The houses were half hidden in the cornfields and orchards around them. They were real houses, built generally of small logs set upright, with wattled walls plastered over and whitewashed. The roof might be of rude clapboards, with saplings tied lengthwise over it for a wind brace. There would be doors, maybe windows, but no chimney. The Cherokees did not at first take up the white man's contrivance of fireplace and chimney; the smoke went out through a hole in the roof. Since the houses were too drafty and cold for winter habitation, each dwelling had a "hothouse" conveniently near. This was a small, earth-covered shelter with one tiny door, which could be entered only by crawling; in it the Indian family "holed up" during cold weather, almost like hibernating bears. In the straggling, informally arranged community, there might occasionally be a two-story house. This would probably belong to some chief or to the resident white trader.

But green and pleasant though the town might be, and sociable, merry, or gravely courteous its inhabitants, inevitably the time did come when the war drums beat, the war songs resounded, the women screamed their taunts, and the wild scalping cry, keen as a panther's shriek, filled all the valley. For the Cherokees, like other Indians, were first of all warriors, and they were most indomitable in their warfare. The American pioneers knew the Cherokees in their grimmest aspect, as fighters. From the standpoint of American history, the most important single fact about the great nation of the Cherokees is that they stood squarely across the westward path of the oncoming settlers, thwarted their advance into the Tennessee Valley itself, and prevented the valley from being completely occupied by the white man until nearly three-quarters of a century after the first settlement was made in East Tennessee.

# CHAPTER V

# The Carolina Traders and Their Empire

ALTHOUGH Virginia's interest in the western country was mild and spasmodic during the century preceding settlement, the first recorded exploration by Englishmen of the country west of the mountains originated in the Old Dominion. It came straight to the Overhill Cherokee country and resulted in the first known navigation—as it happened, an involuntary navigation—of the Tennessee by an Englishman.

In 1671 Abraham Wood, a business associate of William Byrd I, had a trading post, called Fort Henry, at the falls of the Appomattox (now Petersburg). From this place, in 1673, Wood sent out an expedition, headed by one James Needham, to investigate the country west of the mountains. Needham had arrived at Charles Town (now Charleston, South Carolina) three years before and had explored the back country with Henry Woodward of Charles Town, from whom he probably got the notion of entering the Tennessee region.

On his journey Needham took with him eight Indians, among them an Ocaneechi, named Indian John, and an illiterate youth, probably indentured to Wood, named Gabriel Arthur. From Abraham Wood's letter, written after Needham's death to the treasurer of the Lords Proprietors of Carolina, we get the details of this early adventure.

Needham probably started from the Yadkin River and crossed the mountains by a trail used later by Daniel Boone. He then passed the French Broad and came to a palisaded Cherokee town on the Little Tennessee. The Cherokees had a hundred and fifty canoes on the river, each one "made sharpe at both ends like a wherry" and capable of carrying twenty men. Needham's packhorse was a curiosity to them; but they had sixty excellent flintlock guns which they had been using against the Spanish in Florida.

After making friends with the Cherokees, Needham left Gabriel Arthur with the Indians and went back to Wood's post to prepare for a second trip. Just as he was starting out on the second trip, he had trouble with the Ocaneechi, Indian John. In the ensuing fracas Indian John shot Needham "near ye burr of ye eare," ripped the heart from his body, and, looking toward the English plantations, cried derisively to his more timid Tomahitan companions that "he vallued not all ye English." Led by Indian John, the party then hurried on to the Cherokee country to dispose of Gabriel Arthur, but Arthur was saved from death at the stake by the intervention of the Cherokee chief. This worthy appeared, gun on shoulder, just as fire was about to be applied to the brush heaped around young Arthur. He cried out, challengingly: "Who is that that is goeing to put fire to ye Englishman?" A Waxhaw Indian sprang up and shouted, "That am I." Whereupon the chief calmly shot the Waxhaw and set Arthur free.

Young Arthur was adopted into the tribe and was taken with them on several raids against the Florida Spanish and against the Indians of the north. On another journey he went with them by canoe down the Tennessee to hunt bear, wild hogs, and beaver. Thus he became the first white man of record to navigate the river. Afterward he escaped, to tell the story preserved in Abraham Wood's letter.

James Needham undoubtedly deserved the tribute paid

him by Wood: "Soe died this heroick English man whose fame shall never die if my penn were able to eternize it which had adventured where never any English man had dared to attempt before." The other side of the venture is suggested in Wood's rueful addition to his epitaph: "And with him died one hundered and forty-foure pounds starling of my adventure." Heroic individual enterprise plus commercial speculation—thus early, in 1673, the two themes of western expansion appear. Wood's encomium is the epitome of many such ventures. At the same time, so far as Virginia was concerned, the Needham expedition was an isolated incident. The Byrds and their successors were interested in the Indian trade, but they were soon far outdistanced in the Tennessee country by their Carolina competitors. And Carolina's real competitors were the French, whose coureurs de bois were pushing in from north and south.

Jean Couture, one of these coureurs de bois, must be put down as the first European known to have made a complete trip up the Tennessee, from its mouth to somewhere on its upper reaches. Couture served under Tonty, La Salle's lieutenant, but after La Salle's death grew discontented with the strict regulations of the Montreal authorities and left the French service. At some time before 1696 he went up the Tennessee by canoe to the Overhill Cherokee towns, and thence through the mountains to Charles Town, where he offered to guide interested speculators to the western country, which he described as a region full of gold and pearls. Nothing came of this offer, but in 1700 Couture served as guide for a party of Carolina traders who went overland to the Tennessee and thence down the river to the Mississippi. This was a more or less official exploratory venture, prompted by Carolina's desire to find ways of checking the French advance as well as to extend their growing Indian trade. Undoubtedly other coureurs de bois, like Couture, deserted the French service for the Carolina interest, for on an early eighteenth century French map a suggestive legend is written along the line of the Tennessee: *Route que les François tiennent pour se rendre à la Carolinne.* But there were other French coureurs and traders who did not go over to Carolina. From Louisiana the French began to feel their way toward the Tennessee Valley, and even to make bold approaches to the Cherokee towns.

Among the Carolinians were farsighted men who had grand schemes for opening the Tennessee route into the western country. By 1700, their traders had already crossed the Mississippi, which they reached by a southerly route running through the Creek country to the Chickasaw nation. But this overland route, with its numerous river crossings, was difficult for their caravans of pack horses and Indian burden bearers. Furthermore, the friendship of the Creeks was an uncertain quantity. If they developed the Tennessee route, they would portage only between the headwaters of the Savannah and the Hiwassee; the rest would be by boat. If the friendship of the Cherokees were assured, Carolina would have a powerful Indian ally against a possible Creek-French combination.

Thomas Nairne and Price Hughes had good ideas as to how this goal might be attained. Nairne, who was Indian agent for the proprietors of the Carolina colony, recognized the key position of the Cherokees; they were, he declared, Carolina's "only defense on the Back parts." He wished to organize the Cherokees into expeditions, led by chosen Carolina traders, which would harry the Louisiana French and "persuade" the coastal Indians. Smaller tribes, like the Natchez and the Chickasaws, could be urged to remove into the neighborhood of the Tennessee River. On the Tennessee itself he visualized the establishment of trading depots, eventually to be protected by forts. He had picked out a good place for one such depot, at a "low riff of rocks"—evidently Muscle Shoals. Furthermore, he deemed that the fur trade of the northwest

might be diverted from French markets to Charles Town, by
way of the Tennessee River. Unfortunately, Nairne's backwoods diplomacy was spoiled by Charles Town intrigues
against him, which resulted in his imprisonment for a while.
He repaired his political fences and got out of prison again,
only to be swallowed up in the great Indian uprising of 1715,
known as the Yamassee War. During this disturbance Nairne
was captured by hostile Indians and burned at the stake.

Price Hughes, an able Welshman, was a friend of Nairne
and shared Nairne's ideas about the development of the back
country, but he differed in that he wanted to establish not
only trading depots but actual settlements. He had a plan for
founding a colony of Welshmen in the Mississippi Valley, and
in the interest of this plan and of Carolina expansion he engaged in much personal exploration of the country. He visited
the Cherokees and navigated the Tennessee. Returning, he
wrote to his brother-in-law: "I've been a considerable way to
the Westwd. upon the branches of the Mesisipi, where I saw
a country as different from Carolina as the best parts of our
country are from the fens of Lincolnshire."

Hughes's plan was the first really definite scheme for
British colonization west of the Appalachians. While his letters and petitions were being slowly mulled over in London,
Hughes kept busy in the back country. He extended the
Carolina trading posts, he renewed and strengthened Carolina's old and valuable alliance with the Chickasaws, he even
temporarily persuaded the Choctaws to flop over from the
French to the British side. Venturing at last too deep into
French territory, he was arrested and taken to Mobile. There
he was subjected to a kind of third-degree treatment by Bien-
ville, the French governor, who interviewed the spirited
Welshman for three days before letting him go. Setting out
alone for Charles Town, Hughes was attacked and killed by
a party of Tohome Indians.

So the great schemes, for all their intelligence, came to

nothing. If any of them had succeeded, it is possible that the English settlements might have advanced from Carolina to the Tennessee River, or beyond, during the first half of the eighteenth century. But probably the Yamassee War, which raged so fiercely as to imperil the very existence of the Carolina colony, would have impeded and delayed any sort of plans for western colonization. When the war was over, the surviving traders returned from the beleaguered colony and its outlying forts to their homes among the Indians, and Carolinians began all over again the slow process of establishing their trade empire. It would have to be a trade empire, not a planned settlement, at least for the time being.

The half century from about 1715 to 1765 is a rather obscure period in the history of the Tennessee Valley, as it is, for that matter, in the history of all the trans-Appalachian part of the South. Except for Verner Crane, John Alden, and a very few others, our historians have preferred to dwell upon the second half of the eighteenth century, when western settlement actually got under way, and they have neglected the earlier period. It is hard to realize that, before the day of the long hunter and the pioneer settler there was another frontier, quite different from the later one that we know so well. In the South this older frontier, the frontier of the traders, was chiefly the domain of Carolina, and Charles Town was its capital. And the story of the Tennessee River during this early period is largely the story of Carolina's persistent attempts to get a foothold in the Cherokee country. The Carolinians aimed to provide the Tennessee with what it has always notably lacked—a mouth opening on the ocean, or, in other words, direct access to a seaport. They wanted to develop a trade route leading from the Carolina upcountry directly through the mountains to the Tennessee. To that end they learned and practiced a backwoods diplomacy which had no parallel in later times. The Carolina trader was the instrument and agent of this diplomacy.

The picture of the typical frontiersman, entrenched in our minds by history and tradition, will not give us much insight into the Carolina trader. He was a frontiersman too, but not a long hunter, a settler, a squatter, or a land speculator. The difference between the "old traders" and the pioneers was fundamental. The traders were interested in the Indians as Indians; their lives and hopes depended upon their ability to take the Indian point of view; and they were, in fact, prone to "go native" and prefer the Indian way to the white way. To the pioneers, on the other hand, the Indian was an obstacle, to be eliminated by fair means or foul. The means did not greatly matter, because the Indian was an inferior, a savage who deserved little more consideration than a buffalo or a tree. With this contempt, of course, there soon came to be mixed a certain admiration, at first grudging, later wistful and almost regretful.

Among the earliest Carolina traders were men of an extraordinarily high type, with gifts of statecraft that set them apart from the rapscallions and semi-outlaws whom the near approach of the settlements finally brought into the Indian trade. Men like Nairne and Hughes were persons of substance and ambition. The complex frontier situation evoked in them a wide range of talents. They did not sit at home in their Georgian mansions and countinghouses while their hirelings went abroad among the savages. They went deep into the wilderness, learned the languages and ways of the Indian nations, and exerted their genius to win among the Indian chiefs a prestige which was the envy and despair of their French rivals. As everyday matter of fact, they carried in their heads the names and locations of tribes and towns, their feuds and alliances, their key personages, their local mores, their political and strategic possibilities. They were economic geographers, who knew the pattern of rivers, mountains, paths, fertile savannas, and had calculated their future worth. They were frontier diplomats, skilled in artifice and persuasion;

and they were also men of war if need arose, born to command, swift and ruthless in attack. Nearly Indian themselves, they often led armies of Indians. A few white men, accompanying and leading a large party of Indian warriors—this was the typical expeditionary force of the earliest times. And on the home front they were colonial politicians, whose views had a continental range. They could sit in council, argue in assembly, and frame a petition and take it to court. They studied the devious politics of Queen Anne's court, in fact, no less shrewdly than the politics of the forest. Except for a few great planters of Virginia, who as yet moved a little slowly, there were no leaders quite like them anywhere else in the American colonies.

Of second rank, but no less remarkable, were the traders who habitually lived among the Indians, and came to Charles Town only to market their peltries and to refit for the next trading year. Some of these were "factors," located at permanent stations—then called "factories"—and responsible to a Charles Town employer. A factor at an important post might have under his supervision assistant factors at more distant towns. Others were independent traders, or "traders on their own account." Once the Indian trade was fully organized and became a matter of prime concern, all traders were licensed and supervised by the provincial government, the more rigidly as time went on.

The independent trader, who predominated among the Cherokees, represents the type of frontiersman with whom the Indian tribes of the Tennessee Valley were best acquainted in those years. He is the "old trader" of whom Adair loves to talk. Since the Indian trade was first of all a business enterprise, these traders were businessmen who had to understand the ins and outs of an extremely risky calling. If they were shrewd and lucky enough, they might accumulate wealth and return permanently to Charles Town to set up as merchants or planters. But they might easily run into debt, in which case they were careful not to return to Charles Town, lest they find themselves in the debtors' prison. Or they might, like the great majority, neither accumulate nor lose, but go on from year to year, contentedly arriving nowhere in particular, and becoming ever more Indian.

These men also were frontier diplomats, whose job it was —from the standpoint of Charles Town—to keep the Indians in a good humor generally and well disposed toward the government and themselves. They were the eyes of the colony. It was their duty to observe and report promptly all important news: the death of chiefs, the succession of new chiefs, the presence of visitors of any sort, the raids carried out and the scalps taken. They were required to calculate and report the number of "gun men" in each tribe. They were charged with noting the best Indian hunters, that these might be rewarded by the colony in some special way, with a bonus or a medal. When occasion arose, the trader was invariably the "linguister," or interpreter, for traveling embassies and distinguished visitors. He was also a guide and a scout and a war leader.

The records tell us the names of many such traders, but provokingly little about the individuals. Eleazar Wiggan, for example, was with the Overhill Cherokees as early as 1711 and was known to them as "the Old Rabbit"—perhaps an affectionate tribute to craft and wiliness; but we know little of him, or of David Dowie, or William and Joseph Cooper, or Robert Bunning. Ludovick Grant stands out more clearly. A Scot of a ruined Jacobite family, he perhaps chose the highlands of the Cherokees as a wilderness substitute for his own lost highlands, and became a man of great influence among the Cherokees. He appears at several crises, and was evidently a man of education and judgment. We know most of all about James Adair, who generally lived with the Chickasaws, but visited also among the Cherokees and other tribes. And we know most about Adair because in his *History of the*

*American Indians* he left a unique record of his wanderings, his observations of Indian life, and his views of their world.

There was only one Adair, and he should not be taken as completely representative. Yet it changes all conventional notions of the old frontier to realize that Adair existed and that his book was possible. To Adair, apparently, it was not so remarkable as it may seem to us that he should sit down among his "old friendly Chikkasah" and write a long systematic study of the Indian tribes of the South. His purpose was to trace out analogies between the life of the ancient Hebrews and the life of the Indians. He was no less concerned to correct much prevalent misinformation about the Indians, disseminated by writers who had never been among them, and to express himself freely on Indian affairs and colonial policy. To accomplish this, he had freshened up his knowledge of the Hebrew language; and though he regretted that he was far away from libraries and the conversation of the learned, he was able to produce a work that he was not ashamed to present to the distinguished friends and patrons, acquainted like himself with Indian affairs, who appear in his dedication: Sir William Johnson (whose name was in the manuscript dedication, but who died before the book was published); Colonel George Groghan, George Galphin, and Lachlan McGilwray. Such men had often urged Adair to use his opportunities for firsthand observation (or so he represents in his modest dedication), and like him had been disgusted with the "fictitious and fabulous, or very superficial and conjectural accounts of the Indian natives" which had been imposed upon the public. His own book might be speculative in its accounts of origins. But in its substance it contained nothing but what he had seen and experienced during his forty years among the southern Indians.

It was not easy for him to do his writing by daytime, for his Indian friends were suspicious of writing and would always want to know what he was doing. He had to conceal his work. We should probably imagine him as using the night hours for composition. With the wind in the pines, and Indian dogs clamoring at the moon, how often he must have turned away from the wilderness scene at his door, lit a candle at the low-burning fire, sharpened his goose quill, and begun a new page. In his memory were the vivid incidents of the day just past, when he had heard the Indian orators exhort their people to hold fast to the old faith and reverence their fathers. Were these people savages? Were they not more truly religious, more genuinely civilized, than the merchants of Charles Town and the schemy colonial politicians? Why was it that the Indians deemed the whites an accursed people and despised them for their ignorance and contempt of the laws of God? To the whites, the Indians were alien and outcast; but to the Indians, the whites were barbarian, and they themselves were the chosen of God. The Indian faith was nearer the ancient Hebrew faith, in both precept and example.

When the manuscript was finished, Adair took it to Charles Town. The forthcoming publication of his book, by subscription, was announced in the *South Carolina Gazette* and the Savannah (Georgia) *Gazette*. He made a trip to New York to arrange for publication, and while there took occasion to visit his friend Sir William Johnson, at Johnson Hall, in the Mohawk Valley. That was in 1768. But not until 1775, after the manuscript had been revised, did the book appear, and then it was published in London. It was the first book written west of the Appalachians—though nobody then thought of it in such a way. That distinction, notable though it is, is the least of its distinctions. Nothing else of its day and time, or of our day and time, is quite like it.

Yet the author of this book was only a trader—a younger son, probably, of a Scotch-Irish or English-Irish-Scotch baronet who like many other younger sons came to the forests of the west to seek his fortune. And Adair was as

good a trader and frontiersman as he was a writer. Undoubtedly he was as skillful in getting a pack train across a difficult
ford or in making a "talk" as were his less literate contem-
poraries. Like them, he took an Indian wife and became in
many respects an Indian. Like them, he could wage war or
peace as occasion required, he fell in debt, he quarreled with
the Charles Town authorities, and had ideas about the conduct of frontier business which Charles Town did not always
accept. Nevertheless, Charles Town benefited much from his
diplomatic skill, for it was probably Adair's genius that kept
the Chickasaws in firm alliance with the English and so put
a major obstacle in the way of French advance up the Mississippi. If Adair was thus capable, we may infer that among
the other traders of the better sort were men of Adair's type,
of as good an origin and education, if not of as much genius,
who shared his views and inclinations, but did not sit down
in the wilderness to write a book.

There were very many others, less able, nameless or all
but nameless. Before 1715 about one hundred traders are
mentioned in the public records of Charles Town for their
services to the colony—or for their misdemeanors; and about
as many more are named from 1715 to 1732. In the earliest
period, English names predominate, with an occasional Scotsman or Irishman. Later the Scots predominate: Campbell,
Gillespie, McGillivray, McIntosh. Since the traders, like the
coureurs de bois, invariably married into the tribe where they
lived, it is easy to understand why the pioneers, in their
troubles with the Indians, so often found themselves confronted by redheaded warriors or by chiefs with names
like Weatherford, McGillivray, and Ross, or were blessedly
snatched from the torture stake by the intervention of "beloved women" with names like Nancy Ward.

Although the frontier diplomacy of the Carolina traders
was masterly, it was probably no better, where individuals
were concerned, than French diplomacy. The supremacy of

Carolina over France rested, in the end, on the excellence of the English goods exchanged for peltries and on the capacity of the Carolinians to deliver the goods, at a fair price, in quantity and with regularity. The Indians often frankly declared that they liked the French extremely well, maybe better than the English; but they preferred English goods, and furthermore could always get English goods.

English goods had substance. The exchange of raw materials for manufactured products did not mean an exchange of valuables for mere baubles, as romance sometimes makes out. Baubles there were in truth—ribbons, bracelets, glass beads, ruffled shirts, laced hats, and petticoats; and mirrors for Indian warriors to hang around their necks in order to keep their make-up and hair ornaments straight. But guns are not baubles, and English blankets are not gewgaws. The trade offered, to Indians of the Stone Age, guns, blankets, bullets and powder, knives, hatchets, hoes, kettles—all well worth, in Indians' eyes, the trouble of trapping or shooting game and curing the skins. According to a schedule of prices of 1716, the Indian got a gun for thirty-five skins; a pistol for twenty; a hatchet for three; a knife or pair of scissors for one; a duffield blanket for sixteen, a yard of strouds for eight; a broadcloth coat, laced, for thirty. The price of liquor is not stated in the schedule but, unfortunately for the Indians, the liquor could be had; the tradition of the American bootlegger goes back to Indian times.

Goods were carried by trains of pack horses, or sometimes, as in De Soto's fashion, by Indian burden bearers. A trader might have fifteen or twenty pack horses in his own train. And several traders, joining forces for safety and companionship, might unite their trains into large caravans. William Bartram in 1777 saw such a caravan in the Creek country, and has left a picture of it that we may take as typical of any of the trade regions:

They seldom decamp until the sun is high and hot; each one having a whip made of the toughest cow-skin, they all start at once, the horses having ranged themselves in regular Indian file, the veteran in the van and the younger in the rear; then the chief driver with the crack of his whip and a whoop or shriek which rings through the forests and plains, speaks in Indian commanding them to proceed, which is repeated by all the company, when we start at once, keeping up a brisk and constant trot, which is incessantly urged and continued as long as the miserable creatures are able to move forward; and then come to camp, though frequently in the middle of the afternoon, which is the pleasantest time of the day for traveling; and every horse has a bell on, which being stopped when we start in the morning with a twist of grass or leaves, soon shakes out and they are never stopped again during the day. The constant ringing and clattering of the bells, smacking of the whips, whooping, and too frequent cursing of these miserable quadrupeds, cause an incessant uproar and confusion, inexpressibly disagreeable.

When such trains returned in the spring to the factories, or trading depots, to Charles Town itself, the horses carried bundles of peltries from the winter's hunting, gathered wherever there was a trader with goods to exchange. The peltries were mainly deerskins, for southern beaver and other furs were inferior to the fine thick pelts of the north. The Charles Town colony exported to England, often for re-export to Germany, enormous quantities of deerskins. In one year, from Christmas, 1706, to Christmas, 1707, the Charles Town merchants shipped abroad 121,355 deerskins; and their average was generally well over fifty thousand a year. If these figures represent what the none too ambitious Indians were willing to hunt down, cure, and deliver to the trader, we may infer that the herds of deer in the Tennessee Valley and other regions during those years must have rivaled in numbers the buffalo of the plains; and the slaughter of the deer in time had results like those of the slaughter of the buffalo.

No account like Bartram's exists to give the flavor of quite another kind of caravan familiar in those times: a war party of Indians, headed by a few white men, hurrying back from a raid against some enemy tribe, and guarding a group of Indian captives destined for the Charles Town slave markets. The Indian slave trade, although now almost forgotten, was an important item in Charles Town's early economy, and it had a tremendous influence on what happened in the back country. In 1708, Charles Town had, out of a total population of about 10,000, 1,400 Indian slaves and 2,900 Negroes. After that time, as Indian troubles increased, it was too dangerous to keep Indian slaves at home, and they were exported to New England and to the West Indies, where they were in demand. But the Indian slave trade remained a dangerous business, even though, as a Carolinian sophistically argued, it served to "lessen their numbers before the French can arm them" and was "a more effectual way of civilizing and instructing them than all the efforts used by the French missionaries." If the Cherokees attacked the Creeks and took captives to sell, then the Creeks were certain to reciprocate upon the Cherokees, and so *ad infinitum*. The resulting enmities did the more respectable kind of trade no good, for intrigues that turned tribe against tribe often had a double edge. The Tohome Indians who killed Price Hughes had felt the brunt of the slave-catchers' raids and took a deadly revenge.

There were other dark aspects of the Indian trade. Traders often abused their privileges, and thus brought the better sort of traders and white men in general into disrepute. The trade itself, even at its best, was a kind of corruption. It brought the Indian tribes into the white man's power. Once they became dependent upon guns, axes, and blankets which they must "buy" and could not make, they lost their self-sufficiency and put themselves at the mercy of an economy and a politics which they could not understand. The threat of withholding trade was a club that the white man brandished. No trade meant a return to flint arrowheads and skin clothing, and the Indians had so far changed their way of life that they did not relish this idea.

And so, despite many difficulties, the Charles Town frontier policy gained ground. In a vague, unreliable way the Cherokees conformed to English devices for handling political and commercial relations. In particular, though no one chief could exercise unchallenged authority over all Cherokee towns, or even over one town, they fell in with the British idea of channeling important negotiations through some old chief, revered for personal reasons, on whom the queer white men conferred the title of "emperor." And they tolerated or welcomed the trader, who might become the chosen friend of a great chief and occupy the best house in town.

CHAPTER VI

# The Brilliant Idea of
# a Scottish Baronet

THE safety of this Province does, under God, depend on the friendship of the Cherokees," declared the assembly at Charles Town in 1718. It was three years after the outbreak of the Yamassee War. The colony had been saved from extinction and had wreaked its vengeance on the offending tribes, driving some of them back upon their allies, the French and Spanish, and scattering other fragments deep in the western interior. A ring of hastily built forts, strategically covering the borders of the colony, protected them from another large-scale invasion. The Virginians had sent aid, though there had been much argument about the conditions attached to it. Indeed, all the colonies were more or less alive to the danger of an Indian attack which might be carried out on a grand scale from Albany to Charles Town; and the royal government at London, at last fully impressed with the menace of French encirclement, was beginning to shape a unified Indian policy and to listen to pleas for support.

For some time the Carolinians had counted the Cherokees as their best friends and staunchest allies, but they had tended to take the relationship for granted. Cherokee friendship, they felt, was guaranteed, not only by the trade itself, on which the Cherokees, far distant from the French and

Spanish, had learned to depend, but by other substantial causes. The Creeks, on the south, were hereditary enemies of the Cherokees, and the two nations harassed each other continually. Under the earlier Indian policy, the Carolinians had attempted to quiet such feuds; but now it seemed in their interest, for a while at least, to let the feuding go on. They might, as one Carolinian said, "hold both as friends, for some time, and assist them in cutting one another's throats without offending either"—a Machiavellian strategy, which had ticklish aspects. And the Cherokees were also inveterately engaged in wars with the French Indians of the Illinois country. That also seemed to make them impenetrable to French influence. Nevertheless, these old assurances did not seem any too reliable when matters got into so fluid a state as they were after the Yamassee War. They must at all odds make certain of the Cherokees, and this they proceeded to do by every means in their power. And so the remote Overhill Cherokee towns on the Little Tennessee began to entertain a procession of visitors such as that country had never seen before. The ceremonial tobacco pipes and the eagle-tail fans were brought out at frequent intervals to greet the white man's embassies, and the most amiable expressions of mutual regard were exchanged.

The assurances of friendship given by the Cherokees had the ring of sincerity; but the mind of the Cherokees, ever prone to new things, always stood a little too wide open for the comfort of the Carolinians. Patient watching, and much honeying and wheedling, were necessary to keep the assurances alive. There were constant rumors of the growth of French influence among the Cherokees. There was always a tendency for them to divide into two parties. In 1730, five years after the chiefs of the Overhills had told Colonel George Chicken, the colony's agent, that "they could not live without the English," the Long Warrior of Tennessee was contrarily arguing for peace with the French Indians, while

Moytoy, head warrior of Great Tellico, was still firmly pro-English and stood against him. There had also been hints of a scheme to massacre the traders. The Carolinians felt that adjustments within their far-flung trade empire were still delicate and precarious, and for preservation required the exceeding tact that could come only from an expert acquaintance with Indian psychology.

Yet at this crisis there appeared on the scene an astonishing figure who knew nothing whatever about Indian psychology and customs. Sir Alexander Cuming had no tact and no experience with Indians. He had only the self-assurance that comes from sublime ignorance and impervious egotism. He was a speculator, a confidence man, and a defaulter. But he had a gift of brag that the Indians liked; and as a bluffer, he was a sheer genius. Nothing could have prepared either Cherokees or Carolinians for his abrupt intrusion into the scene or for the success of his personal and very unofficial embassy. Nothing, even yet, fully explains the Cuming episode. He seems to have hypnotized everybody; the Charles Town officials, the traders and Indian agents, the Cherokee people and their chiefs, and finally the court and the government of George II.

What this inspired fool did was to rush into the middle of things and, while experienced frontiersmen held their breath, easily obtain from the Cherokees, "on bended knee," their apparent submission to the Great Man on the other side of the Great Water.

Sir Alexander was a Scottish baronet, of somewhat decayed circumstances, who may have pictured himself as a kind of John Law, able to float a "bubble" of speculation in Carolina as Law had done in Louisiana. He came to Carolina because his wife, he said, had dreamed a dream. Upon his arrival at Charles Town, he took pains to impress himself upon the colonists as a man of great estate who had come to engage in a vast promotional enterprise which would do won-

derful things for them. His first step as promoter was, naturally, to borrow money. The first notes were short-term
notes. He paid these promptly and established his credit. Then
he plunged. "He then erected," says a contemporary Carolina account, "a Loan Office of his own, signed great quantities of his Notes and emitted them upon Loan at 10 per
cent Interest, the Borrowers mortgaging their Estates to him
for Security . . . buying up with them abundance of Gold
and Silver and a great Deal of Country Produce which he
shipt away continually. He set up three Offices in different
Places. . . . He also bought several large Plantations, and built
a Stone House with Walls three Foot thick, and strong
Doors and Windows which he called his Treasury."

Just before the crash came, or, in eighteenth century
language, before the "bubble" broke, Sir Alexander left
Charles Town for England. He left in state, on a man-of-
war, the center of adulation and wonder, with seven Cherokee chiefs in his train. Only after this well-timed departure
was one of his bits of paper protested. The men of Charles
Town had been thoroughly bilked. His treasure house, when
broken open, disclosed nothing but empty boxes, old iron,
and rubbish. He had carried off fifteen hundred pounds
sterling of good Carolina money, and few people were entitled to laugh at the victims because Sir Alexander had
played no favorites—he had taken in everybody who had
money to invest.

His journey to the Cherokee country was made before
these melancholy disclosures, while Sir Alexander was still in
his glory. The trip was his own idea entirely. He had no
authority from the colonial government, and his mission, as
he openly acknowledged, was completely unofficial. In fact,
it was not at first a mission, but an excursion or junketing
trip, to give him an opportunity for scientific exploration, for
botanizing and mineralizing and collecting natural curiosities. With him went an impressive number of Charles Town

worthies, among them Colonel Chicken and George Hunter, and all the experienced "old traders" that could be got together. In all, there were at least a dozen in the party, besides the flamboyant Sir Alexander.

His daring scheme came to him suddenly at Keowee, after there had been much talk of the disposition of the Cherokees and of the necessity, doubtless, for committing them still more thoroughly, somehow, to the Carolina interest. He told no one about his mad idea. If he had done so, the Carolinians would certainly have stopped him, or tried to stop him, for what he had in mind was against all reason.

One night when three hundred Indians had gathered in the townhouse, Sir Alexander took charge of proceedings. In process of his "talk," with Joseph Cooper interpreting, he abruptly called on the chiefs to drink the king's health on bended knee, and thus to acknowledge King George's sovereignty over them, and their readiness to obey him in everything. The interpreter was appalled; yet he was caught; and had to go on and interpret without change of countenance, although he felt sure that his last moment had come; the proud Cherokees would refuse, would indeed angrily spring up and murder them all, then and there. But strangely enough, the Cherokees were overawed. They agreed without demur to a proposition which nobody had ever thought to put to them, and thus made "a Submission they never made before, to God or Man." The promise was in stern language, for Sir Alexander admonished them that if they violated it, they "would become no People."

Sir Alexander had not only risked a refusal, the results of which might have been disastrous. He had also gone armed into the townhouse, in complete violation of all Indian proprieties. He had, indeed, three cases of pistols and a gun and a sword under his coat. When one of the traders protested, and informed him that such things were never done among the Indians, Sir Alexander answered "with a wild look, that

his intention was if any of the Indians had refused the King's
health to have taken a brand out of the fire that burns in
the middle of the room and have set fire to the house. That
he would have guarded the door himself and put to death
every one that endeavored to make their escape that they
might have all been consumed to ashes."

The wild man had observed that the townhouse had
only one narrow door. If the Cherokees refused, it was his
desperate plan to force them to submit, or else, like Samson,
to go down with them in the ruins of their temple.

It was a fool idea, but it worked. The amazed Carolinians were too good at frontier diplomacy to betray their real
feelings to the Indians. They were ready to use their advantage, even though it was gained by bluff and deceit. And the
Cherokees, perhaps because they felt themselves more flattered than they had even been, were sure that a great man
stood before them, a worthy representative of the Great Man
across the water, and to every suggestion of Sir Alexander
they responded with unheard-of docility.

Suspecting that the testimony of this dramatic night
might not be believed by the cynical, Sir Alexander took
care to have the Carolinians sign a written declaration of
what they had witnessed. He next sent messengers throughout the Cherokee nation and summoned all the headmen of
the Upper, Middle, and Lower towns to meet him at Nequassie on an appointed day. Then he moved on, everywhere continuing to gather his minerals and herbs, and everywhere, too,
repeating the substance of his talk at Keowee. It was like a
triumphal procession. The speed with which the supposed
tenderfoot covered ground made the frontiersmen's tongues
hang out; the ease with which he won the Indians left them
open-mouthed.

Coming over the mountains to the Little Tennessee, Sir
Alexander stopped at Great Tellico, and made friends with
two important chiefs, Moytoy and Jacob the Conjurer. Moy-

toy told Cuming that it had been generally talked about among the towns that he, Moytoy, would be made "emperor" of the nation. But, he modestly added, now that Sir Alexander was arranging everything, "it must be whatever Sir Alexander pleased."

The great ambassador's horse went lame at Great Tellico. He left the beast in care of William Cooper, and rushed on, with Ludovick Grant, to Tennessee town. Here the party was joined by Eleazar Wiggan, and the "Old Rabbit" witnessed an undreamed-of sight: the "King" of Tennessee, like all the rest, did homage, before Sir Alexander, to King George. Returning the same night to Great Tellico, he was stroked with eagles' tails by the Cherokees in a great celebration.

The greatest celebration was still to come. Sir Alexander returned to Nequassie on the appointed day, and with him swarmed a host of the Overhill Cherokees, their company "always increasing," says the annalist, as the march went from town to town. It was "a Day of Solemnity the greatest that ever was seen in the Country; there was Singing, Dancing, Feasting, making of Speeches, the Creation of Moytoy Emperor, with the unanimous Consent of the head Men asembled from the different Towns of the Nation, a Declaration of their resigning their Crown, Eagles Tails, Scalps of their Enemies, as an Emblem of their all owning His Majesty King George's Sovereignty over them, at the Desire of Sir Alexander Cuming, in whom an absolute unlimited Power was placed, without which he could not be able to answer to his Majesty for their Conduct." Again Sir Alexander repeated his talk, and again the Cherokee chiefs swore obedience on bended knees. Again, too, the farseeing Sir Alexander made the Carolinians sign a written document as witnesses of the occasion. At Nequassie, Sir Alexander received the "crown of Tennessee" which he had asked for, from Moytoy and Jacob the Conjurer. The crown, reported the somewhat sarcastic Ludovick Grant, a little later, resembled a wig, and was made of "Possum's hair dyed Red or Yellow."

Sir Alexander now conceived one more brilliant idea, the most brilliant of all the numerous ideas that forever were crowding an altogether too fertile brain. It was the one idea out of his vast stock that was destined to affect favorably and permanently the destinies of the white man in the Tennessee Valley.

He invited the Cherokee assembly to send a delegation of chiefs with him to England, to visit the Great Man across the water. With very little hesitation, the Cherokees accepted the invitation. Who would go, was the only question. Moytoy could not go. His wife was ill. There was a little holding back among others, for it was a long journey, and they might not get back in time for the hunting season, and if they did not, what would their families eat? Oukounaco, the "White Owl," of Tennessee town, was the first to signify his willingness, and six others followed suit. Oukounaco was the youngest of the group, but, as events were to prove, he was the most important historically. For what he saw in England convinced him of the power of the British Empire, and in subsequent years, under his new name, Attakullakulla, or Little Carpenter, he consistently turned his influence toward peaceful relations. He was probably the best friend the white men had among the Cherokees.

Within a month the party was on the great water. Sir Alexander's Charles Town bubble was bursting, but he did not care. He was bound for bubble headquarters.

In London, Sir Alexander and his train of Cherokees were tremendously feted. They were the sensation of a capital which was just beginning to reap the fruits of empire and therefore was not yet jaded with a surfeit of exotic visitors. The reception of the Cherokees was probably a shade more politic than the reception of Schuyler's Mohawk warriors, twenty years before, for the demands of colonial diplomacy were beginning to penetrate the wigs of King George's ministers. The Cherokees were presented to King George, kissed the hands of his sons, and were entertained by his Majesty at dinner. His Majesty presented them with a purse of a hundred guineas and gave them lodgings in Covent Garden. They were taken to fairs, to military parades (an extremely politic diversion), to the theater, to an exhibition of archery, and to an eighteenth century form of a Kiwanis dinner, given by the merchants who were interested in the Carolina trade. They had their portraits painted, unluckily not according to the law of nature, but in civilized dress because the Duke of Montagu, who paid the artist, so specified. And to make the entertainment completely significant, one of the Indian princes had his pocket picked, or rather his rings picked off his fingers, by an expert at the art, "the infamous Jenny Tite," who, though pursued by a constable and a posse, was unfortunately not apprehended.

Presently came the climax for which all this was a preparation: the treaty of friendship and commerce. In order that the treaty might be couched in language to which the Cherokees were accustomed, Sir William Keith, who happened to know the right idiom and who also happened to be in England, was brought in to draft it. In glowing rhetoric, abounding in references to the love of the Great Father for his good children and subjects, the powerful and great nation of the Cherokees, the treaty affirmed the eternal friendship of the English nation for the Cherokee nation, but it also subtly recorded the agreed fact that the Cherokees were now subjects of the king, and hence brothers of the English, and must perpetually fight for them, never against them. Above all, it gave the English exclusive trade rights with the Cherokees. And what did the Cherokees get out of it? At the end of every article of the treaty, the consideration is recorded, in quasi-Indian idiom:

That the Chain of Friendship between him and the Cherrokee Indians is like the Sun, which shines here and also upon the great Mountains where they live, and equally warms the Hearts of the Indians and of the English: That as there are no Spots or Blackness in the Sun, so is there not any Rust or Foulness in this Chain; and as the great King has fasten'd one End of it to his own Breast, he desires you will carry the other end of the Chain, and fasten it well to the Breast of Moytoy of Telliquo, and to the Breasts of your old Wise Men, your Captains, and all your People, never more to be broken or made loose, *and hereupon we give two Pieces of Blue Cloth.*

And so on, beginning with trifles, but in steadily increasing lavishness: "and hereupon we give twenty guns" . . . "whereupon we give 400 lb. weight Gun Powder" . . . whereupon we give a Box of Vermilion, 10,000 Gun Flints, and six Dozen of Hatchets."

At the end, after a declaration that the agreement shall bind all parties "as long as the Mountains and Rivers shall last, or the Sun shine," the consideration is at last, truly symbolic, after the Indian fashion: "whereupon we give this belt of wampum." But to the symbolic exchange of presents, understood by the Indians and all primitive peoples as the concrete representation of an oath, and therefore essentially a ritual, the Englishmen had added a reward, a price, a bribe, and had thus introduced a mercenary element quite out of tone with the proceedings. The treaty of friendship was in effect a bill of sale. Civilization was beginning its subtle work.

For the Cherokees, Oukah Ulah delivered an answer, which, like Sir William Keith's sonorous periods, also resounded with rhetoric. It was, however, true rhetoric of the sort in which the Indian chiefs were practiced, and here and there were sly overtones of reference, of which Sir William Keith would have been incapable. Oukah Ulah accepted the terms of the treaty: "We have come hither naked and poor as the Worm of the Earth; but you have every Thing, and we that have Nothing must love you, and can never break the Chain of Friendship which is between us."

At the conclusion of his talk he laid a bunch of feathers on the table and said: "This is our Way of Talking, which is the same Thing to us, as your Letters in the Book are to you; and to you, beloved Men, we deliver these Feathers, in Confirmation of all that we have said."

He referred also, though not by name, to Sir Alexander. "There was a Person in our Country with us, he gave us a yellow Token of Warlike Honour, that is left with Moytoy of Telliquo. He came to us like a Warrior from you; a Man he is, his Talk was upright, and the Token he left preserves his Memory amongst us . . .

"We have look'd round for the Person that was in our Country; he is not here, however we must say, he talk'd uprightly to us, and we shall never forget him."

In this politely indirect way Oukah Ulah referred to the mysterious absence from the proceedings of their friend, Sir Alexander. The dignitaries had tried to explain, as best they could, that Sir Alexander was unavoidably detained, but the Cherokees were uneasy and displeased.

Although they for some time declined to sign the treaty, on account of Sir Alexander's absence, they finally did so. But long afterward James Adair learned from the interpreter at the proceedings that the Indians, alone in their lodgings late that night, debated whether or not their spokesman Oukah Ulah and the interpreter should be put to death. For to the articles of the treaty in which the English laid claim to their land Oukah Ulah had answered with the sacred Cherokee formula *toeuhah*, or "It is true." They did not mean really to acknowledge sovereignty, and they had, at this time, no idea of selling their lands.

As for Sir Alexander, he was indeed unavoidably detained. Sir William Keith, the idiom man, and his Excellency,

Robert Johnson, governor of the colony, had been put forward to supersede him, and Sir Alexander had been quietly suppressed. A mere Scottish baronet was not eminent enough for an occasion so important. And furthermore, news had come from Charles Town of Sir Alexander's broken bubble and the empty treasure house. And above all (for the broken bubble might have been ignored) Sir Alexander had become a pest, annoying the king and the Board of Trade with his wild schemes and with his suggestions for reforming the government of the colony. He had in fact nominated himself for the governorship, as being the one person capable, from the evidence before their eyes, of managing the Indians.

The infatuated man never gave up this idea, but returned to it in 1748 with a Zionist scheme, in which he himself figured as the Messiah destined to lead the Jews into a new Canaan. He proposed to settle three hundred thousand Jewish families in the Cherokee mountains, with himself, of course, as leader and chief financier. To meet the expenses of this colonization plan, he offered to raise a subscription for a half million pounds, on which capital provincial banks would be established in the New World. Although "some of the most learned Jews" gave ear to his proposition, it came to nothing, and in his later days his progress was steadily downward. He experimented in alchemy and attempted the transmutation of metals. He fell into debt, and was imprisoned. He died penniless and unrewarded, a poor brother of the Charterhouse.

The Cherokees returned safe, under the wing of the Carolina governor. They had been gone about a year. They had missed the hunting season, but of course they had their presents of powder and ball, of hatchets, and gun flints, vermilion, and red and blue cloth.

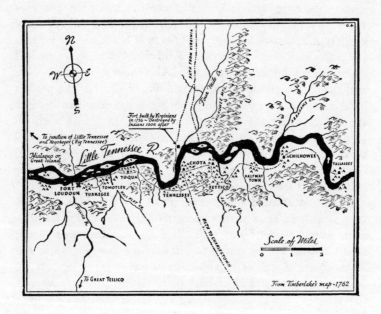

CHAPTER VII

# Captain Demeré Builds Fort Loudoun

O<small>N THE</small> south bank of the Little Tennessee, **not**
many miles from the point where it enters the Big Tennessee,
are the meager ruins of a fortress, the sole visible relic in all
the Tennessee country of the French and Indian War. A narrow ridge runs down to the waterside and breaks off sharply
where the river bends. Looking southeast from this ridge, a
visitor sees today a pleasant amphitheater of low-lying fields,

94

one of the great bottoms where both Indians and pioneers
loved to dwell. It is ringed by low, wooded ridges, and beyond these lie the towering mountain ranges through which
the Little Tennessee has dug its ravine. Northeast, toward
Maryville and Knoxville, are the rolling lands of the valley
of the Tennessee. On the northwest is a smaller bottom, en-
closed in the bend of the river. The main road between Knoxville and Chattanooga is but a mile away in that direction.
To the west is a higher ridge, of which the lower ridge is a
projection.

Old ramparts, overgrown with weeds and saplings, outline an enclosure that follows the narrow ridge to the bluff
and slants off down the slope to the river and the cultivated
fields. Within, a few low heaps of rubble, hardly discernible
in the thick brush, mark the sites of old chimneys and
hearths. Some courses of new rock along the ramparts and
a few incompleted structures of doubtful import among
the weeds tell the tale of a modern reconstruction, by the
WPA, which failed like its original. The only firm thing
here is a tablet set up by the Colonial Dames, which speaks
austerely through the pokeberries and horse weeds the name
and legend of the place.

More eloquently than any tablet, the neglected ruins of
Fort Loudoun suggest its tale of gallantry and misfortune.
Some ill chance, fateful as an Indian's curse, lurks around
the spot. The ruins are a monument to South Carolina's
dream of empire and to the men and women who at her
bidding faced siege, massacre, torture, and captivity in these
surroundings. Here was made colonial South Carolina's last
and most determined attempt to control the Overhill Cherokees and to keep mastery over the Tennessee waterways. If
South Carolina had succeeded, the first permanent settlement
within the present borders of Tennessee would have been at
Fort Loudoun. South Carolina failed, as it happened, but if
South Carolina had aspired less boldly and built no fort at all,

then French influence would have been strong on the Tennessee and in the Overhill Cherokee country, and the southern phase of the French and Indian War would have been a different story. The spot is one of the fields of decision of American history.

For more than a quarter of a century after Sir Alexander Cuming's visit, Carolina prestige ran high among the Cherokees. Their flourishing trade empire was guarded by two great bastions, held by Indian allies. The western bastion, between the Tennessee and the Mississippi, was held by the Chickasaws, who wore themselves out in their unyielding struggle against the French. In their high mountains flanked by rivers, the Cherokees defended the eastern bastion, and from it swept down the Tennessee in their pirogues, to harry the Illinois country. On the southern flank, the new colony of Georgia, erected for philanthropic purposes, was an element in the grand strategy of the frontier, since it served as a buffer between South Carolina and the Spanish.

Yet there was never a year without spells of uneasiness. The subtle French were extending their persuasions inland from Fort Toulouse and threatened to get a foothold in the Tennessee Valley itself. There were signs of restlessness among the Overhill Cherokees; and, in particular, something bad was stirring in the town of Great Tellico, which was developing into a seat of chronic disaffection.

One disturbance, of a peculiar kind, was put down by traders and Indian agents under the usual head—French influence. But it was not that; it was the presence in the Cherokee country of a utopian socialist named Christian Gottlieb Priber.

Like Sir Alexander Cuming, this Priber fascinated the Cherokees, but for entirely different reasons. Priber, an idealistic German from Saxony, was not for the English interest, or the Spanish, French, or the nonexistent German interest.

He was purely and simply for the Indian interest against all comers. His doctrine was: America for the Indians, Tennessee for the Cherokees. With the Cherokee nation as his base of operations, he proposed to organize the southern tribes into a confederation of, by, and for the Indian people. It would be a "Kingdom of Paradise," a wilderness utopia, with a republican form of government and a thoroughgoing communist order of society. Priber was the first radical to make an appearance in the southern mountains.

As soon as the traders reported Priber's designs, the Charlestown authorities were naturally disturbed, and determined to lay hold of him. Ludovick Grant, the trader resident among the Overhill Cherokees, was directed to seize him and bring him to Charlestown. It was soon evident that the Cherokees would not be pleased, and Grant desisted. Next, the authorities sent up a Colonel Fox with a small posse. But he too failed. It was as hard to arrest Priber among the Cherokees as it would be, in Adair's phrase, "to struggle with the Pope in Rome."

Later, however, when Priber was indiscreetly visiting among the Creeks, he was captured by some English traders, who took him, with all his manuscripts—and he had many—to Frederica. There he was kept in prison until his death. His manuscripts, which included a journal and a dictionary of the Cherokee language that he had been compiling, all eventually disappeared.

Like most idealists, Priber undoubtedly suffered from some misrepresentation by persons who were not competent to explain his views. They would have been perfectly understood by Rousseau, but there was no Rousseau at Charlestown. The Carolina view was that the evil Priber did lived long after him. For years after Priber's stay among them, the Overhill Cherokees were more difficult to get along with, and Great Tellico remained a permanent trouble spot.

The French, though they did not have Priber in their

employment, were keen enough to use to their advantage the disaffection he had caused. To Great Tellico, especially, they sent their agents, among them one of the most precocious schemers who ever plotted against the English. This was the Chevalier de Lantagnac, a shadowy, boyish figure who flits mysteriously across the pages of colonial history. Apparently he was a first-class spy, who, after ingratiating himself with the Carolina authorities, got their permission to live and trade among the Cherokees. After staying with the Cherokees five years, he slipped away to Fort Toulouse, and from that time on acted as French liaison agent and agitator among the Overhill Cherokees. He was in touch with the chiefs of Great Tellico and even made arrangements for the delivery of munitions of war, which were to be used, if occasion offered, against the English.

Such disturbances, together with other considerations, impressed upon the Charlestown authorities the need of a fort in the Overhill country. Governor James Glen had planned such a fort long before it was actually built. If the Carolinians did not control the Cherokees by some means stronger than the diplomacy of agents and traders, the French would push in. There was also a desire to forestall the Virginians, their trade rivals, who were beginning to see opportunities in the Tennessee Valley. At times the rivalry of South Carolina and Virginia seemed only a little less intense than their mutual hostility to the French. The outbreak of the French and Indian War in 1754 drove the two colonies into an awkwardly united effort, but did not end the distressing quarrels between Governor Glen of South Carolina and Governor Dinwiddie of Virginia.

In 1754, Governor Glen built Fort Prince George at Keowee. The officer in charge of construction was Captain Raymond Demeré, of Frederica, Georgia. The new fort among the Overhills, far to the northwest, was to be a joint project of Virginia and South Carolina. The British govern-

ment allotted ten thousand pounds for expenses, but, to
Glen's disgust, put the actual cash into Dinwiddie's hands.
Glen, who wanted a really splendid fort, asked Dinwiddie to
surrender seven thousands pounds, but Dinwiddie sent only
one thousand; he wanted most of the money for the Braddock expedition, which seemed more important to Virginia.
The quarrel between the governors reached its height in 1755.
In that year Glen called a council of Cherokee chiefs at Saluda
just at the moment when Virginia was trying to enlist Cherokee warriors to help in the expedition against Fort Duquesne.

When no Cherokee warriors turned up for the northern
campaign, Dinwiddie blamed Glen for being instrumental in
Braddock's defeat, and sent complaints against him, sizzling
hot, to the British government. Glen decided to act inde-
pendently, raised funds in Charlestown, and marched for
the Cherokee country with a fort-building expedition of
which he had taken personal command. He was too late. The
express recalling him and announcing the appointment of
William H. Lyttelton as his successor, reached him en route,
at the frontier post known as Ninety-six. He turned the
command over to Captain Raymond Demeré, who was again
in charge of building operations, and entered his coach, to pass
out of colonial politics forever.

In the months that followed—the months of June, July,
and August, 1756, which were the right months for building
a fort—Captain Demeré had much leisure to contemplate the
situation. It was melancholy and confusing. They had
changed governors on him, and the new man took his time
about giving new orders, meanwhile taking care to cancel
all the plans of his predecessor. Demeré had to discharge the
militia and go with his small contingent of regulars (the
King's Companies) to Fort Prince George, there to await
orders. He spent his time in repairing the defenses of Fort
Prince George, which were now in ruinous condition, and in
reassuring the delegations of Cherokees that kept trickling

down from the Overhill towns and near-by regions, full of complaints and questions, avid for presents of frilled shirts and matchcoats and for rum if it could be got. Alarming rumors came over the mountains about the hostility of the Creeks, the raids of the Shawnees, the activity of the French, the double-dealing of the Cherokees.

More annoying, in some ways, than rumors was the news that Major Andrew Lewis, of Virginia, had actually arrived in the Overhill country, with a sizable contingent of workmen, and was already building a fort of some sort opposite Chota itself. This was the project in which South Carolina was supposed to have co-operated. The Virginians had expected to find South Carolina men on the ground when they arrived. Not finding them, they went ahead anyhow, on their own. As it later turned out, the Virginia fort, a bare stockade, was a mere token performance, intended to enlist Cherokee aid for the fighting in the north; it was never named, and never garrisoned; and the Cherokees soon tore it down. Nevertheless, for the time being, despite Major Lewis's friendly and informative letters, Captain Demeré could get little encouragement out of the situation. "The Cherokee," Lewis wrote him, "are like the devil's pig; they will neither lead nor drive." And presently the major himself came to Fort Prince George, en route to Virginia by the long way, because he had had news of an ambush on the easier path up the Valley, and his men, who were workmen rather than soldiers, were hardly the right force to meet a determined enemy.

Lewis's talk was full of foreboding. He had had much ado to stop the Little Carpenter from sending Demeré a letter telling him to return to Charlestown. He had heard also that the Little Carpenter had vowed to take away the guns of an advance party that Demeré had sent up to his town of Tomotley; and that he would strip them of their clothes, let the sun tan their white skins, and would treat them as slaves.

It was Lewis's opinion that the Cherokees wanted a fort, yes,
but only to be assured of getting ammunition and goods at
no cost. They probably planned to massacre the Englishmen.
The fort would not be secure without a garrison of at least
five hundred men. Thus opining, the major departed, by the
safe route.

Demeré had had a visit from the Little Carpenter, just
before the advance party went up. At first all went well. The
Little Carpenter exuded advice and good cheer. The advance
party, he declared, must be his personal guests. But a few
days later he found some rum and got savagely drunk. He
shouted menacingly, and threatened Demeré with a bottle.
When the captain showed a firm front, the Little Carpenter
changed his tune and apologized. He had asked the people of
Keowee, he said, to scratch him with gar's teeth to make him
remember to be polite. Outwardly serene, Demeré accepted
the apology, but had many inward misgivings as he watched
the chief leave for the north with the advance party. Could
he really trust the Little Carpenter? And what of the other
great chiefs? What of Old Hop, the so-called emperor;
Oconostota, the Great Warrior, war chief of the Overhill
towns; Willenawah, or Big Eagle; Outacite, or Mankiller,
otherwise known as Ostenaco and Judd's Friend? All were
supposed to be friends of the English, but were they, really?
Beyond him, to the north, lay the wooded ridges of the
Twenty-four Mountains which must be passed to reach the
Overhill towns. Behind him, far to the south, was his pleasant home at Frederica, where his timber investment was going to ruin and his finances were falling into disorder from
lack of attention. But he could only bite his nails while the
summer months slipped away, and wish that Governor Lyttelton would make up his mind.

In late August the tardy governor sent up the militia
who were to do the actual construction work—two companies of provincials under Captains John Stuart and John

Postell. With the regulars, Demeré had a force of about two hundred men. There was a quartermaster, one John Chevilette, but not much in the way of supplies. Demeré would have to get corn from the Indians, but he had only a slim stock of goods to offer in exchange. With the aid of Chevilette he requisitioned beef cattle from the neighborhood, persuaded the unwilling traders to furnish pack horses, and made ready to go.

Along with the troops came a professional military engineer, a German named John William Gerard de Brahm, who had lately been employed in fortifying Charlestown. Evidently Lyttelton would permit no simple frontier fort of palisades pierced by loopholes. He wanted a handsome affair of bastions, traverses, and bulky ramparts, with chevaux-de-frises on the outside and barracks and officers' quarters on the inside. The idea was all right, but De Brahm was not the kind of man to work with the militia. Besides, he had professional doubts that he did not hesitate to announce: the fort was too far from any support; its line of communications was so tenuous as to be practically nonexistent. All true, but what was the use of talking about it? Worst of all, the extent of De Brahm's authority was not clear. Did he command troops, or was he merely in charge of engineering operations?

For armament, Lyttelton had sent up twenty cannon and two cohorns, or mortars. These would be very impressive to the Cherokees, but how were they to be transported over the roadless mountains? Demeré did not attempt to solve this problem at the moment, but left the artillery at Fort Prince George.

On September 21, 1756, Demeré finally marched, not by the direct route over the Twenty-four Mountains, but by the easier though longer way, along the divide to the Hiwassee Valley, then northeast to Great Tellico and Tomotley. Even this, he wrote Lyttelton, led through a "dismal and wild kind of country. . . . Twelve resolute men by way of ambuscade might cut off 100, there being such mountains, narrow passes, dismal and dangerous places."

Arriving in the Overhill towns on October 1, the expedition was greeted with ceremonial rejoicing, and Old Hop at once paid Demeré a visit. "This is the spot [Tomotley]," he said, "where I first chose to have a fort built, and afterwards you may build another for yourselves wherever you choose to fix. I have one fort at Chote [the Virginia fort]. I want another here, then do you fix on a spot to build one for yourselves that a Gun being fired at one may alarm all three. The Place pitched upon by your beloved man [of the advance party] is too remote."

Then with a glance at the red coats and the handsome uniforms of the officers, he added: "I see you and your warriors are well-dressed in red Clothes. I am naked and ragged. I hope to be enabled to appear like a man that I may set with you without disgracing you."

This broad hint was the beginning of a continuous hold-up. The chiefs must be supplied with presents, and Demeré was much embarrassed by the paucity of his stores. He put them off as best he could, and filled his letters to Lyttelton with urgent requests for matchcoats, frilled shirts, checked shirts, guns, blankets, flaps, and mirrors.

Meanwhile, there was a first-class quarrel about the location of the fort. De Brahm was finical, and rejected the site chosen by John Pearson, the surveyor, and the advance party; he wanted a fort that would command the river, up which he apparently thought French boats might come at any moment. The Indians, too, had their ideas about location. As the argument waxed hot, the German, in a fit of dramatized anger, snatched his own pistol from its holster and, offering it to Demeré, begged the captain kindly to shoot him through the head. "I told him," reported Demeré, "that he might blow out his own brains if he would." The site chosen was a compromise, which partially satisfied both De Brahm and the Cherokees, but not Demeré. Nevertheless, he pitched camp at Tomotley, a mile and a half away, and the work began. From beginning to end, it went badly.

De Brahm's design was too magnificent. In that isolated spot the labor and materials available were not sufficient to complete it before winter. The engineer had mapped out an elaborate fortress of the approved polygonal shape, with breastworks 21 feet thick and projecting bastions—all named for members of the British royal family—in which cannon were to be mounted. The narrow, rocky ridge afforded room for only two bastions on its crest. The rest of the fort slanted curiously down the southern slope of the ridge and sprawled across the low ground by the river. So the King's Bastion and the Prince of Wales' Bastion, on the crest, were considerably higher than the Duke of Cumberland's Bastion on the slope and the still lower works in the flat. Within the main enclosure there would be barracks, powder magazine, and storehouses. Instead of a conventional abattis, de Brahm ordered that the ditches protecting the ramparts be planted with thorny locust shoots which, when grown up, would prick the naked skins of attacking Indians.

Demeré, with most of the officers and soldiers, regarded the plan as a hideous mistake and a waste of time, but he had to defer to the governor's special appointee. Nevertheless, he complained to Lyttelton that the lower part of the fort was open to fire from the ridge. Indians could fire into it even with short-range trade guns, and could do deadly execution with rifles. The low ground would become a loblolly when the rains began. The ditch was a mere trace. The jeering Cherokees were already calling it a fort to keep cows and horses in. His only consolation was the fertile river bottom north of the fort, where they could plant a corn crop in the spring if they were still alive then.

While the work limped along, Demeré concerned himself with the problem of immediate defense. The Cherokee

towns were seething with rumor. Every chief who visited
Demeré whispered that some other chief was in French pay.
Lantagnac, the agitator, was frequently reported as visiting
Great Tellico. French John, another agent, came even into
Chota, pretending to be old Hop's slave. *"C'est un Esclave
voluntaire,"* Demeré wrote sarcastically. Old Hop visited the
English camp one evening to tell a fearsome story of how the
French were preparing to send their Indian allies to attack
the fort, but broke off his narrative when the Little Car-
penter was reported to be approaching. Later on, through
Captain Stuart and Lieutenant Wall, Demeré got more com-
plete information and advice.

"He says," wrote Demeré to Lyttelton, "he is old and
Lies upon a bad Bear skin, and as for the White People they
take care to Lye upon good clean Cloth though in the Middle
of the Woods and in fear of nothing. . . . That if he had
seen any Women amongst us he would have imagined that
Dallying with them had employed us, but as he saw none he
knows not what we have been doing. Now he says . . . make
a wooden Fort immediately and then go on with your works
. . . He says for his own part that his Life is not more than
an Inch long and he knows not how soon a bullet may kill
him, [but he] cries within himself to see in what a Defence-
less Condition we seem to be in." Furthermore, the old chief
warned that, though the Little Carpenter and Standing Turkey were his nephews, they were not dependable, neither
were his own sons. Only the Great Warrior, Oconostota,
could be counted on, because, drunk or sober, he always told
the Indians to love the white people.

The threat of attack seemed so great that even De Brahm
yielded to Demeré's entreaties, and they erected two rows of
light palisades on the ridge for a temporary defense. At the
same time, in his lodgings at Tomotley, De Brahm undermined morale by telling the Cherokees that they had no obli-
gation to pay for goods but should receive them as a just

right. He was secretly preparing to leave the job before it was done; in fact he was boasting that he would eat his Christmas dinner in Charlestown.

On November 10 Demeré celebrated the king's birthday by firing a salute from the three light swivels that they had got over the mountains. One gun was overcharged and burst, taking off half the face of Corporal James Hill, of which the corporal died the following morning.

By November 25 provisions were very low, and Quartermaster Chevilette was in disrepute. Demeré issued rations from the reserve stock of wheat flour and beef suet, and told the grumbling provincials that they would not starve. They still had horses, and "horse beef," he assured them, was very good. He had eaten it before this, and he was ready to eat it again with them.

At the end of November, twelve of the cannon left at Fort Prince George were brought up. This feat of transportation was accomplished by Trader John Elliott, a hard, cantankerous character with whom Demeré had been quarreling prodigiously over certain casks of rum that Elliott had illegally brought into the Cherokee country. Demeré finally solved the rum problem by sending a detail to stave in the casks, and he forgot his irritation with Elliott when the cannon appeared. Elliott lashed each gun crosswise over a pack saddle and tied it with belts around the horse's belly. Some horses were killed when the guns caught against trees, twisted, upset the animals and broke their backs. Twelve guns were brought over the mountain path nevertheless, and the only problem was how to mount them.

Shortly before Christmas, 1756, the quarrel with De Brahm reached a climax. The engineer pronounced the fort finished and made ready to leave, over the furious protests of Demeré and his officers. De Brahm told the militia companies that he was through with them and that they would now be discharged; that they were under his orders, not Demeré's, and could not be punished for desertion. Then he slipped away.

Rising from sickbed, Demeré was barely able to prevent the mutinous provincials from streaming off through the wintry woods. Ordering the drums to beat assembly, he paraded the troops under the bleak December sky, read them the Articles of War, and warned them grimly of the consequences of deserting in the face of the enemy. The seat of the disorder, he discovered, was in Postell's company, and he reprimanded Captain Postell in private. Then, with a good commander's instinct for the practical, he put all the troops to work upon the fortifications and began to drive them hard.

Demeré did not attempt, however, to carry out De Brahm's ambitious design. Abandoning the camp near Tomotley, he set up a makeshift camp within the enclosure and began to erect a line of heavy palisades. Despite torrential rains that almost drowned them in their improvised quarters, the labor sped. Huts were built. The forge was turned into a guardhouse. The cannon were drilled for mounting, though the metal was so hard that the guns had to be heated red-hot before the smiths could make a hole. Three-horse trucks with wooden wheels were made to haul trees from the forest for palisades and boards. A charcoal pit was dug to burn charcoal for the smithy. Wooden troughs were hewn out to hold salt beef. Sawyers were put to sawing three-inch planks for gun platforms. Clay kilns were built to burn pine wood and make tar; the hot spicy juice of pine ran down in little rills and congealed into tar—their substitute for axle grease. The hedgemaker put rich soil into the ditch for planting the locust shoots. Everything hummed. The grumbling stopped. The amazed Cherokees crawled out of their hothouses to marvel at the energy of the white men who went singing through the snowy woods to cut great trees or stood knee-deep in muddy water to set palisades.

Meanwhile Demeré took care that De Brahm should not lack an answer to whatever misrepresentations he might offer in the governor's warm house at Charlestown. A dignified protest was dispatched, signed by all the officers. We may judge its wording from a missive earlier addressed to De Brahm but probably also intended for the governor's eye:

Can you call this a fort? No guns or platforms; no barracks; no guards; no necessary houses or drains; no requisition for the health of the garrison; no houses for the officers but miserable hovels built at their own expense, altho' denied by you a little dirt to clay the walls with; no store houses capable of holding any quantity of provisions; in short, nothing yet deserving the name of fort.

The outworks which you say are near finished are no ways defensible, the breast work being in places not three feet high. Nothing but palisadoes can hinder a man from galloping into the fort ahorseback . . .

Lyttelton ignored Demeré's request that a competent person be sent to survey the condition of the fort. He did send word, however, that the fort must be named in honor of the Earl of Loudoun, who had arrived to take command of the British forces in America. (And about the same time— to the confusion of later historians—a fort on the distant Virginia frontier was also named "Loudoun.")

By early April the palisades were in place, loopholed and formidable. For better defense, they were set to incline outward. The fort had two large gates, one opening toward the river, the other toward the "front"—that is, probably toward the Indian towns south of the fort. The gates were locked at night, as much to keep the soldiers in, Demeré wrote the governor, as to keep Indians out. There was a sally port in the higher part of the wall. Other work was well under way, and soon it would be time to plant corn. On the whole it was a good job, Demeré felt, and he took pride in reporting excellent progress to Governor Lyttelton.

He was surprised to receive a tart rebuke instead of commendation. Why, asked the governor, had he not finished the fort according to De Brahm's plan? Once more Demeré attempted to explain his difficulties, including the needs of immediate defense. He wrote that he was putting all hands to labor on the breastworks, but the outlying works, isolated from the fort proper, were still under water. As a final touch he added: "I am sending De Brahm's false plan of the fort. Perhaps your Excellency may have occasion for it."

And during all these months the task of conciliating the Cherokee chiefs went on perpetually. Demeré made special

efforts to improve relationships with Great Tellico, which still reeked with subversive tendencies. Since Demeré could not himself visit the town, he sent Lieutenant Wall to distribute presents and hold a talk. The Cherokees received Wall with an Eagle-tail Dance, led by Chief Mankiller, whose loyalty had been suspect, and the situation temporarily looked favorable.

But at Chota, French agents were still sneaking in, spreading rumors and offering flattering proposals. Let the Cherokee chiefs beware of visiting Charlestown, they whispered. The governor would give them fine coats, to be sure, but those coats were *poisoned*, and when the bedizened warriors set forth on the home trail, the coats would "do their business." Poison and disease might be hidden in food, too. Worse still, the French spread the tale that the officers of Fort Loudoun allowed the Cherokee women to be taken to the fort before their husbands' eyes, for the use of the soldiers.

A little later, disloyalty broke out in the garrison itself. Lieutenant Wall and a soldier named John Brown were caught in the Creek country, hundreds of miles to the south, in the act of deserting to the French at Fort Toulouse. Brown, who turned king's evidence, said that Wall had boasted he would "put the French in a way to take Fort Loudoun"; and that, if he could get back to the fort with an attacking party, he would catch that old rogue, Quartermaster Chevilette, and "would make him dance with the rattles, which is the custom when a prisoner is burnt."

Despite such anxieties, as the summer months of 1757 drew near, Captain Demeré felt that his position was stronger in every way. The fort at last was a fort, not a labor camp. The corn was growing. He was able to whet the Cherokees into active raids against the insolent enemy. The Little Carpenter led a war party to attack the new French fort on the Ohio, and similar war parties went off to other points. In June, Demeré sent a lieutenant and thirty men to ambush and kill a party of Shawnees who were visiting, as they often did, at Great Tellico. The detachment returned with three scalps and a good report. Old Hop said that, though his hands had formerly been clean, he was now "bloody all over"— that is, committed to fight. Pressing his advantage, Demeré offered Old Hop five hundred weight of leather if he would surrender the person of the agitator, French John; but French John fled to Tellico and could not be secured. In August, some of the Tellico people, led by a half-breed named Savannah Tom, killed and mutilated a white woman who was on her way to join her husband at Fort Loudoun. Captain Demeré demanded satisfaction from the Cherokees, and persuaded some of the chiefs to go with his men on a punitive expedition against Savannah Tom and his adherents.

While these enterprises were in progress, Captain Paul Demeré, the brother of Raymond, arrived with a contingent of fresh troops to relieve the militia companies and to take over command of the garrison. It was a relief that Captain Raymond Demeré had long desired and sought. Before departing, he tried to persuade the provincials to re-enlist, but they refused, to a man, and soon were "all gone in a great hurry." The captain bade good-bye to his brother and turned south, with his own small party, to try a new route home over the Twenty-four Mountains, which would avoid the danger spot at Great Tellico. As he climbed the ridge and looked for the last time on the valley of the Little Tennessee, he must surely have vowed that his first request of the governor, on arriving at Charlestown, would be to strengthen the garrison of Fort Loudoun. His own brother Paul commanded that post now, and nobody knew better than he, Raymond Demeré, that it was the most dangerous post on the Carolina frontier.

# CHAPTER VIII

# The Siege and Fall of Fort Loudoun

Fort loudoun now faced the green world of the Little Tennessee. Twelve cannon overlooked the palisaded bastions. Imposingly they pointed across the savannas and cornfields toward the forest of oak and hickory and poplar and down the clear ripple of the shallow river where pirogues came and went. The British colors rose to the morning gun and sank to the evening gun. Drums sounded the Grenadiers March for the parade, beat the tattoo at dusk, and rolled for reveille while mists marked the curve of the river and many smokes rose from Tuskegee, near by, and from more distant Tomotley. The gates creaked open, the guard changed, red-coated sentries walked post, bayonets fixed. Through the gates flocked Cherokee women, laughing, chattering in their soft forest tongue, carrying baskets of garden truck and wild fruit or of many-colored fish, fresh-caught in the weirs. An old trader passed, his beard thick, his shirt greasy with bear-oil, his Cherokee wife trudging behind him. Through the gate, too, came Old Hop, limping and withered, but stately; or Oconostota, tall and strong, his face pitted from small-pox, a plain-spoken man but every inch the Great Warrior; or the frail, almost delicate figure of the Little Carpenter, clad in a new shirt, frilled and fine, a present from his "brother," the Great Man Charlestown—the lobes of his ears, distended by silver bangles, drooped to his shoulders, and the shrewd eyes glinted appraisingly below the bare egg-shaped dome of his head where the scalp lock bobbed.

Captain Paul Demeré, stiff and straight in handsome regimentals, strode out, with a lieutenant and a linguister, bound for Chota and a talk. The sentries saluted with a clang. Inside the crowded enclosure, soldiers, waiting for the morning details, chaffed one another as soldiers will: *Where was you last night, Luke Kraft? Same kind of place you was in, I reckon, Fred Mouncy!* The clink of the blacksmith's anvil began. He had many guns to mend—Indians were always breaking their guns. Crows flapped up and circled slowly among the trees by the river, near which a dull clattering sound arose fitfully. It was hardly soldiers' work, but the corn-guarding detail had to be on the job at day-dawn if they wanted to eat next winter. But the hoeing was done, the corn was laid by, and soon would come the Green Corn Dance of the Cherokees. Orders or no orders, sergeant or no sergeant, there were soldiers who meant to be there—best time in the world to find you a loving Indian gal.

Across the river to the east ran the Virginia Path, the way Cherokee war parties took when they went to join General Forbes on the Virginia front. Sometimes you could see them, no longer clad in greasy checked shirts and motley dress, but stripped, feathered, and armed as Indians should be. To the south, along the winding riverbank, straggled the Indian towns: Tomotley, Toqua, sacred Chota, and farther south, moody Settico. To the west, behind the ridge that over-looked the fort, ran the Tellico River and the path to Great Tellico, which stood ominously athwart the path to Charles-town. On the north the Little Tennessee—then called the Tennessee—ran through the knobs and canebrakes to its junction with the Hogohegee, the Big River, not yet known as the Tennessee, beyond which lay an unknown country traversed only by hunters or war parties bound for La Belle

Rivière and the French posts and Shawnee towns of the north.

Thus it was on the utmost frontier, in August of 1757. As the new commander, Captain Paul Demeré, surveyed his post, he must have deemed it a strong-looking place, well armed, and well, though not sufficiently, garrisoned. The Cherokees were quiet and seemed friendly. As stores accumulated and traders came, the fort more and more assumed the air of a settlement. Some of the soldiers' wives came up from distant South Carolina, to be with their husbands. After a while, children were born—the first English children born west of the mountains. One winter there was, for a time, a preacher to baptize these children and to read the gospel. In fact, there were visits from two preachers, both Presbyterians —John Martin and William Richardson. Their missionary zeal met little response among the Cherokees, and they soon departed.

In three years from that August the fort was lost, and the entire garrison killed or captured. The French and their allies, long feared, did not accomplish this. It was the Cherokees who rose in great blood-anger. The story of this, the first war between the Cherokees and the English settlers, is one of the strangest and most tragic in the annals of frontier warfare. And there is nothing else in American history that quite parallels the fall of Fort Loudoun, although the pattern of its fate is woven of old melancholy themes: an exposed position, insufficiently held, attacked by a foe superior in numbers; the lethargy of governments; delay in sending relief; a gallant defense; then disaster.

The fall of Fort Loudoun was determined by far-off events. The cause of the Cherokee war was not, after all, the machinations of the French, although their agents eagerly whetted on the Cherokee warriors. It was a slowly growing irritation; an ingrained schismatic impetuousness which the great chiefs could not control; the folly of new traders who brought all white men into contempt among the Indians; the shock of encounter with white men who were not traders at all—the back-country settlers of Virginia and the Carolinas; and the itching of young warriors to steal horses and take scalps, and of all warriors to avenge the dead.

Incidents occurred which deepened in gravity as they multiplied.

Cherokee warriors who went to help General Forbes on the second expedition against Fort Duquesne discovered that the general did not know how to treat his allies. He would not, the Little Carpenter complained, so much as give them a little paint! Straggling home, in discontented bands, these warriors caught themselves some horses in the Virginia back country. But these were not the horses of traders. They belonged to Virginians who did not like to have their horses caught up by passing strangers—especially by Indians. All Indians were alike to these men, who not only seethed with wrath against horse thieves, but were perfectly aware that Virginia and South Carolina, however unwisely, paid a bounty for scalps—meaning French Indian, or Shawnee, scalps. These grim men went after their horses and got them. While they were about it, they took scalps—Cherokee scalps. For a scalp was a scalp.

When news of these troubles reached the Cherokee towns, there was mourning, and the women made reproachful songs. The war poles went up. Hastily, Governor Lyttelton covered the bones of the dead with presents, to dry the tears of his brothers. Still, Cherokee relations were none too good.

The Little Carpenter and his band straggled home, too. General Forbes was fool enough to order the Little Carpenter and his band to be arrested as deserters, deprived of weapons, and sent under guard to the Virginia frontier. This was a gross insult to the last survivor of the great chiefs who had gone across the water with Sir Alexander Cuming to visit the king. The Little Carpenter discreetly allowed himself to be appeased, but the incident rankled, none the less.

In 1759, alarmed at the hostile attitude of Settico and Great Tellico, Governor Lyttelton reinforced the garrison of Fort Loudoun and stopped furnishing ammunition and goods to the Cherokees. The embargo only whetted the zeal of the war faction, who felt sure of French supplies. Taunted and harangued by the Mortar, a visiting Creek chief, the warriors of Settico broke loose and took twenty-two scalps in the Rowan County and Yadkin settlements. This, the first hostile act, was patched up by the Little Carpenter, who apologized for the heady young warriors and brought to Captain Demeré the scalps that had been taken. The captain ordered them buried.

In the winter of 1759, a mad act by Lieutenant Coytmore rekindled hostilities. He had been transferred from Fort Loudoun to Fort Prince George. With two officers he visited the wives of certain Cherokee warriors who were away on the warpath and brutally assaulted them. A little later, the officers repeated the rape.

The Lower Towns were in a tumult. The Overhill towns, though greatly disturbed, were still pacific.

Governor Lyttelton called out the militia and prepared to take command of an expedition against the Cherokees. Just at this moment thirty-two Cherokees, headed by Oconostota, appeared at Charlestown for a peace talk. At the feet of the governor, the Great Warrior laid deerskins, and offered white wampum in token of amity. The governor behaved badly. Avowing his determination to go to the Cherokee country, he upbraided the warriors and said that if satisfaction were not given him for the murder of the settlers, he would take satisfaction. He challenged Oconostota's right to speak for the Overhill towns, and when the chief arose to reply, stopped him rudely and broke off the council. This was a mortal insult, and the Great Warrior did not forget it.

Starting for the Cherokee country, Lyttelton took along Oconostota and his Cherokee delegation, nominally to guarantee their safety against rash reprisals by the settlers, but really as hostages. The Cherokees felt themselves to be simply prisoners. Already they could anticipate the cold pressure of the fetters that the French had often told them the English were preparing. At Fort Prince George, twenty-eight of the "hostages," including Oconostota and other chiefs, were imprisoned in a hut which had formerly housed only six soldiers.

Lyttelton took the view that the Indian killers of settlers were murderers under English law. Summoning the Little Carpenter, he reminded the old chief that under the treaty made in the days of Sir Alexander Cuming, the Cherokees had promised to deliver up to English justice any Cherokees guilty of acts of violence. He would release the imprisoned warriors, he said, only if the Little Carpenter brought him the "murderers" that the Cherokees were sheltering. The Little Carpenter pleaded that some of the more prominent chiefs be released to assist him in his search for the guilty. Accordingly, Lyttelton released Oconostota and three other chiefs. A treaty was then signed, and the Little Carpenter actually persuaded two of the guilty "murderers" to surrender. He could do no more, and went home to stay. All the Cherokees who were not confined took to the woods. War was preparing. The treaty was worthless.

Smallpox broke out at Fort Prince George, and Lyttelton's army became disorganized and mutinous. He disbanded the expedition and went back to Charlestown.

By February of 1760, the Cherokees were raiding the back country, killing traders everywhere, attacking cabins and stations. Fort Loudoun was not yet directly imperiled. In that quarter the Cherokees held back. But Oconostota and his warriors appeared at Fort Prince George and demanded the release of the hostages. Being refused, he attacked the fort, and held it in close siege, while smallpox raged within.

On February 14, Oconostota came to the parade ground,

passed over some letters from Fort Loudoun, and again demanded the hostages. Lieutenant Coytmore, who was now in command, once more refused. Two days later, the chief sent two women to ask for another parley. Although warned of the danger, Coytmore went to the riverside with Ensign Bell and the linguister Foster. Oconostota came to the opposite bank. He carried a bridle in his hand. When asked where he was going, Oconostota replied that he was going to catch a horse and ride to Charlestown to ask for the release of the hostages, and that he wanted a white man to go with him. Coytmore said he would try to find a man. At this, Oconostota swung the bridle around his head and turned away. It was a signal. Thirty warriors fired from ambush. Coytmore received a mortal wound in the breast. Ensign Bell was shot through the leg, linguister Foster in the buttocks. The wounded men carried Coytmore to the fort while the Indians were reloading, but the lieutenant survived only a few days.

Inside the fort, the soldiers crowded to the hut and demanded the lives of the hostages. Ensign Miln argued with them and promised to put the hostages in irons. But when the sergeant brought ropes and shackles, the Cherokees refused to submit. The soldiers, rushing into the hut, were met with tomahawks and knives that had been concealed in the earthen floor. In the turmoil, a soldier was mortally wounded, another injured. In a few moments the maddened garrison killed every Cherokee in the hut. And through this act the war changed from an affair of sporadic raids to total conflict. The killing of the hostages was the doom of Fort Loudoun.

While the Cherokees besieged Fort Prince George and other points in the south, Fort Loudoun, far beyond the Twenty-four Mountains, was cut off from support or relief. It was as if the green forest closed impenetrably around it. Only occasional bits of information trickled through, brought by some hardy trader or friendly Indian.

The first hostile movement against Fort Loudoun was an attempt, led by Ostenaco and Willenawah, to kill the beef cattle of the garrison. Captain Paul Demeré frustrated this attempt, drove the cattle into the fort, slaughtered them, and salted the meat down. The Cherokees then surrounded the fort and fired into it from a distance, while the garrison prepared to hold out until some relief could arrive.

Meanwhile, Lyttelton had been superseded by Lieutenant Governor Bull. Before leaving office, Lyttelton sent urgent appeals for help to Virginia and North Carolina and to General Jeffrey Amherst, commanding in the north. Virginia ordered Colonel William Byrd III, who was already in the back country of Virginia with George Washington's old regiment and other militia, to march to the relief of Fort Loudoun. Byrd obviously did not relish the task. He moved down the Valley with scandalous slowness. In the words of James Adair, "The Virginia troops kept far off in a flourishing parade," while Fort Loudoun suffered and perished.

General Amherst promptly sent 1,500 British regulars by sea to Charlestown, under Colonel Archibald Montgomery. With his regulars and a small body of South Carolina militia, he set out in June, 1760, to relieve Fort Loudoun. The Scottish light infantry of Montgomery's command were better adapted to forest warfare than the heavily accoutered troops that were slaughtered at Braddock's defeat. The friendly Indians of the towns nearer Charlestown were attracted by "their sprightly manner of dancing, their dexterity in the use of arms, and natural vivacity and intrepidity," and were eager to join the Scottish warriors in the field. The eastern band of the Chickasaws, in fact, were ready to supply a group of scouts, led by no less a person than James Adair. But Montgomery did not know how to use these resources.

After an exhausting march, he quickly relieved Fort Prince George and burned the near-by Cherokee towns. But the look of the country ahead appalled him. "It is next to impossible," wrote Montgomery's aide, Major James Grant, "for us to think of proceeding over the mountains; the whole country is the strongest and most difficult I was ever in. A few men, properly conducted, might retard the march of an army."

Nevertheless, after peace overtures failed, Montgomery pushed ahead. At the Crow's Pass, near Echoe, on the head-waters of the Little Tennessee, the Cherokees not only re-tarded but stopped the advance. The army was ambushed in a dangerous ravine. Before Montgomery could extricate his troops, he had lost 140 killed and wounded. Bewildered, his troops in disorder, faced by the impassable mountains, Montgomery retired with speed to Fort Prince George, and thence to Charlestown. From there he retired to New York. "Tell it not in Gath," wrote the angry editor of the *South Carolina Gazette,* "nor publish it in the streets of Askalon, that the army which came here under command of the Hon. Col. Montgomery, and penetrated into the heart of the Cher-okee country, NEVER WERE DESIGNED to go to Fort Loudoun, but expected to effect the release of that garrison by a PEACE, the roads being horrible, etc."

Meanwhile Fort Loudoun held out, but the garrison were faced with starvation. They had not even the satisfaction of shooting at the enemy. The Cherokees kept out of range, but lurked near the fort and cut off nearly all attempts at communication.

In one letter that slipped through, dated May 16, 1760, Captain Paul Demeré wrote that provisions would last a month at the rate of one pint of corn per day per soldier. A month later the ration was reduced to a quart of corn per day to three men. Some food was brought in by Cherokee women who were wives or consorts of the soldiers. When Willenawah threatened to kill these women, they laughed and gave the taunting reply: "If you kill us, our relatives

will kill you, according to our law." To encourage these
feminine allies, Lieutenant Governor Bull managed to send
up, by "two bold fellows," some gay ribbons and paint.

The situation had its curious features, since even the
Little Carpenter himself paid visits to the fort and occasionally smuggled in food. In June he took dinner with Captain
Demeré. When asked for news, he said that he had none,
that the Indians hid everything from him and called him
the white people's friend. Nevertheless, he warned Demeré
that a seeming withdrawal of the Cherokee warriors was only
a ruse. In spite of the warning, the fort's doctor and another man ventured out, and were killed and scalped near
the gate.

From the Little Carpenter, too, came word that Montgomery's relief expedition had started. The garrison spent
two months in hope and suspense. Finally the news of Montgomery's defeat reached them. As if in confirmation, Cherokee warriors pranced before their eyes, out of gunshot, and
displayed the scalps of Montgomery's men. They shouted
that their hands were sore with the labor of killing and
scalping so many.

The garrison now felt "abandoned and forsaken by God
and man." No answer came to the messages they sent to the
Virginia troops. Their food was gone. Soldiers began to
threaten to desert the fort and try the perils of the forest.
Demeré kept such protesters close in hand, but allowed four
men, not of the garrison, to slip away. After long wandering, these were picked up, in a starving condition, by Byrd's
scouts.

On August 6, Demeré held a council of war, which decided that the fort could not be held any longer. They must
seek terms of surrender. To Demeré's first approach Oconostota returned a curt refusal: "We are sure of the fort and
all that are within it." Suspecting that John Stuart's prestige was greater than his own, Demeré then sent Stuart to

Chota to negotiate. The dolorous mission returned with regular Articles of Capitulation, done in precise eighteenth century style, providing for a surrender with the honors of war:

1st, That the Garrison of Fort Loudoun march out with their arms and Drums, each soldier having as much powder and Balls as their officers shall think necessary for the march, and what baggage he may choose to carry.

2nd, That the garrison be permitted to march for Virginia, or Fort Prince George, as the Commanding Officer may think proper, unmolested, and that a number of Indians be appointed to escort them, and to hunt provisions for the march.

3d, That such soldiers as are lame, or by sickness disabled from Marching, be received into the Indian towns, and kindly used until they recover, and then be returned to Fort Prince George.

4th, That the Indians do provide the Garrison with as many horses, as they can conveniently, for their march, agreeing with the soldiers or officers for payment.

5th, That the Fort, Great Guns, Powder, Balls, and spare arms be delivered to the Indians, without any fraud, on the day appointed for the march of the troops.

Signed:

Paul Demeré

Cunni X Catogue
his mark

Ouconnostote
X
his mark

It may seem extraordinary that the Carolina men, no matter how desperate their condition, should ask terms of their savage adversaries. It seems hardly less remarkable that terms should be granted and a surrender conducted according to the usage of civilized armies. In a last letter to the governor, carried by the trader Charles McLemore, Demeré explained that he had no choice but to surrender. Since the Cherokees would not attack the fort, but merely blockaded it, there was no chance for a gallant fight. They could not cut their way out, for although they had ammunition, they did not have enough food for the march, much less for a running battle through the mountains. Demeré and his officers might also have reflected that the garrison had lived on friendly terms with these Cherokees for three years—had visited back and forth with them, married their women, smoked tobacco and sat in council with their chiefs. They hoped that "honorable surrender" might not prove to be a ruse, the prelude to easy slaughter, and would take their chances with treachery if allowed to keep their arms and march slowly. Perhaps they thought the surrender of the fort would appease the Indians. The army could be well on the road before the Cherokees finished celebrating their victory. In his last dispatch Demeré said that they flattered themselves that the Indians "meant them no harm"; that their demeanor was reassuring.

On August 8, Demeré turned over the cannon, 80 small arms, and 1,000 pounds of ammunition. All this booty the Cherokees carried in triumph to Chota. The next day the garrison, with all other men in the fort and the women and children, began the march for South Carolina. The escort duly appeared. It consisted of Oconostota and several other prominent chiefs and warriors. Despite exhaustion, the Carolinians marched fifteen miles the first day along the path to Charlestown and made camp in the evening two miles from Great Tellico, near Cane Creek. Here the escort, making various excuses, vanished into the night. It was a bad sign.

As the advance guard set out next morning, they saw the woods were thronged with Indians painted for war. Stuart ran toward the camp, which was just breaking up, and gave the alarm. It was too late. From ambush close by, the Cherokees poured a deadly fire upon them. Demeré was wounded at the first volley. The Cherokees at once singled him out, and—so the tradition is—scalped him alive and made him dance for them, after which they cut him down and dismembered his body. When Demeré fell, Ostenaco went among the Indians crying, "Stop, we have got the man we wanted."

But the massacre continued. All the officers except Stuart were killed, and so were twenty-three privates and three women. Many more were wounded. The others threw down their arms and were taken as prisoners to the various Cherokee towns. The Cherokees afterward claimed that they had no intention of killing more than a number equal to the number of hostages confined and killed at Fort Prince George.

In the days immediately following, the prisoners were humiliated, beaten, and made to dance with rattles in the fashion of victims intended for the torture stake. According to John Stuart's account, given after his escape, eighty of the prisoners suffered death, either by torture or otherwise. At Settico, Luke Kraft was burned at the stake, and his comrade Fred Mouncy was compelled to stand by and watch the slow death. At Chota the prisoners were forced to dance before the Creek chief, the Mortar. Yet as soon as the first frenzy died away, the survivors were well treated, and when, at the end of the war, negotiations were completed for their return, some chose to remain with the Cherokees and lead from that time on the Indian life.

# CHAPTER IX

# Stuart's Escape and Timberlake's Mission

At the beginning of the massacre of the Fort Loudoun garrison a Cherokee named Onatoy seized John Stuart by the arm and led him across Cane Creek, away from the slaughter. By Indian law he was now Onatoy's prisoner. The next day Onatoy took him into Fort Loudoun, which the Cherokees had occupied, and led him to the Little Carpenter—perhaps at Stuart's suggestion. The old chief had not taken part in the attack. He gave Stuart a friendly greeting and proceeded to ransom him from his captor. For ransom he gave all he had with him—rifle, coat, all his clothing but his flap. Thus naked, he conducted Stuart to Demeré's house, which he had taken for his own.

Oconostota now demanded that Stuart join the Cherokees in a renewed attack upon Fort Prince George. Stuart could write letters to the commandant, Oconostota said, and he could also direct the firing of the cannon of Fort Loudoun, which the Cherokees proposed to lug over the mountains for the siege. A number of the Fort Loudoun gunners would be taken along. If Stuart agreed to this, he would be set at liberty. If he refused, and if the gunners also refused, then Oconostota declared that he would burn the prisoners, one by one, in sight of the garrison of Fort Prince George. Oconostota's animus was increased by the fact that the Cherokees, in looting Fort Loudoun, discovered much powder and ball buried within the enclosure, in violation of the terms of surrender.

Confident that the Indians could never transport the cannon over the mountains, Stuart put the chief off with excuses. Then he appealed to the Little Carpenter.

The Little Carpenter told his fellow chiefs that his captive, Stuart, was getting weak and needed deer meat. He arranged for Stuart to go on a hunting party with him—a party in which he managed to include three other prisoners, two warriors, and three squaws to do the cooking. For nine days they wandered by a devious path toward Virginia, and finally reached the camp of Major Andrew Lewis, who had been sent forward from the main body of Virginia troops to meet refugees from Fort Loudoun. Stuart returned to Charlestown by way of Virginia, and when his health was restored, occupied himself with searching out and recovering survivors of the Fort Loudoun massacre.

Stuart's prestige among the Indians was now very great. The British government soon appointed him superintendent of Indian affairs for the South. It would be his task to restore trade and to get tribal affairs into order. And that was all right. But it also became his lamentable duty to attempt to enforce the Royal Proclamation of 1763, which forbade settlement west of the headwaters of rivers flowing into the Atlantic. And that was not all right. In the end, it would bring Stuart into conflict with the people for whose cause he had fought at Fort Loudoun.

The Little Carpenter, returning from Major Lewis's camp, found himself an outlaw among his own people for the time being. During his absence with Stuart the Creek chief, the Mortar, broke open and plundered his house. The Little Carpenter stood alone, but when the tide turned, the Cherokees were glad to use his services as ambassador.

The tide quickly turned. The French, despite continued

efforts, were unable to follow up the advantages offered by the fall of Fort Loudoun. A French boat, laden with supplies, set out up the Mississippi and Ohio and then up the Tennessee, with the purpose of establishing a depot at Fort Loudoun. The boat was stopped and all but overwhelmed by the tumultuous waters of the Suck. The supplies were unloaded, and a trading post was established, far below the original destination, near present-day Chattanooga.

And now General Amherst sent a second expedition, this time of two thousand soldiers, to march against the Cherokees. This force, augmented by the Carolina militia, was commanded by Lieutenant Colonel, formerly Major, James Grant, who had been Montgomery's aide on the previous expedition. Back he came, over the old route, and again the Cherokees prepared an ambuscade near the scene of Montgomery's defeat. But this time Grant had Chickasaw scouts and light infantry to cover his flanks. He pushed forward, regardless of losses. The Cherokees ran out of ammunition. They regretted, too late, that they had wasted much powder and ball in victory celebrations; and they had left at home the bows and arrows, the weapons of their ancestors, which might have served them. They faded into the forest. Grant did not pursue, but ravaged the Middle Cherokee towns. Within a few days he burned fifteen towns, cut down fifteen hundred acres of crops, and drove five thousand Cherokees into the mountains to subsist on roots and berries.

The Overhill towns were not touched by this invasion, but the Cherokee nation as a whole was greatly weakened. In the negotiations that followed, the Little Carpenter played a leading role. He refused Grant's demand that "Four Cherokee Indians shall be delivered to Colonel Grant to be put to death in front of his camp; or four green scalps be brought to him in the space of twelve nights." When this repugnant clause was eliminated, peace ensued, and continued unbroken until 1776.

The Virginia troops had meanwhile moved slowly down the Valley and entered the present borders of Tennessee. Near Long Island of Holston River they erected a stout fort, which they named Fort Robinson. Although afterward abandoned, this fort was symbolic of the foothold that Virginia gained—it might be said—at South Carolina's expense. Once having found the path to the Tennessee country and seen its lands, the hardy Virginians and the token force of North Carolinians with them were not thenceforth going to be restrained, as individuals, by royal proclamations or treaties that might forbid entering and settling. Furthermore, they had seen the waters of the great stream that might lead them into this region.

And so the voyage of Lieutenant Henry Timberlake, in the late fall of 1761, down the Holston and the Tennessee to the Overhill towns was the herald of many voyagings to come, from the direction of Virginia. Timberlake was with the Virginia troops at Fort Robinson at the time of the visit of a Cherokee delegation. Byrd had been replaced by Colonel Adam Stephen as commanding officer. The Cherokees requested that some ambassador be sent back with them to explain the treaty and make friends with their people. Timberlake volunteered for this ticklish and, it might well be, dangerous mission.

The gallant Virginia officer wrote and published a *Memoir* of his journey—a remarkably fine narrative, done in a sprightly and charming eighteenth century prose, in which he inserted, at an appropriate point, his own translation of a Cherokee war song, rendered in elegant couplets of the type made fashionable by Alexander Pope. The book reveals the dashing personality of its author, but it also records in meticulous detail the customs of the Cherokees. Timberlake also goes into the record as the first voyager to complain against the difficulties of navigating Tennessee water and of poling and paddling upstream.

Timberlake took the river route against the advice of the Cherokee delegation, who preferred to journey overland. In his dugout canoe his companions were an interpreter named John McCormack and Sergeant Thomas Sumter—afterward General Sumter of Revolutionary fame. Starting on November 28, 1761, with the Holston at low stage, Timberlake's party almost immediately lodged on a sand bar. From that time on their progress was continually interrupted by the pushing, pulling, heaving, and wading with which later voyagers became familiar. They had two guns with them, but soon broke the firing apparatus of one, and lost the other in one of their struggles with the river. They were near to starving until Timberlake at last achieved makeshift repairs of the broken gun. With this weapon, after one miss, McCormack killed a large bear, on which they subsisted for the rest of the trip. The weather turned cold, and the river froze. They had to break their way through ice and to contend against snow, hail, and rain. With a thaw there came higher water, and they cruised rapidly past the French Broad and on to the mouth of the Little Tennessee. Here they encountered a hunting party of Cherokees who escorted them upstream to the Cherokee towns. When Timberlake's hands got sore with poling, the chief, Slave Catcher, ousted his wife from his own canoe and took Timberlake on board as a passenger.

After resting at the Slave Catcher's house, Timberlake went on to Tomotley. On the way he paused to view the ruins of Fort Loudoun; for it was now in ruins, since, by order of Oconostota, the Cherokees had burned it to the ground. He was welcomed by Ostenaco and escorted to Chota, where the peace articles were read and Timberlake had to smoke pipe after pipe of tobacco until he was ready to collapse with nausea. At Settico he was entertained by an Eagle-tail Dance, which was performed to the sound of drums taken from Fort Loudoun, mingled with some of Indian make.

As they approached [wrote Timberlake], Cheulah, singling himself out from the rest, cut two or three capers, as a signal to the other eagle-tails, who instantly followed his example. This violent exercise, accompanied by the band of musick, and a loud yell from the mob, lasted about a minute, when the head-man waving his sword over my head, struck it into the ground, about two inches from my left foot; then directing himself to me, made a short discourse (which my interpreter told me was only to bid me a hearty welcome) and presented me with a string of beads.

On his trip down the Tennessee, Timberlake made a map of the river, which unfortunately was lost. But his remarkable map of the Little Tennessee, showing the exact location of the Cherokee towns, survives today, and is still an accurate guide to the sites of the towns.

After a stay of some months, Timberlake journeyed back overland to Williamsburg, Virginia, attended by a large company of chiefs and warriors, whose entertainment offered a considerable problem to the governor. From Williamsburg he voyaged to London, taking with him Ostenaco and two Cherokee warriors. The visit of this Cherokee delegation created a sensation quite equal to the Cherokee visit of some thirty years previous. The poet Goldsmith was among those who waited long in the anteroom for the privilege of seeing Ostenaco. When he was finally admitted, the chief seized him and embraced him with such cordial intimacy that the poet found his cheeks covered with vermilion. Sir Joshua Reynolds painted the portraits of the warriors. They had an audience with the king and were taken to see all the sights.

Timberlake, however, found himself much embarrassed by the doings of some high-grade flunkey or racketeer to whom he refers as "Mr. Caccanthropos." This person cheated him mercilessly in the handling of the expense accounts of the Indians, and then accused Timberlake of charging admission to the throngs who came to see the Indians. Thus, although the visit was a diplomatic success for the English government, it turned into a personal disaster for Timberlake. He came off badly at court and at the hands of London society. Neither crown nor colony ever reimbursed him for the personal expense he had undertaken in promoting and carrying out the visit. A second visit, made in 1764, with another Cherokee delegation, left him still deeper in the hole. He wrote and published his book, seemingly, in an endeavor to recoup his finances. But he died before it appeared in 1765. The last sentence of his book is a commentary on his grievous situation, and it reflects a sentiment which by that time was beginning to occupy a number of distinguished minds, impressed like Timberlake with the contrast between the Noble Savage and civilized man: "My circumstances are now so much on the decline, that when I can satisfy my creditors, I must retire to the Cherokee, or some other hospitable country, where unobserved I and my wife may breathe upon the little that yet remains."

Men who saw the Cherokee country, in those times, had just such a hankering to return. Many did return, and many more came besides. The old frontier of the trader was passing away. The new frontier of squatter and settler was beginning.

In 1760, Daniel Boone, adventuring alone from his home on the Yadkin River in North Carolina, visited the Watauga country and carved on a beech tree his famous legend: "D. Boon cilled a Bar on tree in the year 1760." The following year he was with the North Carolina militia that joined the futile Virginia campaign for the relief of Fort Loudoun. After that campaign Boone, with a few friends, adventured again in the wolf-infested hills near the present Abingdon, Virginia.

More and more of the "long hunters" went out from

the back country to camp in the wilderness and to bring back —if they were not robbed by the Indians—a rich garner of peltry and bear fat. Elisha Walden, for whom Walden's Ridge was named, was a long hunter. Stephen Holstein, or Holston, for whom the Holston River was named, was a similar adventurer, but was more distinguished for his dimly recorded early navigations than for his hunting. The long hunters, staying out months at a time, explored the inviting country of the Upper Holston, but, wary of Cherokee interference, kept away from the Overhill towns and preferred the Cumberland and other more northern valleys for their most ambitious expeditions.

When they came back from a long hunt—and, despite the peril, they generally came back—they told their tales. The ears of prospective settlers were not the only ears that listened. Men of high place, schemers associated with the Loyal Land Company of Virginia and similar speculative groups, listened too, and formed connections with the long hunters. In North Carolina, for local reasons, there was less interest in large-scale speculation for the time being. Nevertheless, Daniel Boone himself was soon in the employ of Judge Richard Henderson of North Carolina, whose keen brain was already shaping up one of the greatest land speculations of all time.

The men of southwestern Virginia were filtering slowly down the Valley of Virginia. Between them and the Holston Valley there was no physical barrier of any importance. They had only to take the ancient Indian path and press on into the new lands claimed but not occupied by the Cherokees. This they did. The men of North Carolina, although they were faced on the west by a lofty, unexplored mountain barrier, found gaps in the ranges and joined the great migration.

## CHAPTER X

# Rally in the Canebrake

IF THE great migration had been free to pursue the easiest, most natural route, it would certainly have continued southwest down the main valley and up the tributary valleys of the Holston-Tennessee system. Then it would have branched north into Middle Tennessee from the region of the Great Bend and would have pushed south into Alabama and Mississippi. But the actual pattern was not at all like that. The settlements inched very slowly down the Tennessee Valley. It was 1798—after Kentucky and Tennessee had become states—before the official Indian boundary could be set even as far south as the Little Tennessee. The Great Bend was settled, partly from the Deep South, partly from Middle Tennessee on its north, a long time before the land between Chattanooga and the Hiwassee River was cleared of Indians. Meanwhile, an island of settlement began in Middle Tennessee in 1780, and another one in Kentucky some years earlier. Both "islands" were reached by a roundabout northern route —the difficult Wilderness Road—that led away from the Watauga settlements, away from the Tennessee Valley, northwest across the Cumberlands and through Cumberland Gap, and so on around.

The Cherokees caused all this trouble. Their formidable resistance to the natural southwestward march delayed and successfully turned aside one of the great folk movements of

American history. Thus they exerted tremendous influence upon the culture of two great states throughout a decisive period of their history. If these facts are remembered, pioneer history, otherwise a tangle of unintelligible raids, massacres, battles, treaties, begins to straighten out. The major problem of the settlers was not—much though the modern historian would like to have it that way—their economic condition, their political rights, or the greed of land speculators. It was purely and simply what to do about the Cherokees, upon whose lands they were intruding and who resented the intrusion. Either the Cherokees must be bought off or they must be driven off. Both methods were tried. Neither was a complete success.

The first settler within the present bounds of Tennessee was William Bean, who built a cabin and cleared land in the Watauga Valley in 1768. In the next year he brought his family from Pittsylvania County, Virginia, and soon his kin and neighbors joined him with their families. The most important early addition to the Watauga settlement was the sturdy Scotch-Irishman James Robertson—"Father of Tennessee"—who visited the Watauga country in 1770 and was captivated by its beauty. He returned to North Carolina, and, while crossing the mountains, got lost, and almost perished of starvation and fatigue, but survived to bring a group of North Carolinians to Watauga. The removal of the North Carolinians may have been prompted in part by the bloody strife then current between the "Regulator" group and Governor Tryon, but it now seems unlikely, as was once thought, that many Regulators migrated at this time. Meanwhile John Carter and Joseph Parker set up a store on the north side of the Holston below the junction of its forks and thus founded the "Carter's Valley" settlement. Farther east, also on the north side of the Holston, Captain Evan Shelby of Maryland and his brother John started a third nucleus of habitation; and Jacob Brown, with some North Carolina families, entered

the Nolichucky Valley. Thus, within a decade after the fall
of Fort Loudoun, four settlements had been established by
the rapid infiltration of small groups. They gained in population with every year.

It was not only a westward movement but a part of the
general drift of population from north to south along the
Valley of Virginia, and it caught up wanderers from Pennsylvania and Maryland as well as from points close by. The
main impetus came from Virginia; and Virginians of English
extraction were in a considerable majority among the early
settlers. But with the stream, too, came the Scotch-Irish, or
Ulster Scots. These constituted about one-fourth of the early
population—though some historians, impressed by the promi-
nence of Scotch-Irish leaders, have been tempted to reckon
their numbers much higher. In truth, whatever they lacked
in numbers, they made up in zeal and energy. Their Presbyterian divines, learned and firm, at once took the lead in
matters religious. There were also Germans from Pennsylvania and the Virginia Valley, and a few Irish, Welsh, and
Huguenots. John Sevier, it seems, might have been of Hu-
guenot ancestry—"Xavier" having been Anglicized into
"Sevier." And almost from the outset there were Negro
slaves.

The greater number of these pioneers were educated, or
at least literate, as the numerous signatures to their various
early petitions attest. They were independent and fearless,
and they had for leaders men of genius, capable of most
shrewd guidance in public affairs. Of those who came from
the old back country of Virginia and North Carolina, it is
likely that many were experienced frontiersmen who had
hunted the wild game and raised cattle on the open range in
the forested valleys to the east and who expected to continue
these pioneer pursuits in the new country. There was a rowdy
element too—outcasts, ne'er-do-wells, and mere thugs. Of
such it was commonly said in those days: "Oh, he'll soon take

poplar and push off!" That is, he would leave by canoe or flatboat for the Natchez country or elsewhere. If he did not, the rowdy one might find himself confronting a stern judge, for the settlers established courts and jails almost as soon as they arrived.

At that time the western extension of the Virginia-North Carolina line had not been laid out, and the settlers erroneously assumed that they were on land claimed by Virginia. When at last, after some confusion, the boundary was surveyed, they felt piqued and cheated to discover that they were living in the western extension of North Carolina. The situation was puzzling, since North Carolina paid little attention to them, while Virginia continued for some time, despite the survey, to exercise jurisdiction over the North-of-Holston people. The Wataugans, being devoid of other government, proceeded, under the arrangement known as the Watauga Association, to institute a simple constitutional government of their own. This experiment frightened Lord Dunmore, the royal governor of Virginia, into foreboding exclamations about their "dangerous example."

The Wataugans had more urgent matters to consider than his Lordship's opinions. In the various surveys and treaties which were being busily prosecuted it was all too evident that the Tennessee settlers were not being taken fairly into account. The treaties were being made over their heads, with John Stuart, as representative of the crown, looking after the Indians, and the representatives of Virginia and North Carolina looking after the land speculators, who generally managed to be present at treaty talks and even to conduct them. It was not clear how the settlers could obtain titles to the new lands, which were encumbered—to say nothing of Cherokee rights—by a bewildering crisscross of British and colonial claims dating back to the seventeenth century. Furthermore, Alexander Cameron, who was Stuart's resident deputy to the Cherokees, brusquely warned the Wataugans to vacate their holdings, since their unauthorized presence was obnoxious to King George and displeasing to his Cherokee wards.

The question of titles and jurisdictions could wait, but the Indian question could not. The Wataugans now took a most remarkable step. Who devised the strategy, we do not know. We know only the fact that the Wataugans disregarded Virginia and North Carolina, ignored John Stuart and the British crown, and went over Alexander Cameron's head. They sent their own emissaries to Chota, and there, despite Cameron's startled opposition, negotiated an arrangement with the Overhill Cherokees. It was an extraordinary arrangement. For a consideration of about a thousand dollars the Wataugans obtained from the Indians a ten-year lease of the lands they had settled. To waive the question of purchase and become, instead, the tenants of Cherokee landlords was a shrewd move. Under this *modus vivendi* the settlements would be temporarily secure; and tenancy might easily merge into possession. More than that, the Wataugans had hit upon a secret that could form the basis of future policy. They had learned—no doubt to the great annoyance of John Stuart—the true state of affairs among the Overhill Cherokees.

If the Cherokees had been all of one mind and had resolved to fight, and if furthermore they could have been assured of supplies, they could have wiped out the settlements or made the region too dangerous to be inviting. But their long experience with South Carolina had accustomed them to negotiation. They may not have realized that frontier diplomacy was entering a new phase—that possession of land, not trading privileges, was now the white man's goal. They could hardly know that the new negotiators were no longer colonial-minded, were indeed Americans, about to throw off colonial restraints.

As for Stuart and Cameron, the official protectors of

Indian interests, their position rapidly became weak. The British administration of Indian affairs was still unrealistically organized around the trade in furs. The home government, remembering Pontiac's conspiracy in the North, was apprehensive about the revival of French influence and did not understand that the prime need of the moment was an orderly policy for the settlement of unoccupied Indian lands. Stuart's treaties and Cameron's threats carried no real force. Virginia and North Carolina would never oust the settlers from their unauthorized occupancy. It was useless to ask them to do so. And Stuart could never quarter British troops on the border to police it and to expel intruding settlers. If he so much as made a gesture toward trying that, men of high place in Virginia and North Carolina would seek—and would get—his political scalp. Those men wielded great influence, they were interested in western lands, and they were already connected in some way with the adventurers in the Tennessee country. Stuart could do little but talk.

Older chiefs, like the Little Carpenter, may have understood how unfavorable the situation was from the Cherokee point of view. They had visited the provincial capitals and knew how great were the resources of the white men. They remembered the defeat of 1760. Through traders they may have gained some inkling of the political situation. At any rate, they counseled peace. The real danger to the settlements came from a party of younger chiefs, of whom Little Carpenter's son, Dragging Canoe, was soon to become leader. This party stood for no compromise and wanted to make war on the settlements. But now they had to be content with objection and argument. A systematic attack on the settlements would provoke a withdrawal of British trade. Without British trade they would run short of munitions of war, unless they proposed to depend—as no Cherokee now did—on bows and arrows and flint-headed tomahawks. Even the irreconcilables were not that primitive. While they wished to cherish their Indian ways and to bar the white man from the vast hunting grounds where deer and bison yet roamed, they had no thought of doing without the traders' wares.

The years between 1769 and 1776 therefore offered special opportunities to the Tennessee settlers. Having tried the technique of direct negotiation and found it good, they worked hard to improve Indian relations. At intervals, to be sure, some unruly settler would break loose, kill a Cherokee without provocation, and so bring on a diplomatic crisis. William Crabtree killed "Billey," a kinsman of the great chief Ostenaco, while Billey, with other Cherokees, was peacefully attending the Watauga races on a certain day of jollification. It was then necessary for James Robertson, at some personal risk, to hurry to Chota and calm the ruffled feelings of Billey's relatives with presents and soothing talk. It was also advisable to punish the white offender—if he could be detected and caught!

The record proves the success of this policy. Although the Watauga settlements suffered from raids by Shawnees and other northern Indians and in 1774 found it good policy to send a detachment of twenty Wataugans, under Captain Evan Shelby, to take part in the Point Pleasant campaign, far to the north, they remained at peace with the Cherokees until 1776.

In 1775, Richard Henderson of North Carolina launched one of the most astonishing enterprises of the times—the great Transylvania Company. Up to this moment Virginia had been grand headquarters for land companies that aimed to grasp the west, but as yet the Virginia companies had done no actual colonizing. Now Henderson of North Carolina leaped ahead of all competitors.

Significantly, it would seem, he followed the example of Watauga in ignoring colonial authority and making a private arrangement. Himself a jurist, he took care to secure certain vague legal safeguards. From Lord Mansfield, an English judge, he obtained an opinion (not, however, delivered from the bench) that a private purchase of Indian lands might be valid, since there was precedent for it in English law. Next he visited the Overhill towns, ingratiated the chiefs, and arranged for a representative of the Cherokees to inspect the houseful of goods that his company had assembled in North Carolina as the purchase price of the lands they sought. The Little Carpenter passed on the goods and adjudged them sufficient. A squaw came with him, too, to examine the stuff from the woman's point of view. It was announced that the treaty talk would be held at Sycamore Shoals on the Watauga River.

In January, long before the appointed date, Cherokees were camping expectantly at the treaty ground. By March, twelve hundred Indians had assembled, and a throng of settlers were there too, anxious to miss no detail of the great occasion. Before this large and picturesque audience, on March 14, 1775, Richard Henderson began the talk. With him were his partners of the Transylvania Company, well equipped with documents, and most of the prominent men of the Watauga country. Before him were the Indian chiefs and warriors of both factions. The chiefs were probably attired, not in Sioux war bonnets, as the ignorant painters of historical murals would picture them, but in handsome eighteenth century matchcoats and ruffled shirts above their leggings, bangles in the drooping lobes of their ears, gorgets of metal or beads low on their necks, a British medal or two on their coats, tribal tattooings or slashes on cheeks or foreheads, individual symbolic designs painted on their faces. Near by, for all to see, was the houseful of goods. Joseph Vann was the official interpreter, but both sides retained other interpreters to check his translation of the proceedings.

After the regular preliminary courtesies and some jockeyings over irrelevant questions, prolonged in leisurely Indian fashion for a whole day, the negotiations finally came to the real point. Henderson proposed to buy from the Cherokees, for goods worth ten thousand pounds sterling, most of Kentucky up to the Tennessee River and all the part of Tennessee drained by the Cumberland River. It was a major portion of the ancient "hunting ground" of the Cherokees, an area of about twenty thousand acres. The Little Carpenter made an amiable speech. Other chiefs joined in. It looked like smooth sailing.

Then Dragging Canoe stepped into the circle and began his appeal to the Cherokees. The gist of his speech survives to us, though rendered in summary only, and wrongly attributed by the historian Haywood to Oconostota—who was no speaker at all. In the richly metaphorical rhetoric of the Indian orator, Dragging Canoe depicted the ancient glories of his people before the white man began his encroachments. Other nations of Indians, he pointed out, had yielded to the white man's desire for land and had already "melted away like balls of snow in the sun." "Where now are our grandfathers, the Delawares?" he asked. Let not the Cherokees imagine that if they yielded what Henderson now sought, it would be enough to satisfy the greedy Long Knives. The white men would press for more and more until they would demand the very homes in which the Cherokees and their forefathers had lived. He called upon his nation to oppose the treaty. Treaties were for old men. "As for me," he said, "I have my young warriors. We will have our lands."

The fierce oratory of Dragging Canoe broke up the meeting for that day. Henderson's side hastily brought out food to divert the minds of the Cherokees from the Canoe's bitter onslaught. Doubtless the feast was the barbecued meat of cattle that had been cooked all night over pits of coals. The Cherokees partook, but then withdrew to hold their own council, and the issue seemed in doubt.

What was said in council we do not know. Perhaps the old chiefs pointed out that the land which was to be sold lay to the north, away from the beloved country of the Tennessee Valley. Perhaps the near presence of the houseful of goods had its effect. At any rate, on St. Patrick's Day, March 17, 1775, the Little Carpenter, Oconostota, and Savanucah (the Raven) affixed their marks to a formidable indenture, worded in the intricately repetitive language of English law, which conveyed to Richard Henderson and his associates the great tract they desired. Multiple copies of the deed had been prepared, which caused some confusion, but the chiefs finally signed all copies.

Still Henderson was not done. He had, he said, some more goods which had not been exhibited, for which he wished to buy a pathway for access to his lands from the Watauga settlements. Dragging Canoe again angrily objected, but was again overruled. The old chiefs sold Henderson his "Pathway to Kentucky." Then Dragging Canoe spoke a final sentence which, though differently reported by various witnesses, has the same ominous ring in all the reports. In the deposition of Samuel Wilson it is reported thus: "The Dragging Canoe told them it [Kentucky and Middle Tennessee] was the bloody Ground and would be dark and difficult to settle it." With this warning he left the treaty ground.

When the main transaction was over, the Wataugans came forward and seized the opportunity to buy from the Cherokees the lands that they had earlier leased. Carter and Parker bought their Carter's Valley land, and Jacob Brown got his immense tract on the Nolichucky River. The Cherokees were in a selling mood. When it was all over, then and only then was rum distributed.

There was a great hullabaloo when the news of Henderson's purchase reached the several colonial headquarters. Cameron ordered the arrest of Henderson. The governors of Virginia and North Carolina published furious proclamations. All to no avail. Henderson was soon gone into the wilderness he had purchased, and no officer could take him.

Furthermore, it was the eve of the American Revolution, and colonial authority was failing rapidly. Eventually Virginia and North Carolina voided the Henderson purchase; but they also conveniently assumed that his purchase voided Cherokee claims, and each state awarded the Henderson group two hundred thousand acres as a consolation prize.

Anyhow, the way to Kentucky had been opened. A stream of settlers now began to pour westward, excited by Henderson's advertisements. One such, published in the *Virginia Gazette*, read, in part:

The Fertility of the Soil, and Goodness of the Range, almost surpass Belief; and it is at present well stored with Buffalo, Elk, Deer, Bear, Beaver &c, and the Rivers abound with Fish of various Kinds. Vast Crowds of people are daily flocking to it, and many Gentlemen of Rank and Character have bargained for Lands in it; so that there is a great Appearance of a rapid Settlement, and that it will soon become a considerable Colony, and one of the most agreeable Countries in *America*.

Out of the buoyant hopes of this brief moment, perhaps, came a song, "Shoot the Buffalo," that lingers yet in the folk memory of the descendants of the Tennessee pioneers. Its simple lines, sung to a variant of a familiar Irish air, catch up and blend, as in one cry of exultation, the lush promise of the wilderness, the tales of the long hunters, the restless ambition of the pioneers, and echoes of Indian bird-and-god myths.

But in the Tennessee Valley, though the swelling population of the Watauga country threatened to overflow to the southwest, the way was closed, was dammed up by the Cherokee nation. And now the valiant men of the frontier would have dire need to rally in the canebrake, and also to watch the canebrake, where at any time painted warriors might lie in wait.

Within a year after the Treaty of Sycamore Shoals the

## Shoot the Buffalo

Rise you up, my dear-est dear, and pre-sent to me your hand, And we'll take a so - cial walk to a far and dis - tant land, Where the Hawk shot the Buz - zard and the Buz - zard shot the Crow. We'll ral - ly in the cane-brake and shoot the Buf-fa - lo! Shoot the Buf - fa - lo! Shoot the Buf - fa - lo! Ral - ly in the cane-brake and shoot the Buf-fa - lo!

old chiefs gave way to the younger element, and the Cherokees armed for war. The outbreak of the Revolution made a
Cherokee war certain, and Dragging Canoe would be the war
leader. The conditions at last were right from the Indian
point of view. British authority, far from restraining the
Cherokee warriors, now egged them on to fight, began to
supply them with munitions, and made them a part of its
grand strategy.

The British plan of campaign in the South called for the capture of Charleston (which had now discarded the colonial spellings "Charles Town" and "Charlestown") by the troops of Sir Henry Clinton, who approached from the sea. Charleston would become a base for operations against the Carolinas and Georgia, and, as a part of those operations, it was intended to turn the Indians against the back country. John Stuart, miserably afflicted with gout and frustration, escaped in the nick of time to Florida and managed to confer with Clinton. "I do not despair of getting them [the Indians] to act for His Majesty's service," he told Clinton. Stuart also talked with a Cherokee delegation and between January and July, 1776, sent one hundred and sixty horseloads of ammunition to the Overhill towns. His deputy, Cameron, and his brother, Henry Stuart, were active in the Overhill country. In October, 1775, John Stuart instructed Henry to inform the Cherokees that "want of trade and ammunition is entirely owing to the bad designs of the Rebels." He added insinuatingly, "You will understand that an indiscriminate attack upon the Province is not meant, but to act in execution of any concerted Plan and to assist His Majesty's troops and Friends in distressing the Rebels. . . ."

The Cherokee attack, when it was delivered, was not a characteristic Indian attack. It was well timed and planned. It revealed some conception of maneuver. It could hardly have been a purely spontaneous uprising.

The settlers, perfectly aware of what was going on, made ready to fight. Since they must now perforce look to the east for help, they petitioned North Carolina to be incorporated into its government, and so became Washington District—later Washington County—of North Carolina. Although they could hardly spare any riflemen, they sent a small contingent to aid in the defense of Charleston, and these frontiersmen were soon engaged at Sullivan's Island. At home, the settlers rooted out Tories, built stockaded forts, and, through sympathetic traders, maintained espionage among the Cherokees. So warning of the attack came to Lieutenant John Sevier, on the Nolichucky, almost as soon as it was launched. The word came from Nancy Ward, the famous "peace woman" of the Cherokees. She was the Little Carpenter's niece, and she slipped the message to trader Isaac Thomas, who escaped at the last moment and brought it to Sevier.

The Cherokees moved almost like a disciplined army, in three divisions, each with a definite objective. One division, under Dragging Canoe, struck the North-of-Holston settlements at Long Island, and there, at the Battle of Island Flats, took place the first engagement of the Revolutionary War in the West. Abram of Chilhowee's division moved on the Nolichucky and Watauga people. A third, under the Raven, mopped up Carter's Valley.

Warned by scouts, the North-of-Holston riflemen left their rude defenses at Eaton's Fort and came to meet Dragging Canoe's force. Dragging Canoe attempted to outflank them. As the pioneers changed front and reformed their battle line—it was a quarter of a mile long—the Canoe urged his followers on with the cry: "The Unakas [whites] are running. Come on and scalp them!" In the battle that followed, Dragging Canoe was badly wounded in the thigh and had to be carried off the field. The Cherokees were repulsed, with thirteen dead and many wounded, and withdrew from the conflict. It was a sharp defeat. The settlers had no men killed, and only a few wounded.

In Carter's Valley, from which the inhabitants had largely fled, the Indians burned and plundered.

In the Watauga country, the settlers fell back into Fort Caswell, near Sycamore Shoals, and there were besieged, while the Cherokees pillaged cabins all around and cut off stragglers. They captured Mrs. William Bean and took her to Chota, where the intervention of Nancy Ward saved her from death at the torture stake. A young man, James Moore, was less fortunate. He was burned to death in Tuskegee, within sight of the ruins of Fort Loudoun.

The Cherokees attacked Fort Caswell at daybreak, when some of the women and girls were milking outside the fort. They screamed and ran for shelter. One of them, Catherine Sherrill, made a circuit to escape the Indians, but could not climb over the lofty palisades. Lieutenant John Sevier reached down and brought her to safety. It was a first meeting, and, though Sevier was a married man at this time, it got a romantic coloring in Tennessee tradition. Four years later, after John Sevier's wife died, he married "Bonny Kate" Sherrill. The Cherokees held Fort Caswell in close siege for two weeks, ravaged the neighborhood, then retired with their booty. The Cherokee attempt to fight in armies had failed, and Dragging Canoe never tried it so systematically again. He fell back on guerrilla warfare, and bands of Cherokee raiders continued to trouble the settlements.

No longer did Virginia stand "far off in flourishing parade" as when Fort Loudoun fell. The Virginia authorities actually had intended to anticipate the Cherokee attack and strike first, in concert with other states. They were not quick enough, but now Virginia troops under Colonel William Christian moved rapidly in. At Long Island, where Fort Patrick Henry had been built, they were joined by a unit of North Carolina troops. In September, gathering up the Watauga and Nolichucky fighters, Colonel Christian moved against the Overhill towns. He had eighteen hundred well-equipped troops, all infantry except a unit of light horse under John Sevier. The Cherokees, torn by quarreling factions and demoralized by their previous defeat, fled to tall timber. Despite several alarms, it was a bloodless campaign. Christian occupied the vacant Overhill towns without a battle. He then inflicted what was, in the view of some of his men, very mild punishment, for he burned only the notably hostile towns—Tellico, Chilhowee, Settico, Tuskegee. He spared sacred Chota. Evidently he wished to conciliate the more pacific element of the Cherokees, if possible. A few old chiefs crept out of hiding and came to a parley. They agreed to meet Christian and representatives of Virginia and North Carolina at Long Island for a treaty the following summer. This, the Treaty of 1777, was held, but it was meaningless, since neither Dragging Canoe nor his followers took part in it. Dragging Canoe's faction had withdrawn from the Overhill towns to the region of present-day Chattanooga. With his young warriors the Canoe would carry on the fight.

Now, although the Wataugans must watch the Indian frontier and meet the British foe to the east and south, they still had time for politics and government. Their representatives went to the North Carolina legislature. The state of North Carolina, at last officially awake to its western interests, opened a land office in Washington County at which the settlers could purchase the lands they had already bought from the Cherokees. James Robertson became North Carolina's agent to the Overhill Cherokees, and stayed at Chota, to watch the diminished Overhills and hearken for news of Dragging Canoe.

Like other prominent men, Robertson had private business as well as public responsibility on his mind. Further advance down the Tennessee Valley was not practicable. But the Cumberland country could be reached by way of the Wilderness Road—and perhaps also by the water route, down the Tennessee and up the Cumberland, if luck was kind. Very likely he had discussed such possibilities with John Donelson and Richard Henderson at the Treaty of 1777. Probably his mind dwelled on his prospects while he sat in the townhouse at Chota and smoked with the old chiefs. Maybe, between puffs, he prompted Oconostota or Attakullakulla to tell him more about how the land lay at Muscle Shoals, or how things were at the French Lick, on the Cumberland, from which Cherokees and Chickasaws had driven the Shawnees so long ago.

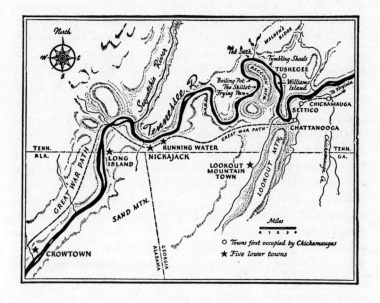

## CHAPTER XI

# The Voyage of the Good Boat
## *Adventure*

THE winter of 1779-80 was one of the coldest ever known in the Tennessee country. Snow began to fall in November, and as winter drew on, the great cold deepened. It was a season when the hardiest pioneer might have wished himself a bear, to curl inside a hollow tree and suck his paw,

149

or a Cherokee, to crawl inside a hothouse and stay there. Yet in this winter, forbidding though it was, took place the most famous of all voyages on the Tennessee River, perhaps indeed the most famous voyage in the annals of the pioneers. In the midst of the cold, Colonel John Donelson of Virginia launched his flagship, the *Adventure*, on the Holston River near Fort Patrick Henry, to lead westward a great flotilla of flatboats and pirogues, loaded with men, women, children, and household goods. Their destination was the French Lick, on the Cumberland River, which they would reach after navigating the entire length of the Tennessee and then making the still more difficult passage upstream by way of the Ohio and the Cumberland. An advance party of men, led by James Robertson, had set out for the French Lick during the preceding fall, by the overland route across the Cumberland plateau and through Kentucky. It was their task to build cabins and prepare the place for habitation. The Donelson party constituted the nautical division of a planned migration of considerable size, from the East Tennessee settlements to what would later become the city of Nashville.

We know with some definiteness just who the Donelson party were and what happened to them, because Colonel Donelson wrote a brief account of his exploit. This he entitled *Journal of a Voyage, intended by God's permission, the good boat Adventure, from Fort Patrick Henry, on the Holston river, to the French Salt Springs on the Cumberland river, kept by John Donelson.*

Historians pause reverently when they come to the Donelson journal. Their gift for exegesis and summary goes to pieces, and they content themselves with verbatim quotation and little comment. Leland D. Baldwin, for example, in *The Keelboat Age,* says that the journal "presents a starkly realistic picture of river immigration that no modern pen could hope to equal," and then speaks no more but only quotes.

Certainly the journal is an American classic. No one can read it without feeling that Donelson's prose style, no less than his courage, was fully equal to the occasion. If he really "kept" the journal while his fleet was cruising down the Tennessee, with hostile Indians shooting from the bank, and boulders, eddies, and reefs clutching at him in the stream, then it is a thousand pities that he did not live longer and write more. The colonel had remarkable gifts, at which we of today can only wonder. Yet for all its vivid excellence, the journal tells less than we should like to know, and it indulges in no explanation whatever. It is a bare chronicle, for which a context has to be supplied. That context is to be derived partly from frontier history in general, partly from the story of Richard Henderson's colonizing schemes, and also, to no small extent, from the occurrences of the year preceding Donelson's voyage.

After the Treaty of 1777, the submissive faction of the Cherokees, having rebuilt their devastated towns on the Little Tennessee, maintained a grudging semblance of peace. But Dragging Canoe was far from even a technical peace. With Ostenaco, Willenawah, and other prominent chiefs, and all the war-minded Cherokees that would follow, he retreated deeper into the wilderness and founded new towns in the mountainous country where the Tennessee begins its twisting furrow across the Cumberland ridges. Settico arose again, under its old name, and other names found new sites in the valley where the city of Chattanooga now stands.

Here they were better located than ever for the purposes of war and pillage. They commanded the river, above and near the difficult Narrows. From their mountain fastness they could go out in mischievous bands to harry isolated cabins and "stations," and then could quickly retire into their secure retreat. They were well placed to receive supplies of goods and ammunition from the British agents in Florida. Their numbers were swelled by warriors from the neighboring

Creeks; and they were joined also by renegade whites, some of whom were fugitive Tories, and a mixture of other elements, Indian and Negro. The Tennessee settlers called them "Chickamaugas" to distinguish them from the more pacific part of the Cherokees, and added terms of eloquent abuse— "banditti," "outlaws," "pirates." By the end of 1778, Dragging Canoe commanded a thousand fighting men and was preparing to drive once more against the western settlements.

To forestall this attack, Governor Patrick Henry of Virginia, in co-operation with Governor Caswell of North Carolina and the Tennessee frontiersmen, organized a bold counteroffensive. The commander of the expedition, Colonel Evan Shelby, rendezvoused his Virginians and Tennesseans, probably six hundred men in all, at the home of James Robertson on Holston River. There he assembled a fleet of pirogues and canoes made from the neighboring forests with ax and adz. The plan was to move quickly with the spring tide down the Tennessee River and strike the Chickamauga towns before they were aware of the presence of danger. When this blow had been struck, a part of the troops, under Colonel John Montgomery, would float on down the Tennessee and join George Rogers Clark in fighting the British in the Northwest.

In mid-April, with the river at floodtide, Shelby's men sped to their objective, and found the Chickamaugas unready. There was no fighting. In two weeks' time they overran and devastated eleven of the Chickamauga towns, including the new Settico, which they struck first of all. Montgomery's contingent went on. The others, after crossing the river and destroying their boats, marched back up the west bank of the Tennessee. They brought with them huge quantities of booty: horses, which were especially welcome for the return trip; and ammunition and goods sent by the British for their Indian allies. For the first time in history, a military expedition had used Tennessee water for transport.

Yet Dragging Canoe would not own himself conquered.

Some of the Chickamaugas came back from their mountain hide-outs and reoccupied a few of the burned towns. The majority, at Dragging Canoe's direction, moved still farther down the Tennessee to a more secret and impregnable retreat. The Five Lower Towns, as they were called—although, because of shifts of occupancy, there were really more than five—made full strategic use of the windings of the river. Tuskegee Island town commanded the entrance to the Suck. Dragging Canoe's own town, Running Water, and the nearby town of Nickajack, lay just below the Narrows. Long Island town and Crow town were still farther downstream. For many years after this the pioneers of Tennessee and Kentucky were very painfully aware of the existence of the Five Lower Towns, but it was long before they could discover just how to approach them for an attack.

Colonel John Donelson could hardly have known much about the re-establishment of the Chickamauga towns. He did know, however, that Shelby's onslaught, in the April preceding his own voyage, had weakened the Chickamaugas and that many of the towns had been burned. Therefore, although every moment of those days was a dangerous moment, the month of December, 1779, could reasonably be deemed one of the least dangerous periods. The extreme cold itself was a protection, probably, since war parties were not likely to dare its rigors. And of course the winter was the season for high water and swift movement on the Tennessee.

Besides, Donelson had a schedule to keep. James Robertson had visited the French Lick early in 1779 with a small group, and had marked the place for settlement—doubtless in agreement with the plans of Richard Henderson. Robertson had planted a corn crop, fenced it in, and left three men to guard it while he returned to the Holston country to complete arrangements for the migration. Only the skilled hunters and Indian fighters would make the westward trip over-

land in the fall, by the untraveled route that Robertson intended to use. The boats of the Donelson fleet would carry the women and children, and whatever household goods could be put on; and they would also offer some degree of shelter and safety. Before leaving East Tennessee, Robertson told Donelson that, if opportunity allowed, he would examine the country between the French Lick and Muscle Shoals. If there was a practicable overland route from Muscle Shoals to the north, he promised to leave some message or sign at the head of the Shoals, in order that the voyagers might disembark there and save themselves the hardships of the long pull all the way around. With such considerations in mind, Donelson gave the order to push off.

Bleak indeed must have been that setting forth. Three days before Christmas it was, and only cold cheer in sight. At Fort Patrick Henry the river was low, and weather was making. On board Donelson's flagship, the *Adventure,* were at least thirty persons—men, women, and children. Among the women was Donelson's fifteen-year-old daughter, Rachel, she who afterward married Andrew Jackson. The other boats, no doubt, were equally crowded, if not with notables, certainly with the ancestors of notables. For the Donelson fleet has the same relation to the history of the old Southwest that the *Mayflower* has to New England: it carried historic persons and the begetters of historic persons. Assuredly they were all most uncomfortable in December, 1779.

The *Adventure* was probably a large flatboat of a type afterward familiarly known as a "broadhorn." She was built at the "Boatyard" (modern Kingsport) of heavy timber, with a hull of squared logs and sides well bulwarked against gunfire. She probably had a roof over a considerable part of the hull, with rude bunks for sleeping quarters, and a stone hearth for the cooking. She was steered by sweeps and propelled by poles when propulsion was regrettably necessary, but was emphatically better adapted to going downstream with the current than to inching upstream against it. The other flatboats resembled the *Adventure,* although perhaps not all of them were as large or commodious. The pirogues were of the common dugout type, but some of them may have had a covering. It was an ungainly, nondescript line of flatboats and pirogues that poled away from the bank and into the current that December morning. There were thirty craft in all, and more would join, downriver.

The first day they went only three miles, to the mouth of Reedy Creek. The river was falling, it was snowing, there was already ice on the water. Donelson made camp in the snow. For all the progress the fleet made from December 22 to February 20 they might as well have stayed in Fort Patrick Henry in possibly greater comfort. But once started, they had to go on—or just stop.

On February 27 they pushed off once more. The *Adventure* celebrated this, the real beginning of the voyage, by getting stuck, together with the boats of Mr. Boyd and Mr. Rounsifer, on Poor Valley Shoals. For an afternoon and a night they lay there, and got off at last only by unloading the passengers into the icy water to lighten the heavy boats. A little farther down, Donelson attempted to land on an island, doubtless to build fires and thaw out frozen feet. The *Adventure* was damaged, and Donelson's company lost part of their baggage, but made camp nevertheless, and were rejoined by the whole flotilla, which had got disorganized and scattered.

March came in, rainy and blustery, with hardly a sign of spring as yet. Beyond the dull green of the cane bottoms were the dark cones of cedars on the lower slopes, or pine groves here and there, among the leafless hardwood forests. Gray sedge grass, sprinkled with young trees and growths of brier and bramble, covered the open savannas near the river; and back of it all they could occasionally see, through the streamers of rain, cloud masses resting on the great mountain

ranges that they were leaving behind them. They were floating down the great valley of East Tennessee, and on either
side of them were the unchangeable shapes of hill and mountain as we see them today.

On March 2 they passed the mouth of the French Broad
River, and now on the Tennessee proper, followed its windings past the high banks on which Knoxville would soon be
built. The current was getting tricky. On the point of an
island, a little above the Knoxville bluffs, Mr. Henry's boat
grounded, and was capsized by the force of the current. The
whole fleet stopped to rescue their wrecked companions,
snatch floating articles, bale out the boat, and help dry the
shivering passengers. Young Reuben Harrison took advantage of this stop to go a-hunting. At night he had not returned. They fired guns to let him know their position, but
no answering shot came to their ears. Next day at dawn
they shot off signals again, and Donelson fired his swivel and
sent out searching parties. But Reuben did not appear to comfort his weeping parents. Donelson left old Mr. Harrison and
others to continue the search, and went on. About ten o'clock
of that day they saw the young man awaiting them by the
water's edge, and Ben Belew took him on board.

On that day, March 4, they passed the mouth of the
Little Tennessee. They were definitely in Indian country
now, and they began to post sentinels at night. For greater
precaution they camped on the north shore, a practice they
had begun four days preceding.

The next day they passed the mouth of the Clinch, and
were joined by a number of boats under Captain John Blackmore, from Fort Blackmore. It was foggy weather now, especially in the mornings, and it was still rainy. Finding that the
fleet was trailing too far behind in the fog, Donelson stopped
the *Adventure* until all boats were reassembled. At camp that
night Captain Thomas Hutchings' Negro man died. His feet

and legs had been frozen, and apparently the resulting infection killed him.

On March 7 the rain ceased, but the March wind began. Blowing from SSW, it kicked up waves. The rough water did not embarrass the heavier craft, but the pirogues had trouble, tossed as they were by the twisting current and the side-slapping waves. It seemed best to put in at the mouth of South Chickamauga Creek, where one of Dragging Canoe's towns had stood.

A year before, or a year later, Donelson would not have camped there. But Shelby's ravages of the preceding spring had left this uppermost of the Chickamauga towns in ashes. Dry weed stalks stood where the townhouse and the cabins had been. Perhaps the children, glad to be out of their narrow quarters for a spell, ran across the desolate cornhills and maybe found a few early violets. And here Mrs. Ephraim Peyton, whose husband had gone overland with Robertson, gave birth to a child.

It must have been a pleasant campsite, for the next morning they did not cast off at dawn, but waited until ten o'clock. Probably the women got a little washing done, and the men put in some cautious hunting and fishing. To the west and southwest they could now see the massive abutments of the Cumberlands, through which the river would soon take them to the Suck and its dangers, and what foes they knew not.

Almost immediately after casting off, it seemed, the swift current bore them past the first Indian town. It was one of the towns Shelby had destroyed, but the Chickamaugas had come back. As Donelson swung the *Adventure* away from the south shore, Indians began to crowd the bank. They called out "brother" and made signs inviting the voyagers to land.

The colonel's son, Captain John Donelson, and a man named Caffrey begged permission to take a canoe and cross over to the Indian side. The colonel gave permission. The rest of the fleet, seeing the *Adventure* draw over to the north shore, began to lay up to that shore also. A canoe full of Indians put out from the south shore and met the two young men in midstream. The canoes turned and approached the *Adventure,* with other canoes following. When the leading canoes came close, a half-breed named Archie Coody sprang on board and introduced himself. The young men, he said, must not cross the river. As he talked, other Indians began to climb aboard. They seemed friendly, and Donelson began to distribute presents. But suddenly more canoes, filled with armed Indians, painted red and black, shot out across the river. Coody ordered his own Indians back into their canoes and urged Donelson to move on quickly. He himself, with one Indian companion, remained on board. Donelson blew a horn and swung the *Adventure* into the current. After a hasty embarkation, the other boats followed. They left the red-and-black warriors behind, but they knew they were entering the gantlet of the Chickamauga towns.

Ahead were mountains, jutting close to the river. The most majestic of all was the great promontory, Lookout Mountain, whose slopes came steeply down to the water. Before they reached Lookout Mountain, Coody and his Indian companion took leave. Smiling agreeably, Coody assured Donelson that they had passed all the towns and were now out of danger, except for the perils of the Suck.

It was a deliberate lie. Soon they approached another town, again on the south side, and again the Indians made friendly gestures, and shouted to the voyagers, as they swung toward the north side, that their own side was better for boats. Here, in the shadow of Lookout Mountain, the first shots were fired at them, and the first casualties occurred. A man named Payne was killed from an ambush on Moccasin Bend, as his boat veered too near the north side, which Donelson was assuming to be safer. But the fleet went by so swiftly that there was no time for the Indians to organize a real attack.

Nevertheless, they were able to pick off the last boat in the line. It belonged to Thomas Stuart, and on board were his family and friends—twenty-eight people. Smallpox had broken out in this group some days before, and by Donelson's orders they always moved last and kept at a distance. The Indians fell upon this straggler and soon killed or captured all the party. The yells of the Indians, the crack of guns, the screams of the women were borne along the gorge to the ears of the voyagers. But the current, now increasingly rapid, prevented any turning back. They could not reach Stuart's boat in time to do any good. An attempt at rescue might endanger the whole expedition. Their only solace was the grim certainty that the smallpox would wreak revenge for them; and tradition says that it did.

As the boats swept toward the entrance to the Suck, they caught glimpses of bands of warriors, going at a dog-trot, single file, along rocky paths that paralleled the river, but presently they rounded the point, entered the ravine of the Suck, and the Indians disappeared from view.

The river now demanded their whole attention. They were in the domain of Untsaiyi, among whose rocks and whirlpools life itself was a gamble. The rains had brought high water, and the eddies and crosscurrents of the narrow gorge sucked and tossed the awkward craft. Men stood at the bow and sides with poles to fend the boats off from rocks and from drifting trees that raced with them on the flood.

The pirogues were more exposed than the flatboats to the fire of the Indians, and they were also tossed more unmercifully by the currents. With these dangers in mind, John Cotton, before they entered the Suck, transferred his family to Robert Cartwright's flatboat and tied his pirogue, still loaded with goods, to the stern of the larger vessel. But the pirogue dashed wildly to and fro, and presently was overturned. The cry for help went up. Donelson, finding a calmer stretch of water and seeing Cotton's difficulty, blew his horn for a landing and pulled over to the north shore, where there was some level ground. As Donelson and his men walked toward the scene of the wreck, they heard again the crack of guns and the whistle of bullets. The heights across the river were fringed with warriors, who were firing down upon them. The Indians had taken a short cut across the mountain while the voyagers were fighting the torrents of the Suck, and now had an easy mark. Hastily they retreated to the boats, leaving Cotton and Cartwright to solve their own problems, and pushed off again.

The Indians, lining the bluffs, continued their fire. In the boat of Abel Gower, James Robertson's brother-in-law, some of the men were wounded, among them the steersman. As the boat drifted helpless, broadside to the current, young Nancy Gower seized the rudder and steered until the men-folks got reorganized. When the flurry was over, Mrs. Gower saw that Nancy's skirt was stained with blood. The girl had been shot through the thigh, and had never whimpered.

At this juncture Donelson noted, in a quick glance, that Cotton's boat was safe after all—though his goods were undoubtedly lost; but Jonathan Jennings's boat was missing.

There was no going back. The current bore them on.

We may infer, from Donelson's phrase, that the Indians "lined the bluffs along" and continued to harass the party until they passed Running Water and Nickajack. Nevertheless, they issued from the Narrows without further harm and entered the long, fairly straight stretch of river between Long Island and present-day Guntersville. Now they were in the Great Bend of the Tennessee and Donelson knew that they were approaching a section of the river in which he had something more than a romantic interest. He studied the scene, no doubt, with a surveyor's eye. Donelson had plans, which dovetailed with the plans of other men, for opening to settlement the pleasant country he now saw. How well the land lay! The mountains were less rugged, and they stood farther back from the river. There would be rich fields in this country. The river widened. The current became more gentle and placid. All the rest of that day and throughout that night they floated without stopping, to put as much river as possible between them and the Indians. And so the next day, and the next night until midnight. Only then did Donelson give the signal to land and make camp. Of Jennings's boat he had no further word, other than it had been wrecked on a rock, somewhere in the Suck.

About four o'clock of that morning they were awakened by a long frontiersman's shout, far in the rear. Down the river came the cry, "Help poor Jennings!" It was indeed Jennings, although in a most bedraggled condition. He came in his boat and most of his company were with him, their clothing cut with bullets, eager for food and for the warmth of the fires, which they had seen from up the river, when they began hallooing.

Jennings had a tale to tell. His boat, he said, was not wrecked. It was grounded on a reef. The Indians, discovering his predicament, turned a galling fire upon the boat. Jennings ordered his wife, his nearly grown son, a young man who accompanied them, and his two Negroes to throw the baggage into the river in order to lighten the boat and get it off the reef. While they were thus engaged, he covered their work with his rifle and vigorously returned the fire of the Indians. Instead of carrying out his commands, the young man and one of the Negroes simply jumped out in a panic; the Negro was drowned; young Jennings and the other young man were wounded and captured by the Indians. Mrs. Jennings also got out of the boat to help push it off. When the boat suddenly started, she lost her balance and was nearly drowned. Mrs. Peyton—she who, only one night before this event, was delivered of a child—stood in the water and helped with the unloading and shoving, with no ill effect to herself. But somehow her newborn infant was killed or drowned in the confusion.

The next day, March 11, Donelson distributed the Jennings family in the other boats. They moved on quietly, quickening their speed by rowing.

The following day, which was Sunday, they heard roosters crowing as they passed another Indian town. They were fired on again. They had run the gantlet, or almost so. But the greatest danger was just ahead—Muscle Shoals.

If Robertson had left a sign, they would disembark here. Donelson landed at the head of the Shoals, on the north bank. While the fleet lay up, he and his best frontiersmen looked for the blazed trees, or the letter stuck in the cleft of a stick that Robertson might have put there.

There was no sign anywhere—not a blazed tree, not a letter, not a cairn of stones. They turned away. Later they were to find out that Robertson had not come to Muscle Shoals at all. He had assumed, because of the great cold, that Donelson would abandon his voyage.

Donelson called a council of war. It was decided that, lacking a sign, they could not with prudence attempt the overland route. They must run the Shoals and go the long way, and they must be quick about starting, if they were to escape the Indians who even now might be following them. As they made this decision, their eyes must have lingered to take in the sweep of the fair country around them: a good valley, with plenty of rich bottom land no doubt, to the north; and on the south a level country, with broken mountains only here and there in the distance.

Cargoes were redistributed to trim the boats. To shoot the rapids safely, their craft must be well balanced. They put off. Before night they were through the Shoals without quite knowing how they had done it. Their salvation was that the river was extremely high. They slid over rocks and reefs with plenty of water to spare. But it was terrifying.

When we approached them [wrote Donelson] they had a dreadful appearance to those who had never seem them before. The water being high made a terrible roaring, which could be heard at some distance among the driftwood heaped frightfully upon the points of the islands, the current running in every possible direction. Here we did not know how soon we should be dashed to pieces, and all our troubles ended at once. Our boats frequently dragged on the bottom, and appeared constantly in danger of striking: they warped as much as in a rough sea. But, by the hand of Providence, we are now preserved from this danger also. I know not the length of this wonderful shoals: it had been represented to me to be twenty-five or thirty miles; if so, we must have descended very rapidly, as indeed we did, for we passed it in about three hours. Came to, and encamped on the northern shore, not far below the shoals, for the night.

The point where they "came to," and doubtless baled out their boats, and thanked Providence, must have been above Florence. The next day they made an uneventful run, but on the morning of the second day from Muscle Shoals, they were fired on by Indians. Five men were wounded. The party made camp near the mouth of a creek, but alarmed by the barking of their dogs, they concluded that Indians were creeping near, and hurriedly broke camp. They fell down the river about a mile and made camp on the north shore. Next morning Donelson sent back young John Donelson and Caffrey to reconnoiter the site of the earlier camp and recover utensils abandoned in their retreat. Asleep by one of the dying fires they found a Negro slave. All the commotion of the preceding night had not awakened him.

The scene of this alarm was near the Creek town of Coldwater, which was attacked seven years later by an expedition commanded by James Robertson. Some members of the Donelson party took part in this later expedition. Sitting around the campfires before they crossed the Tennessee to deliver their attack, they recalled earlier perils and retold the story of their voyage. It was, they said, "one of the most marvellous escapes that had ever been known. . . . The savages were shooting at them from the shores; it was cruel death to land on either shore; they must go forward, trusting in Providence to preserve them."

Donelson made good time on the easy lower reaches of the Tennessee. The lesser shoals and sand bars were covered deep by the high water. In a week they floated 250 miles to the junction of the Tennessee and the Ohio. Very likely (since Donelson records no bad weather) it was a fair March season, with young green beginning to show in the sheltered places, beyond the cane thickets and gaunt white sycamores that fringed the banks. Reaching the mouth of the Tennessee, they landed "on the lower point, immediately on the bank of the Ohio"—that is, at the site, or very near the site, of what would later be Paducah. Here the voyagers pondered their situation, which still had its grim aspects. The heavy boats floated like chips downstream. But to go up the Ohio and then up the Cumberland—that was entirely different.

Our situation [wrote Donelson] is truly disagreeable. The river [the Ohio] is very high and the current rapid, our boats not constructed for the purpose of stemming a rapid stream, our provision exhausted. The crews almost worn out with hunger and fatigue, and know not what distance we have to go, or what time it will take us to reach our destination. The scene is rendered still more melancholy, as several boats will not attempt to ascend the rapid current. Some intend to descend the Mississippi to Natchez; others are bound for Illinois—among the rest my son-in-law and daughter. We now part, perhaps, to meet no more, for I am determined to pursue my course, happen what will.

Pursue his course he did, but it took more than a month to pole, shove, tow, and otherwise persuade the clumsy boats up the Ohio to the Cumberland, and up the Cumberland to the French Lick. They moved laboriously, hoisting makeshift sails when the wind was in the right quarter, and living off buffalo, and wild swan, and "Shawnee salad" (possibly "poke salad"), for they now had no food except what they could obtain from the wilderness around them.

At the very end of March they had the first sign that the journey's end was near, or at least no longer inconceivably remote. They met Richard Henderson, in person, with a party of surveyors. As usual, Henderson was looking after his interests, on the ground itself of his interests: that is, he had been running the line between Virginia and North Carolina. Probably he had a broad smile on his face, and not only because he was meeting Donelson; for the survey had disclosed that the Cumberland settlements did *not* lie on the Virginia side.

Somehow, this meeting does not quite look like pure coincidence.

Henderson gave the voyagers advice and information in great sufficiency. But he had no food to give. Corn, he said, was on the way to the French Lick. He had ordered some sent down from Boonsborough. They went on. At the mouth of Red River, near present-day Clarksville, Moses Renfroe and another group of settlers dropped off. The rest arrived on April 24, 1780, at the French Lick, and climbed the bluffs to the cluster of cabins which was to become a capital city.

In the four months since Christmas, 1779, they had floated a thousand miles. Exactly how many of the voyagers completed the trip, out of the original two hundred or more, we do not know, since Donelson recorded in his journal only the names of heads of families. Out of the company, it appears that at least thirty-three were lost, either through being killed or captured by Indians, or drowned, as the Peyton infant probably was, or frozen, as was the unfortunate Negro. Others—at least nine in all—bore the marks of wounds from Indian bullets. All must have counted themselves lucky to have arrived.

# CHAPTER XII

# John Sevier and the Lost State of Franklin

THE DECADE beginning in 1780 saw the rise of John Sevier, Tennessee's first popular hero. As Colonel Sevier, he was one of the commanders at the famous victory of King's Mountain. He was the first and only governor of the independent state of Franklin, but although Franklin was "lost," Sevier was not. He became the first governor of Tennessee when in 1796 it was admitted as a state, and held the same office five times thereafter. Above all, he was the bane of the Cherokees, and his career was founded largely on his campaigns against them. He is said to have fought thirty-five battles, and from them all emerged scatheless and victorious. Yet he never conquered Dragging Canoe and the Chickamaugas.

To understand this man, one must set aside conventional notions about the frontier. He did not cultivate the broad homespun humor of a Davy Crockett. Rather, he was something of a beau sabreur and may have worn his hunting shirt with a touch of elegance. He was a brave man, but did not have the irascible head-on directness of Andrew Jackson. He was a good politician, but not a speechmaker. A great landspeculator, he was nevertheless ready, like Henderson and Donelson, to risk life as well as fortune. His prestige rested upon military prowess, and he showed a touch of genius in

his use of mounted forces against the Indians. His swift raids
foreshadowed the cavalry methods of Bedford Forrest. The
war whoop he taught his men to use in charging may have
been a remote ancestor of the Rebel Yell. Genial, vivacious,
never aloof, he shared in the merrymakings and hardships of
his followers and, though commanding, moved among them
as an equal. He was also an intimate of William Blount, Richard Caswell, and other master planners, and he shared in their
tremendous schemes. His greatest virtue was that he identified
himself fully with his people and had no ambition that could
not be gratified within the bounds of the wilderness country
that he loved. The nickname "Old Hickory" symbolizes the
personal toughness that became a valuable political asset to
Andrew Jackson, his great rival of later years. But Sevier was
"Nolichucky Jack." He belonged to a place. He belonged to
the river and the valley where he built his home.

The times were made for him, and he was made for
them. The Tennessee frontier was all but encircled by enemies. After the fall of Charleston in May, 1780, Lord Cornwallis launched a campaign of devastation and terror that
swept west and north through the Carolinas. Tarleton's dra-
goons and mixed forces of Tories and regulars under Ferguson harried the backcountry. Although the Cherokee
border required constant watching, and the Tennessee settlements were crowded with refugees from Georgia and the
Carolinas, the men of Holston and Watauga contributed
forces to the Revolutionary battle line far out of proportion
to their resources and numerical strength. In the hard year
of 1780 they fought at Thickety Fort, Musgrove's Mill, and
Cedar Springs, in North Carolina. And in the autumn of
1780 a frontier army, rendezvousing at Sycamore Shoals under Isaac Shelby and John Sevier of Tennessee and William
Campbell of Virginia, rode far across the mountains to seek
out and destroy Major Patrick Ferguson's threatening force
of eleven hundred British and Tories. In a single afternoon

the overmountain men killed or captured all of Ferguson's command, killed Ferguson himself, and thus—in the opinion of many persons competent to judge—tipped the balance of the Revolutionary War in the South. After that, contingents from the western country fought in the bloody battle of Guilford Courthouse, and in the last days of the war were among the forces pressing the British pickets at Charleston.

Always they were having to turn from the British invader to meet the Indian onslaught. The first Cherokee campaign of which Sevier had sole command followed hard upon the Battle of King's Mountain. An Indian attack, planned with the assistance of British agents and undertaken by order of Cornwallis to divert pressure from his own vicinity, was actually being organized while Sevier's mountain riders were tracking Ferguson. It represented once more a general uprising, not merely a drive by the Chickamaugas. Sevier's counterdrive, the Boyd's Creek campaign, was a model of frontier warfare and illustrates the methods that he used again and again.

Forewarned of Indian trouble, Sevier sent a detachment hurrying back from King's Mountain to strengthen the frontier guards. On his arrival in Watauga, he had hardly unsaddled before he was on the move again, with hastily assembled forces, not waiting on the reinforcements that were to come from Virginia. It was to be an offensive campaign. There would be no more huddling in the wretched palisaded forts.

Scouts soon located a considerable body of Indians, and Sevier halted, made a secure night camp, and waited for more of his men to join him. The next day he crossed the French Broad and, after careful reconnaissance, discovered the Indians in ambush near Boyd's Creek. Sevier simulated an attack with a part of his forces to draw the Indians into his counter-ambush. The ruse succeeded, the Indians pursued rashly as the decoys fled, and Sevier's men, who had been organized into three divisions and instructed to execute an enveloping movement, broke cover and closed in for the kill. The envelopment was imperfect only because Major Jonathan Tipton (brother of John Tipton of later fame) misunderstood Sevier's orders and did not wheel the left wing, which he commanded, fast and far enough to complete the encirclement. Thus the Indians were able to retreat through a gap in the line, but they suffered heavy casualties. On Sevier's side not a man was killed, and only three were wounded, among them Major Tipton. The extremely light casualties among the frontiersmen, in this as in other of Sevier's battles, are somewhat difficult to understand. Possibly the Cherokees, who did deadly work in guerrilla raids, failed in open battle because Sevier's quick rush was timed to catch them with unloaded guns, and the Indians had not mastered the technique of firing and reloading under battle conditions.

After this fight Sevier was joined by troops from Virginia and from Sullivan County, and though rations were very short for a time, the army feasted on Indian stores after crossing the Little Tennessee. Again, as in Christian's campaign, the Cherokees vacated their towns and offered no real resistance, although they lined the distant ridges and fired scattering shots. And again there was a punitive burning of towns. Chota was not spared this time, and some of the Hiwassee towns were included for good measure.

In 1781, Sevier's mounted riflemen made an extremely difficult surprise march across the Smoky Mountains and ravaged the Middle towns, in the beautiful "Vale of Cowee," where Bartram, a few years previous, had watched the Cherokee nymphs pick strawberries. But neither this nor the Boyd's Creek campaign touched the true source of Cherokee power, which was far down the Tennessee River, at the Five Lower Towns of Dragging Canoe. Sevier made his first and only campaign against this stronghold in September, 1782.

It turned out to be a peculiar campaign. With two hundred and fifty men Sevier rode to Chota. Before him, at

Chota, appeared Kunokeskie, better known as John Watts—
the son, possibly, of a soldier of the Fort Loudoun garrison—
and offered his services as guide for the march against the
Chickamauga towns. Furthermore, John Watts said, he would
be glad to assist in negotiations, since it was likely that peace
might be arranged. Actually, Watts was loyal to the Chickamaugas and was probably following the Canoe's instructions.
His real purpose was to divert Sevier before he reached the
inner citadel, and perhaps also to lead him into ambush. Apparently Sevier was deceived by Watts's plausible talk. At
any rate, he accepted the Indian's services.

Marching to Chickamauga Creek, Sevier harried the
towns of that neighborhood, which had been reoccupied after
Shelby's campaign of 1779. Then—though the historical
accounts are a little indefinite—he proceeded down the Tennessee River, came close to the entrance of the Suck, crossed
an arm of the river, and destroyed Tuskegee Island town, on
Williams Island. At this point, the story goes, a Chickamauga chief, Bloody Fellow, called out a challenge from the
bluffs opposite. Sevier then recrossed the river and, in the
first battle of Lookout Mountain, defeated, or at least drove
back, the Indians gathered there.

Whether Sevier was deceived by John Watts into thinking he had destroyed all the Chickamauga towns, or whether
he deemed it wiser not to venture farther into unknown and
dangerous territory, cannot be known. But he did not attack
the Five Lower Towns. Instead, after some delay, he turned
far to the south and ravaged the unoffending towns along
the Coosa River. With this wanton destruction Sevier closed
his third Cherokee campaign, which was also the last campaign of the Revolutionary War west of the mountains.

With the end of the war, politics came to the front. The
settlers were faced with tiresomely complicated but very
pressing questions. Under the Watauga Association they had
already enjoyed a kind of independence, and they shared in

the separatist tendencies that were stirring the western border of the new nation. They were naturally responsive to the suggestion that a new state should be set up, which might soon be admitted to the Union if there was no obstruction by North Carolina.

Meeting in convention in 1784, representatives of the East Tennessee settlements authorized the establishment of such a state, to be named—perhaps with an eye to the favor of a great patriot—for Benjamin Franklin. John Sevier was chosen governor, and a temporary constitution, soon to be replaced by a permanent one, was devised. The boundaries of Franklin, although never officially defined, were probably intended to include all of the present state of Tennessee, and perhaps also the Great Bend region and some of western Virginia. In quite an orderly fashion, Franklin proceeded to exercise all the functions of a state. It even authorized a coinage, but its mint, if ever established, apparently never issued any coins. Franklin was a promising creation, and its exultant citizens began rather pointedly to speak of themselves as Franks. In a short time, however, it was in trouble. It was undermined from without; it developed quarreling factions within. By 1788, after four years of ups and downs, Franklin was done as a political entity. Nevertheless, it left a deep impression upon East Tennessee. In later years the people of that region, ever mindful of the Lost State of Franklin, repeatedly made motions to separate from the state of Tennessee.

Considering the ease with which new states were later erected, one may think it odd that Franklin did not speedily become the fourteenth state of the Union. Why it did not is a complex and baffling historical puzzle, the solution of which depends upon whether the puzzle solver is romantic or realistic, an ardent patriot or a skeptical researchist.

The romantic view, which stems in some measure from the older Tennessee historians, argues that the Franklin movement grew out of the natural genius for self-government possessed by the hardy Westerners. John Sevier was their great leader, and he was ready to sacrifice everything save honor in his people's cause. Other patriots, also men of genius, stood with him. In the end Franklin was lost because North Carolina vacillated and played the tyrant. Moreover, there was betrayal from within by folks like rowdy John Tipton, who must surely have been a great villain. The most highly colored statement of this romantic view was written by James Gilmore, a New Jersey man who visited Tennessee during and after the Civil War.

The realistic view holds that the state of Franklin was a grand exploitative scheme got up by a group of land speculators to guarantee security for their deals in western lands. The shrewdest speculator was William Blount, a tidewater North Carolinian of genuine Cavalier ancestry, who preferred to work behind the scenes as much as possible. But other eminent persons worked with him, and naturally this group astutely arranged things so that John Sevier, the military leader, would be the people's choice. John Tipton, in this view, becomes a small gesturing figure—a local politician with an angry sense of being bilked. The state of Franklin becomes a mere convenient instrument which was allowed to wither away when it had served its purpose. The lusty pioneers become the exploited masses, misled by politicians whom, without good cause, they obstinately worship. This point of view has been ably set forth and documented by a Southerner, Thomas Perkins Abernethy. In the end it is no more satisfying than the view of the romantic Yankee from New Jersey, and the harried inquirer may with excellent reason prefer the solid and moderate interpretation of Tennessee's Samuel Cole Williams, who in his book, *The Lost State of Franklin*, wisely takes a middle path.

The bare facts are these. In 1783, North Carolina opened an office, administered by John Armstrong, for the entry of claims to western lands. Since this office was in North Carolina at a point remote from the settlements, and was closed after a few months, it was obviously intended to serve the land jobbers of North Carolina. In 1784, after Armstrong's office had been closed, the North Carolina legislature voted to cede the state's western lands to the national government, with provisions that openly invited the establishment of a new state. The cession, however, met with strong opposition; and within that same year the legislature repealed the act of cession.

The state of Franklin was formed in the few months' interval between the cession and the repeal. The legislature's reversal of position was a shock to partisans of the new state. Sevier was at first inclined to drop the project, but he saw that the movement had gathered much headway, and he accepted the governorship. He afterward said that he was "dragged with the Franklin measures by a large number of the people of this country." He now found himself—if we accept Abernethy's phrase—"the unwilling governor of a rebel state." But he did not behave exactly like an unwilling governor. On the whole he stood firmly with the Franks through the confusing times when North Carolina jealously obstructed the Franklin movement and took good care to look after its own selfish and speculative interests.

Franklin appealed to the Continental Congress, and sent William Cocke to plead its cause for admission to the Union. The plea failed, but at one time it seemed close to success.

The first split within the state of Franklin itself came on the adoption of a permanent constitution. Samuel Houston, a Presbyterian divine who was a graduate of Liberty Hall, in Lexington, Virginia, championed an original constitution which had been devised by Arthur Campbell, of Virginia, and William Graham, president of Liberty Hall College. It was furiously assailed by another clergyman, the Reverend Hezekiah Balch. A fiery public controversy ensued, during which the opposing parties vigorously pamphleteered and agitated. Finally, at the suggestion of Sevier, the convention adopted the constitution of North Carolina—the government against which Franklin was "rebelling."

This rift was deepened by the subtle policy of Richard Caswell, who, as the new governor of North Carolina, strove to placate the frontiersmen with indefinite promises while covertly he undermined their state by authorizing the election of North Carolina officials within the Franklin counties. Two sets of elections were held, and two competing groups of officials sought to exercise authority. The power of the opposition, now led by headlong John Tipton, grew rapidly, and the two groups of partisans began to brawl violently. The prestige of Franklin was further weakened by the Treaty of Hopewell, in 1785, the first held by the national government with the Cherokees. The terms of this treaty negated an arrangement Sevier had made with the Cherokees at the Treaty of Dumplin Creek. It placed in Indian territory some already settled land, narrowed the boundaries of Franklin, and assured the Cherokees, in so many words, that if a settler trespassed upon their land, they might "punish him or not as they pleased."

The last hopes of Franklin faded when the federal Constitution of 1787 made no provision favorable to the admission of Franklin to the Union. Under Article IV, Franklin could not become a state without the consent of North Carolina. This consent of course was withheld until, at leisure, North Carolina ratified the Constitution and at long last really ceded its western lands, with provisions that took care of its Revolutionary veterans and land speculators and that forbade the abolition of slavery, unless the citizens of any new state erected from the cession should give their consent. The Tennessee country became a part of the Territory South of the Ohio River, and finally, in 1796, Tennessee became the sixteenth state of the Union, being the first state to be erected out of a territory of the United States.

Meanwhile, by 1788, the state of Franklin was dead and Sevier was in effect an outlaw. The triumphant Tiptonites began a series of raids and seizures, and Sevier at last gathered a small force and made a belated attempt to restore the authority of Franklin. He besieged Tipton's house and called on Tipton to surrender, with his men. Insolently refusing, Tipton told Sevier himself to submit, manned his defenses, and waited for his partisans to come to the rescue. It was bitter cold weather. Tipton's Sullivan County adherents, arriving in a snowstorm, surprised Sevier's men and drove them back in a small battle which, though halfheartedly fought, caused some fatalities. Sevier was "silent and morose" during the action, and men on both sides fired into the air rather than, kill their fellow frontiersmen.

Party feeling was now intense, and if Sevier had chosen to rally his followers, there might have been a real civil war. Instead, he joined his most faithful partisans, the people who lived south of the French Broad on the dangerous Indian border. There a kind of ghost of the state of Franklin lived on briefly.

During this period a Cherokee named Slim Tom came to John Kirk's house during his absence, and was hospitably fed by the family. A few hours later he reappeared stealthily and slaughtered all his hosts—eleven members of the family. Kirk found the bodies lying in the yard when he came home. This atrocity made occasion for another Indian campaign, and Sevier, though now without authority, summoned his riflemen and fell upon the Overhill towns. It was the least creditable of his campaigns. John Kirk went along, with cold hate in his heart, and with him was his friend, James Hubbard. During a lull in the ravaging, Hubbard hoisted a flag of truce and decoyed Old Tassel and other pacific chiefs into a cabin for a parley. Then Hubbard handed Kirk a tomahawk and urged him to take his revenge. Kirk tomahawked the old chiefs one by one in cold blood. They were unarmed, and they bent their heads unresistingly to the death they saw was inevitable. It was a terrible deed, and it strengthened the Cherokee will to fight. Sevier upbraided Kirk but did not punish him, for the sentiment of the troops supported Kirk.

There was one more sharply dramatic episode before this phase of Sevier's career ended. Samuel Johnston, the new governor of North Carolina, ordered a warrant to be issued for the arrest of Sevier on the charge of treason. Two prominent judges, when applied to, refused to issue the warrant, but a third, less friendly to Sevier, did so. Tipton, with a posse, seized Sevier in his lodgings at Jonesborough and carried him off to Morganton, North Carolina. There Sevier's North Carolina friends made bond for him, and he awaited trial.

What happened next may well be a disputed matter between romanticists and realists, but the traditional story of Sevier's rescue is so true to the spirit of the times that it cannot be discarded as pure fiction. According to this account, Sevier's frontier friends, burning with a sense of injury, resolved to send a picked group to bring the lost leader home. The guiding genius of the band seems to have been Dr. James Cozby, a tall and brawny soldier-surgeon, scarred in many a fight, who had served under Sevier at King's Mountain. The band rode to Morganton, where court was in session, leading with them a fine racing mare than belonged to Sevier. They tied their horses on the outskirts of town, left their rifles concealed in the brush, and with pistols hidden underneath their hunting shirts, walked into Morganton and mingled with the large crowd that was present for the meeting of court. Nathaniel Evans led Sevier's mare to a point in front of the courthouse door, where she could be seen from within, while Cozby entered the courtroom itself. There— according to the reminiscences of William Smith, who knew the actors in this drama—sat Sevier, "as firm and undaunted as when charging the hosts of Wyuca on the Lookout Mountain":

Slowly he turned his head, and their eyes met; Sevier knew the rescue was at hand, but he was restrained from any outward demonstration, by a significant shake of Cozby's head. . . . During a pause in the trial, Cozby stepped forward in front of the Judge, and in that quick and energetic tone, so peculiar to him, asked the Judge if he was done with that man? The question, manner and tone, caused every person to start, to cast their eyes on the speaker, then on the Judge, all in amazement. In the meantime, Sevier caught a glimpse of his favorite mare, standing at the door; taking advantage of the confusion, he made one spring to the door; the next, he was safely in the saddle, and with the speed of thought, was borne from the wondering crowd. "Yes," cries a waggish voice, "I'll be damned if you ain't done with him!" His comrades were not slow to follow him, and, although immediate pursuit was made, a few minutes brought him to the main body, who, with one wild shout of victory, closed in the rear, and bore him on in triumph.

The pursuit was only a gesture. The sympathies of the crowd, perhaps of the court, were with Sevier. The charges against him were not pressed. Before long the trend of events were reversed, and Sevier went to Congress to represent the western district of North Carolina. After that, honors came thick and fast. Not even the enmity of Andrew Jackson, with whom Sevier quarreled and who carried the feud to grotesque extremes, could dislodge Sevier from first place in the affections of the frontiersmen of Tennessee.

North Carolina politics, which wrecked the state of Franklin, finally turned to Sevier's advantage. Certain other bold projects, mysteriously interwoven with the history of Franklin, were wrecked by other causes, still hidden from our understanding by the impenetrable fog of frontier intrigue.

William Blount, John Sevier, and their associates understood perfectly that the course of settlement ought to move down the Tennessee Valley and into the Great Bend, and with perhaps ill-justified optimism looked ahead to the day when an "island" of settlement might be planted below the Five Towns, much as the Cumberland "island" had been planted by Henderson. By means not yet clear, the Blount group in 1783 acquired a claim in the Great Bend and by certain political maneuvers persuaded Georgia to set up a county, called Houston, in the Great Bend. Joseph Martin, John Sevier, and John Donelson were among the commission appointed to govern it, and Donelson was surveyor. Attempts at settlement were actually made, but all were frustrated by the Chickamaugas, who grimly told the intruders to be gone. It was apparent that no permanent settlement could be achieved until Dragging Canoe's warriors were overpowered and their Creek allies, farther south, could be intimidated. One of Sevier's cherished designs was to send the military power of Franklin against the Creeks, in combination with troops from Georgia. But the expedition, though formally planned, never came off.

And there was also the Spanish conspiracy. It would seem that the frontier leaders looked on a Spanish alliance as at least a remote possibility—a last resort if other hopes failed. Even James Robertson was involved to some extent. Gardoqui, the Spanish minister to the United States, and Miro, the Spanish governor of Louisiana, made discreet approaches in high quarters. Two of Sevier's letters to Gardoqui survive, in which Sevier, using very careful language, emphasizes the defense needs of the state of Franklin and the strategic importance of Muscle Shoals. He also suggests that a small loan might be acceptable—to the state of Franklin, of course—and refers to the question, at that time a hot political issue, of keeping the Mississippi open to navigation. It does not seem altogether impossible that Sevier was dallying with the prospect of a Spanish alliance. If so solid and worthy a character as James Robertson could join a movement to name the Cumberland settlements the District of Mero

[Miro] in honor of the Spanish governor, there must have been reason for the frontiersmen to covet Spanish friendship, or to seem to do so. But the Spanish officials did not follow up their approaches, nothing more happened, and the frontiersmen did not, in the end, choose a foreign allegiance.

To emerge from battle and controversy with leadership still accorded him by common consent was John Sevier's achievement. It was no mean achievement, although the methods he used were not always beyond criticism. The skeptical modern may be puzzled to know why the men of the frontier worshiped John Sevier and continued to vote for him, although at times it was against their "interests" to do so. The explanation is plain and easy.

The state of Franklin, as a political conception, was a fine thing, but very likely the average frontiersman did not care much about that or any other government. He had what he wanted—a home in a new, free country, and land that he could hold or exchange for other land if the notion struck him. He liked the wilderness and was not discomposed at the prospect of a fight, whether against Indians or other comers. He admired the man who could lead the fight, and once his devotion was given to that man, would follow him to the death. This personal loyalty overbore all political and economic considerations.

In the Tennessee Valley it was almost as in Homeric days. The frontiersmen followed their leaders as did the Achaeans their hero-kings. Or, to use other terms, it was a country like the highlands of Scotland, where clansmen rose at the call of the chief. Although an advanced and modern form of government was superimposed upon them, the Franks were in principle a group of clans. Family, community, blood ties, battle comradeship counted more than political slogans and theories of government.

Lyman Draper recorded how the pioneers felt about it

when he thus preserved the sentiments of one who fought
under Sevier:

Every man considered himself a soldier. He had his horse and
his rifle, which he knew well how to use, and he was always ready
at short notice to join his fellows in any emergency. All had a
common interest, and that most vital: their homes, their families,
any everything dear to man. Thus there was formed among them
a pride of tacit league and covenant, which all regarded as most
binding.

When fighting came on, everyone fought for himself, officers
as well as men. The best officers were those who fought best; as
among the Indians, the officers were leaders rather than commanders.
Command was always more nominal than real. In fighting, it was
always expected that the officers would lead on; any failure to do
this would be marked as cowardice, and the officers cashiered, not by
court martial but by acclamation.

It would surprise men of this generation to see the power
these leaders exercised over their followers. It was a power conferred by God and nature, much more effective than that on
parchment.

CHAPTER XIII

# Dragging Canoe Blockades the River

Even before the Donelson voyage, a few parties of emigrants left the Boatyard or other points on the Holston and floated down the Tennessee, bound for Natchez or for the Illinois country. And after Donelson, in a thin and fitful trickle, others took the hazard and got through. But as long as Dragging Canoe and his warriors of the Lower Towns held the Tennessee in firm blockade, there could be no such mass emigration down the Tennessee as distinguished the Ohio and its upper tributaries. Settlers bound for Middle Tennessee took the old route through Cumberland Gap and Kentucky, or waited at Southwest Point (Kingston) for a guard to accompany them over the newly built wagon road across the Cumberland plateau to Nashville. Or they went by the Kanawha to the Ohio and sought other regions than Tennessee.

Probably no other spot on the river would have suited Dragging Canoe as well as the place he chose for his capital, Running Water. The site, unmarked today, was on the south bank about thirty miles below Chattanooga. A creek runs through a valley that slopes on a broad front to the river within a closely jutting semicircle of mountains. Just above this valley—where Hale's Bar Dam now stands—the tortuous course of the Narrows ends, and the river turns southward. The townsite faces Sequatchie Valley, across the river, where the Cumberland ridges barricade the north; and on its western flank a high bluff comes almost to the water's edge. The railroad now utilizes the narrow passage between bluff and river where, in Indian times, a trail led to the town of Nickajack, four miles downstream.

At Nickajack, as at Running Water, is a valley backed by wooded mountains. One of its prominent features is the enormous cave that opens in the face of a low bluff overlooking the river but at some distance from it—a bat-haunted cave, ramifying far underground, and roofed at its aperture by gigantic horizontal layers of solid rock. Boulders, broken from this roof, lie tumbled about the cave mouth, and among these, issuing from the cave, flows Nickajack Creek. The Indians probably did not use the cave to any great extent. Their dwellings and fields were scattered along the level ground between cave and river, and extended to the prehistoric townsite now known as Shellmound.

The location of the two towns met all requirements of military security. On the east, the approach was guarded by the defiles of the Suck and the rugged masses of Lookout and Raccoon mountains. No hostile force could come from that direction without becoming involved in the perils of the Suck or being exposed to ambush on the difficult and unknown mountain paths. To the north and west was the Tennessee, which any attacking force must cross; and at that time the pioneers knew no path that led to a crossing in the vicinity of the Five Lower Towns. To the south, at Dragging Canoe's back, were his Creek allies and the mountain wilderness.

If invaders came overland from the east, a canoe would shoot away from new Settico or Tuskegee Island town, and immediately Dragging Canoe's "defense in depth" was set to work, as warriors moved up to the assembly point. If a boat was sighted on the river, a runner hurried overland by the short route, and by the time the voyagers had navigated the circuitous Narrows, an ambush was ready; guileful canoes put out in pretense of friendliness, while other canoes, packed with warriors, hid in the cane thickets. If the voyagers nevertheless got away, they might be caught at towns farther down the river, or pursued and overhauled at Muscle Shoals.

For purposes of offensive warfare, the location was no less excellent. It was a concealed base from which the Cherokees could issue in armies of one or two thousand or in scattered bands, moving by paths known only to them, free from observation, free to choose the time and the place to strike. Furthermore, Dragging Canoe's communications were secure. From British agents in the south there came munitions and trade goods, and the Creeks often sent large parties of warriors. The principal British agent in the Lower Towns was now the trader, John McDonald, grandfather of the famous John Ross of later history.

Dragging Canoe kept in touch with the British in Detroit and with important northern tribes, such as the Shawnees. The great Shawnee chief, Tecumseh, lived in the Lower Towns for two years, while he was developing his scheme for united resistance of all Indian tribes to the Americans. But Dragging Canoe's most important diplomatic ties were with the powerful Creek chief, Alexander McGillivray, and with the Scottish firm of Panton & Leslie at Pensacola, Florida. This firm was in Spanish territory, but the Spanish governors of Florida and Louisiana were content to let this British-owned company furnish the Chickamaugas with munitions and goods. The Spanish policy was to build up the Indian front as a buffer against American advance into the lower Mississippi Valley, and they were glad to ignore an arrangement which did not directly involve them. The Spanish also took care to make presents to the Indians and to fill them with promises and fine words, while simultaneously they engaged in intrigues with the leading men in the Tennessee country.

While distant leaders wove their tangled webs of diplomacy, Dragging Canoe's policy was clear, consistent—and grim. As long as his towns stood firm, the Tennessee could not be freely navigated, and no settlements could be made in the rich lands of the Great Bend. It was even a question whether the established settlements, especially the Cumberland settlements, could survive the intensive guerrilla warfare to which Dragging Canoe and his Chickamaugas subjected them. Federal policy played into Dragging Canoe's hands, since it sought to restrain settlers within boundary lines drawn by treaties and to prevent them from attacking the Indian stronghold, while, at the same time, it failed to provide adequate protection. It seemed to assume that the savage warriors of the Lower Towns could be checked by diplomatic negotiations and Christian admonitions.

All this, to Dragging Canoe, was a guarantee of immunity. Under his blanket, his tomahawk laughed at the white man. His position had but one weakness: the danger of betrayal from within. It was always possible for some trader to whisper his plans for attack. Or some captive, adopted into the tribe, might return to the white people and guide a frontier army to the hidden fastness.

Under William Blount as territorial governor, East Tennessee was actually not so well provided for offense and defense as it had been in the days of Franklin. Although at White's Fort—the future Knoxville—a strong barracks, which was practically a fort, overlooked the river, and troops were quartered there, Blount depended on the regular militia, and no longer on the old volunteer risings. This arrangement did not suit Sevier's style of fighting; and although he was now brigadier general, his campaigns were on the whole less effective. Nevertheless, he built a fort at Southwest Point, at the confluence of the Clinch and Tennessee, and this afforded some protection. The Cumberland settlements, isolated from East Tennessee by the wide stretch of uninhabited mountains, fought their scattered best from isolated log houses or from "stations"—rude stockades with one or more loopholed block-houses rising above the enclosure.

The ferocity of the Indian attacks bred a like ferocity among the settlers. There were Indian haters, like Kirk and Hubbard, who for good cause swore eternal vengeance upon all Indians. There were also scouts like Abraham Castleman and Thomas Spencer, famous for his giant stature, who ranged and fought for the love of it, and became as Indian as the Indians. It was a time of blood feuds, bitter forays, swift rides by pioneer armies that subsisted on the Indian diet of parched corn and jerked meat. Strangely enough, it was also a time when frontier leader and Indian chief at intervals negotiated and exchanged letters in perfect courtesy, the grace of Indian rhetoric matched against the pithy elegance of eighteenth century English.

More than once the territory of the Lower Towns was approached by a frontier army, but the citadel itself was not penetrated. Sevier's raid of 1782 turned aside into Georgia, after reaching Lookout Mountain. In 1788, General Joseph Martin failed miserably at the same spot. Martin, a Virginian who had become Cherokee agent for North Carolina, had set up a residence in the Overhill towns, and had married, partly for political reasons no doubt, a daughter of Nancy Ward. There was pressure on him to do something effective about the Chickamauga band, and he attempted to strike a blow. Starting from White's Fort with five hundred men, Martin moved down the Great War Path to the Hiwassee and thence by a night march to Lookout Mountain, where he hoped to make a surprise attack. Instead, his force was ambushed. Perhaps Sevier would have rallied the men and held them in line. Martin was unpopular, and the frontiersmen distrusted his leadership. After some vain attempts to dislodge the Indians, Martin's troops fled in disorder, crying, "It will be another Blue Licks!" (They referred to a defeat of the Kentucky frontiersmen by Indians led by Simon Girty.)

Meanwhile the Cumberland settlements were not idle. In 1787, James Robertson had crossed the Tennessee at Muscle Shoals with a considerable force and destroyed the Creek town of Coldwater. His right wing, which had been ordered to move up the Lower Tennessee, was ambushed and roughly handled at the mouth of Duck River, and did not reach the scene of action. The destruction of Coldwater did not menace the inner citadel, which Robertson did not yet know how to approach.

In 1792, at White's Fort, William Blount held a full-dress treaty, the most ornate and ceremonious of all the treaties. The governor sat in a marquee; officers were present in glittering uniforms; the chiefs were formally introduced; protocol was carefully observed. But, although the chiefs of the Lower Towns attended this treaty and Blount was hopeful of the results, it did not tame the Chickamauga band.

The Indian depredations went on. The Lower Towns waxed strong. The tale of siege and massacre was never done. The old chiefs, Little Carpenter, Oconostota, Ostenaco, had been gathered to their fathers. At his own request, Oconostota was given a white man's burial. A canoe was his coffin. "I want to be buried," he told William Martin, "and I want my body to face the Long Knife." The peaceful inclinations of Hanging Maw, who had succeeded Old Tassel as leader of the Overhills, were more than canceled by the intensity of the warfare conducted by the bitter-enders: Dragging Canoe, the bitterest of all until his death; and others whose names became bywords in the settlements: Bloody Fellow, Double-head, John Watts, the Glass, Little Owl, Richard Justice, and redheaded Bench.

In widely separated ambushes, the Indians slaughtered the old valiant men of the frontier: William Christian fell north of the Ohio; John Donelson on the Kentucky road; three of the Sevier family near Clarksville; the giant Spencer in East Tennessee. Raiders besieged Nashville for days at a time. Moving once again in armies, they struck Cavett's Station near Knoxville and threatened the territorial capital itself. They cut off travelers and burned cabins. They rose from cane bottoms to kill men at the plow. They took women captive and carried them far away, scratching their legs with garfish teeth to make them hurry. From time to time they made treaties, but always with a tomahawk under the blanket.

The gantlet of the Lower Towns, bristling with weapons, struck at boats on the river and beat down every attempt to settle in the neighborhood. In 1788 the Indians killed thirty-seven out of a party of forty immigrants who were floating down the river near the mouth of Chickamauga Creek. In March, 1790, Major John Doughty of the United States Army, who had been sent by Secretary of War Knox to carry a conciliatory message to the Indian tribes south of the Ohio, and especially to the Cherokees, proceeded up the Lower Tennessee to the neighborhood of Bear Creek. There his party was treacherously attacked by a mixed band of Cherokees and Shawnees. Out of fifteen soldiers in his barge, Major Doughty lost five killed and six wounded, and he had to abandon his mission. In 1791, the Glass, with sixty warriors, ousted a party under Zachariah Cox which, after drifting past the Five Lower Towns at night, attempted to build a blockhouse on an island at Muscle Shoals. In 1794, the Indians wiped out William Scott's party of thirty-three people; they were overtaken at Muscle Shoals after repelling attacks at Running Water and Long Island; all the white people were killed, and their Negro slaves were taken prisoner.

Among many such acts of river brigandage, one of the most notable was the capture and massacre of the Brown family near Nickajack, in 1788. The event had tragic irony in it, since the boy Joseph Brown was spared by the Indians and survived to guide the pioneer army which finally destroyed Nickajack and Running Water. The "Narrative" of Joseph Brown, written either by Joseph himself in his maturity or by some talented ghost writer, is one of the most striking of numerous Indian captivity stories. To the pioneers Brown seemed an avenger specially sent by the Almighty for the ruin of their enemies. His tale was so edifying that it was printed and circulated under religious auspices as a tract to illustrate the efficacy of prayer; but the version given in Ramsey's *Annals,* which is followed here, is more detailed and matter-of-fact.

Joseph's father, Colonel James Brown, was a Revolutionary officer who wished to emigrate to the Cumberland settlements by the water route, as Donelson had done. Aware of the dangers ahead of him, he built an unusually well-protected boat, armored with oak plank two inches thick above the gunwales and provided with loopholes. In the stern he mounted a swivel gun. With him he had his wife, his five sons and four small daughters, and five young men. His two grown sons and the five young men were good marksmen. Seemingly, all that the colonel had to do was to stay in the middle of the river, keep moving, and shoot at sight. But he was good-natured and much too innocent-minded, and he violated all three of these rules.

At dawn of May 9, 1788, the company got safely past the Chickamauga towns. At Tuskegee Island town, just below, Brown made his first mistake. He permitted Cutleotoy, headman of the town, and three other warriors, to visit on board his boat. The visitors dropped off without unpleasantness, and Brown floated on, not realizing that Cutleotoy had sent the usual warning message downriver.

The Tennessee was at high water, and they went quickly through the Suck. As they approached Running Water, four canoes came out to meet them. Others were paddling up within view, through the flooded bottoms, and still more were crowding through the tall cane.

The Indians in the first four canoes had hidden their weapons. As usual, they made friendly signs. They even held up white flags. As the number of canoes multiplied and they crowded nearer, Brown became alarmed. He warned them to keep off, leveled his swivel, and prepared to fire. The Indian spokesman, John Vann, then called out that they came only to talk and visit. He claimed protection under the treaty recently signed and said "they only wished to see where we were going to, and to trade with us, if we had anything to trade on."

Colonel Brown believed the fair words and let them come on board. The Indians began to grab up whatever small articles caught their fancy. To Brown's protests, Vann replied soothingly: everything would be all right; Dragging Canoe, the great chief of Running Water, would make the thieves surrender the stolen property; he would even furnish a pilot to take the boat over Muscle Shoals. Vann's purpose was to maneuver the boat into a position where the Indians could fire into it at short range, from the bank, if resistance developed; but preferably to take the boat without having to fight at all.

The boy Joseph saw what happened, but without comprehending it at the time. A big Indian with a sword caught him by the arm and threatened him. The colonel intervened. The warrior turned and with one blow cut the colonel's head half off. Another warrior flung the body into the river. Joseph was astonished to see his father sink in the water. He had not seen the blow, and ran to his brothers crying that "an Indian had thrown our father overboard, and he was drowned."

It was over quickly. When the boat drew near the upper end of Nickajack, a young warrior named Kiachatalee took Joseph as his prisoner, forced him into a canoe, and, upon landing, turned him over to an old white man who was standing there with his wife. This was Tom Tunbridge, a deserter from the British army. His wife was a Frenchwoman who had for some time lived among the Indians and had once had an Indian husband. "My boy," said Tom Tunbridge kindly,

"I want you to go home with me." The boy consented, on condition that he be brought back to the boat in the morning, for he supposed that the stopping of the boat was only for the night. Before he had walked half a mile with Tunbridge, he heard the sound of guns from the riverside. In his innocence he supposed that his brothers and their companions were testing their rifles, as he had seen them do during the voyage.

But it was the noise of massacre. As the boat drifted near the high, cane-covered bank at the lower end of Nickajack town, Indians concealed behind stumps and in the cane fired into the boat. The women, presumably, and the children and Negroes had already been removed by Indians who desired them as prisoners and who put off with their captives and booty, leaving the field of fire open to their confederates. At any rate the young men were all killed, the others made prisoners.

Meanwhile Joseph found himself the center of a hot dispute. A fat Indian woman rushed up, sweat dripping from her face, and demanded that he be killed. The boy would see everything, she cried. He was little now, but soon he would grow up and become a warrior, he would leave them and guide white men's army to Nickajack. Indians crowded close while the argument went on, and Joseph, who did not understand a word of what was said, waited, mute and uncomfortable. Presently Tunbridge led him on. As they walked, he explained what the old woman had said: that his people were all killed, and she wanted him killed too; that her son would soon arrive to do the killing. But he must not be afraid, said Tunbridge; he must take care not even to seem afraid, and he would not be hurt.

As they reached Tunbridge's house, Cutleotoy, the old woman's son, came up with a party of warriors, and Tunbridge went to the door to argue with them. Joseph remained inside with the Frenchwoman. From the mat where he crouched and trembled he could hear the voices. Much later he learned what the babble meant. Tunbridge argued that it was wrong to kill women and children. Cutleotoy repeated the old woman's warning: the boy must be killed lest he bring an army to destroy them. Tunbridge reminded Cutleotoy that Joseph was the prisoner of Kiachatalee, his wife's son by her Indian husband, and that Cutleotoy had no right to execute him. Since Cutleotoy was a chief, the headman of a town, and Kiachatalee was as yet only a young warrior, Tunbridge's reminder only made him more angry. He brandished his tomahawk above Tunbridge's head and charged him with being "the Virginian's friend." At this threat Tunbridge stepped away from the door and said, "Take him along."

The Indian rushed inside. Joseph felt Cutleotoy's hand on his hair. The Frenchwoman begged him not to kill the boy in her house. Cutleotoy dragged him to the path outside, where ten warriors waited, some of them with the fresh scalps of white men on sticks.

They stripped off Joseph's clothing to prepare him for their sport. Naked, he kneeled in the road and began to pray. The Frenchwoman again intervened and begged them not to kill the boy in her path. It was the path by which she carried her water every day, and would they make it all bloody? They began to talk to one another, and one said, "Let us take him to Running Water and have a frolic in knocking him over." But Joseph, busy at his prayers, knew nothing of what they said. Until his dying day he remembered how salvation came to him in the twinkling of an eye.

As soon as my clothes were off [says the "Narrative"] I fell on my knees and cried, like the dying Stephen, "Lord Jesus, into thy hands I commend my spirit," expecting every moment to be my last. But I had not been on my knees more than one minute when Tunbridge said, "My boy, you must get up and go with them; they will not kill you here," but told me nothing of what was said of having a frolic at Running Water town.

We had not gone more than seventy or eighty yards, when Cutleotoy stopped his men, and said to them, that he could not, and they must not kill me, and it would be as bad for him, as though he himself had done it; for that I was the prisoner of poor Job (the Frenchwoman's son) who was a man of war.

"Now," said he, "I have taken a negro woman out of the boat, and sent her by water to where we live, and if we kill this fellow, poor Job will go and kill my negro, and I don't want to lose her; nor could all the Indians in the nation keep him from putting her to death." Well might he fear poor Job, for though he was only twenty-two years old, and it had been a time of peace since he was a small boy, he had taken the lives of six white men. . . .

Now, when Cutleotoy spoke thus, the thought of my being one day a man, and leading an army there, and having them killed, had given way to avarice, for the old woman, as well as her son, wanted the service of the negro. As I knew nothing of what they were saying, I was on my knees, trying to give my soul to God through the merits of my saviour, and expecting the tomahawk to sink into my skull every moment. At length, the favour given to Stephen in his dying moments, came to my mind: how he saw the heavens opened, and the blessed Saviour sitting at the right hand of God. I opened my eyes, and looking up, saw one of the Indians, as they stood all round me, smile; then, glancing my eyes round on them, saw that all their countenances were changed from vengeance and anger, to mildness.

The chief of Nickajack was the Breath, a generous Indian—"a man of fine mind," Brown's narrative calls him. The Breath was absent from Nickajack when the Brown boat was captured, and when he returned he was angry with his people. He saw to it that Joseph, for his own protection, was adopted into the tribe. From that time until he was ransomed about a year later, Joseph led the life of an Indian boy. He used his eyes and ears. He saw much and remembered everything. He learned what route the war parties took when they went against the Cumberland settlements—across the river at a certain bend, then up the Sequatchie Valley to the ridge where the eagles had their home, then over, and on to the north. When General Martin made his futile attack at Lookout Mountain, Joseph saw Dragging Canoe's warriors take the trail to the east, in hot pursuit.

Time went on, and Joseph was rescued, in an exchange of prisoners brought about by John Sevier, after one of his deadly raids. Joseph's mother and his sisters were also found and exchanged. The youngest of the little girls had grown accustomed to Indian ways and did not want to leave her Indian foster mother. Joseph had to tear her away rudely. As for himself, he had no such reluctance to say good-bye to Nickajack, although he had become rather fond of his "brother," Kiachatalee—"Chat," Joseph called him, for short. So he went back to the white settlements, and in his head he carried a map of paths and towns.

Five years after Joseph Brown was redeemed from captivity, the Indian woman's prophecy was fulfilled. The boy Joseph, now a grown man by frontier standards, led an avenging army to Nickajack and Running Water.

Dragging Canoe died two years before this day of retribution. Singularly enough, he did not fall in battle, but died from an unknown cause after a great Eagle-tail Dance held in his honor, at which scalps of white men were brandished aloft and then symbolically torn by the teeth of dancing warriors. This was in the spring of 1792.

The great raid of 1794, known in Tennessee history as the Nickajack Expedition, was planned and directed by James Robertson of Nashville, although he himself, for reasons of policy, did not lead it or take active part in it. It was, in official language, an "unauthorized expedition," and Robertson was duly reprimanded for it by Governor William Blount. It seems certain that Blount's official reproof was tempered by private satisfaction. Blount winked at the Nickajack Expedition.

Military action, in fact, was long overdue. The settlers had been restrained from earlier attack by two circumstances. One was lack of knowledge of a favorable route of approach to the Lower Towns from the Cumberland settlements. The other was the policy of the Washington administration, which frowned upon any volunteer forays, and yet declined to sanction or support any such large-scale operations as were conducted by General Wayne against Indian foes of the Northwest.

The first of these difficulties was overcome when Joseph Brown moved to the Cumberland settlements. The young man told what he knew. He also went with scouts to reconnoiter the path. It was declared practicable, and Joseph made ready to act as guide.

The other difficulty was circumvented by simply going ahead, without official authorization. Robertson took care, however, to give the proceedings an air of authority. By a series of interesting coincidences, a fine contingent of Kentucky militia joined the Tennessee militia just at the time when Governor Blount ordered Major James Ore of East Tennessee to proceed to the Cumberland settlements with his command of regularly levied troops. Robertson seized his opportunity, appointed Major Ore commander of the three bodies of troops, and gave him adroitly worded orders "to defend the District of Mero against the Creeks and Cherokees of the Lower Towns, which I have received information, is about to invade it, as also to punish such Indians as have committed recent depredations . . . and if you do not meet this party before you arrive at the Tennessee, you will pass it, and destroy the Lower Cherokee Towns, which must serve as a check to the expected invaders."

Ore carried out these shrewd instructions. He had 550 men, all mounted. Leaving Nashville on September 7, 1794, his command marched approximately by the route followed today by the Nashville-Chattanooga highway. They camped

at Black Fox's Spring (Murfreesboro), then at the Old Stone
Fort (Manchester), went over the mountains near the site of
Monteagle, and so into Sequatchie Valley. They reached the
Tennessee River on the night of September 12, three miles
below the mouth of the Sequatchie River, and prepared to
cross the Tennessee about where the town of South Pittsburg
now stands. They met no invading army of Indians, of course.
There was none. It was a swift movement, intended as a surprise.

Their approach was not discovered. They were several
miles to the southwest of Nickajack, on the weak flank
of the inner citadel, and were in a position to carry out a
destructive enveloping attack, provided they could cross the
river under cover of darkness and fall suddenly upon the
towns. The problem was, how to get 550 men, with their
guns and ammunition, across a river "three-quarters of a mile
wide" and swollen by recent rains.

They had brought along two oxhide boats—"bullboats"
of the primitive Indian type—for ferrying the ammunition.
They had no boats to ferry troops, but this lack was no great
obstacle to men of the half-horse, half-alligator breed. Joseph
Brown and three other men swam the river and lit a fire to
mark a landing point. Brown had to swim with one arm,
because he had recently been wounded in the other arm during a brush with some Indians. The oxhide boats went back
and forth all night with loads of guns and ammunition. One
of those who swam back and forth, pushing a bullboat, was
Edmond Jennings, a great hunter and fighter, son of Jonathan Jennings of the Donelson expedition.

The fighting men got over in all sorts of ways. Some
made rafts of canes and small logs, on which they drifted
and paddled across. Others swam. At daylight only 268 men
had got over. The commanders decided to push ahead with
this number. The men left on the north bank moved up the
river to a position opposite Nickajack, with the intention of

cutting off any Indians who might try to escape by swimming.

The attacking force divided into groups which marched so as to converge upon Nickajack from above and below the town, while the center closed in between. Joseph Brown with twenty men went to cut off the retreat by way of Nickajack Creek. The men of the left wing, under the command of Colonel John Montgomery, moved forward through the early morning fog that lay thick among trees and brush, and came upon two isolated cabins. No Indians were stirring there; Montgomery left a squad to watch while the others pushed on.

The battle began at these cabins. A young woman came out and began to pound corn for the morning meal. A young warrior, her husband, presently stepped to her side, put his arm around her waist, and playfully began to help her with the pestle and mortar. Some frontierman's finger, itching to shoot, taut on the trigger, could not resist this target. The rifle cracked, and the young warrior dropped.

The alarm was thus given before the army was fully deployed for the attack. Nevertheless, the surprise was effective. Guarded from observation by the brush and by the patches of corn that grew thick around the scattered cabins, the frontiersmen were close enough to deliver a deadly fire as the Indians ran out. The fighting was easy; the battle soon became a slaughter. The riflemen shot down Indians at their cabin doors, picked Indians off as they ran, or took leisurely aim at the heads of swimmers. In no time they killed seventy warriors, among them the chief, the Breath. They took captive twenty or more women and children; other women and children were killed or wounded in the general confusion.

The frontiersmen sent some of the women captives across the river by boat. Among them was the young woman whose husband had been killed by the first shot of the attack. Seizing her chance, she sprang into the water and began to swim off. As she swam, she wriggled out of her garments and left them floating on the water. "Shoot her! Shoot her!" hallooed the soldiers. "No, don't, she's too smart to kill," cried another, and struck up the aiming rifles. Later, the women prisoners, who had been crowded temporarily into a cabin, were horrified when they lifted downcast eyes and saw Joseph Brown standing at the door. They waited for the avenging tomahawk to fall. One of them begged Brown to remember that the Cherokees, when the situation was reversed, had spared his life. "We are white people," said Joseph Brown. "We don't kill women and children." "Oh, that is good news for the wretched," she said.

When the firing died down, Major Ore hurried his men eastward toward Running Water. There was no time to plan another envelopment. The only approach was along the bank, straight up the Tennessee. Across the river the lofty cliffs of the Cumberland ridges, their topmost rocks touched with morning sun, stood in regular echelons of green and gray-blue, a long series of promontories ranked against the deeper blue and green of the east, broken as if notched where the river wound through them. Mists still hung in the ravines. They pushed on through the canebrake and brush. At the narrow pass between mountain and river, just below Running Water, the rifles of the advance guard began to crackle. The warriors of Running Water had heard the distant firing and were coming to help their brothers, but it was too late. After a sharp skirmish, the Indians vanished into the forest. Major Ore's men burned the deserted town, and that same day recrossed the Tennessee. They had had three men wounded and no men killed. The inner citadel had been taken almost without a struggle.

All Cherokee resistance now ended. The Five Lower Towns joined the Upper Towns in making a firm treaty with Governor Blount at Tellico Blockhouse. Bloody Fellow, who at George Washington's suggestion, had changed his name to Clear Sky, spoke for the Cherokees:

"I want peace," he said, "that we may travel our paths, sleep in our houses, and rise in peace on both sides. I now deliver to you this firm peace talk, that our people will mind their hunting, and that both parties may rise in peace each day. My talk shall be made known throughout the Nation."

Wherewith he handed Governor Blount a string of white beads.

Soon after this time, a song by an unknown composer became current in the South. The tune, a lilting Celtic air, was called "War Department," and the song ran thus:

## War Department

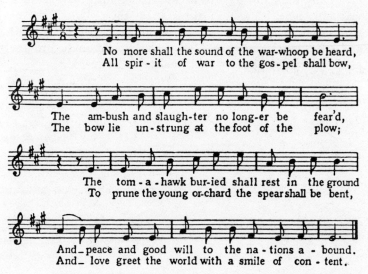

No more shall the sound of the war-whoop be heard,
All spir-it of war to the gos-pel shall bow,

The am-bush and slaugh-ter no long-er be fear'd,
The bow lie un-strung at the foot of the plow;

The tom-a-hawk bur-ied shall rest in the ground
To prune the young or-chard the spear shall be bent,

And_peace and good will to the na-tions a-bound.
And_love greet the world with a smile of con-tent.

Now the Cherokees became farmers and took part of their treaty money in plows, spinning wheels, and looms. They listened to the missionaries—the Moravians in North

Georgia, the Presbyterians and others at the Brainerd Mission near Chattanooga—and became Christian farmers. Their feet were on the white man's path, but they still remained a nation and dwelt in the land of their fathers.

Knoxville, growing into a pleasant town on the high ground between First and Second creeks, became the first capital of the new state of Tennessee, and in its pioneer newspaper, the Knoxville *Gazette*, the problems of peace were up for discussion—among them the question of river transport.

The Tennessee River, so far as the Cherokees were concerned, was now open to traffic—a traffic by which some of their leaders, at places like Ross's Landing, were quite ready to profit. To the south, the warlike Creeks were still warlike; but they did not control the river.

Only the natural perils of the river remained. The Suck was still there. Muscle Shoals was still there. No battles or treaties could remove them. It would be nearly a hundred and fifty years after the Nickajack Expedition before the great natural obstacles would finally be conquered.

# CHAPTER XIV

# Flatboat and Keelboat Days

O N THE Tennessee, as on other western rivers, flatboat and keelboat came into use as soon as the settlers realized
that their rich new lands, which yielded so abundantly, were
also roadless lands. A man could walk or ride the wilderness
path, but he could not haul cotton over it, or timber, or iron.
Even when the first roads were built, hauling was far too
expensive for the average settler who might want to trade in
Philadelphia, Richmond, or Baltimore; and it was out of the
question to haul to and from New Orleans; yet those were
the markets among which the Tennessee settlers had to choose.

They chose New Orleans, and reached it by way of the
Tennessee River, undaunted by the roundabout and dangerous voyage down the Tennessee to the Ohio, down the Ohio
to the Mississippi, and so around the circle to their destination. If the boatman started from the upper Holston, his one-
way water journey might alone amount to two thousand
miles; and he still had to get back home. In retrospect, it does
not seem odd that the Tennessee Valley folks began very early
to take a passionate interest in railroads; or that, after elect-
ing Andrew Jackson to the Presidency, they came to dislike
his opposition to internal improvements at federal expense
and turned against him in favor of the rising Whig party.

They wanted—they hardly knew what. Steamboats by
all means, as soon as steamboats developed, and then river

improvements to help the steamboats through the Suck and over Muscle Shoals. Canals, when canals were popular. Railroads and highways, when the canal idea failed and the river seemed unconquerable. But until such improvements came in, there were only flatboats and a few keelboats, and a hard pull by the long way around.

A flatboat was river transport reduced to bare essentials: a broad-bottomed, boxlike structure, perhaps with a little rake at the bow. It was steered by a board fastened to a long pole, and was steadied in the current by clumsy, oarlike sweeps on each side, called "broadhorns." It was built of green timber sawed from the forest near the stream and put together with wooden pins. The floor planks, two inches thick, rested on six-inch sills, on which studs were fitted to hold rafters for the roof. The roof might be gabled or round; one early observer described it as being "like the roof of a carriage." It covered at least half, or as much as two-thirds, of the boat. The larger flatboats measured up to 20 by 100 feet and could carry heavy loads—300 to 400 bales of cotton. The crudest possible type would be a mere log raft, with a shelter of rough boards, but the better boats might be fancied up considerably, with a pump to take care of leakage, and a brick or stone fireplace with a chimney, for cooking and good cheer.

The records have little to say about how a flatboat was launched. Was it built on a sand flat where the spring rise would float it? Or was it pushed into the river on log rollers? Certainly it did not slide prettily into the water, over greased ways.

In North Alabama, the great poplars that rose eighty or ninety feet to the first limbs were much prized by flatboat builders. Taylor, the historian of Madison County, says that such poplars were split and framed to make "gunwales." Then they were "framed on strong timber levers projecting beyond over a steep bank, and when the great frame had been

well floored and calked it was moved out to the projecting ends of the levers, generally working on rollers, where it was turned over into the stream, bailed out, finished off, equipped with its rowing and steering apparatus, loaded and launched on its long voyage."

Once in the river, the flatboat was manned with a small crew. Five men were enough—or even three for a small boat: one for the steering, and one or two men for each sweep. The motive power was the current, in which and with which you floated. The current was free to everybody, and you could use it with reasonable satisfaction, provided you left on high water and kept your awkward craft away from collision with boulders and from entanglement with the driftwood "rafts" that piled up on the points of islands. Provided, also, you were content to go always downstream.

Flatboat traffic was one-way traffic. Except in short local trips, no flatboat returned to the place where it was launched. If the owner was migrating with his family, he might build his first cabin out of the timbers of his boat. If he was carrying freight, he disposed of his cargo and sold the flatboat for lumber. He came back overland on shanks' mare, or any way he could. After the settlement of the Great Bend, a flatboatman might bring a cargo of East Tennessee produce to Ditto's Landing, Triana, or Cottonport, sell his produce to local merchants, then reload with cotton for the trip to New Orleans. Or he might go all the way through from East Tennessee to New Orleans.

Of course a flatboat was an exceedingly cumbrous affair, and voyaging by flatboat was tedious, and might be very dangerous, especially when the boat was heavily loaded. Davy Crockett, who was no riverman at all, once became part owner of a flatboat load of staves, intended for New Orleans, and decided to go along with his venture. The boat was wrecked on a great "raft" in the Mississippi and began to sink. The redoubtable bear hunter was caught in the narrow cabin, which had only one small window, and that far too small for a man of Crockett's heft. His companions yanked him through anyhow, in the nick of time. Crockett lost most of his clothes, a good deal of his skin, and all of his investment.

The swift eddies and currents of the Suck were a notable danger to flatboats, as to steamboats later on. There were stories about how bad it was to be carried around and around in the whirls of the Boiling Pot. The artist David Hunter Strother, who wrote and sketched for *Harper's Magazine* under the name "Porte Crayon," visited Chattanooga in the late fifties and was entertained by a local boatman with an elaborate version of the tale of the flatboat caught in the Pot!

This was the way of it [said the boatman]. There was a man and his family come from above somewhar, in a flat bound for Arkansaw. He was pretty well loaded with farm-stock, women, children, and truck; and having heard tell of the Narrows, he was afeared to go through by himself, but wanted a pilot. So, after considerin' a while, I agreed to put him through for two dollars. . . .

I never had been through there, but I had heard people talk about the Skillet, and the Sleek, and the Bilin' Pot, and all that; and I thought I could shoot her through, and if I sunk her I'd lose my money—that's all. So we tuck a few drinks and put off, and I takes the steerin'-oar and put her head down, and let her rip. Night come on pretty soon, but that was all the same to me; so we tuck a few more drinks, and let her slide. And we went over some rough places, and, after while, come to a pretty smart current runnin' smooth. "Now she goes it slick as goose-grease!" says he to me. So, by-and-by, we see lights on the shore, and passed by a house where a feller was playin' Old Zip Coon like a saw-mill, and people dancin'. "Here's good fun to you!" says he, and we tuck another dig. So we went on pretty sprightly; and, by jingo, before we got well out of sight and hearin' of that house we went past another, whar they were dancin' to the same tune. "Success to 'em!" says I. "Hand us that bottle; while fun is goin', we might as well have our share." So we drank a mouthful, and before we were done talking about it we went past another place, fiddlin' and dancin' like the rest.

"Mister," says he to me, "this here's the jolliest settlement ever I traveled through—all agoing it to the same tune." "Pears to me," says I, "I hear another fiddle and fellers a laffin'; and presently sure enough, we streaked past another house whar they were goin' it a leetle more extravagant than the others—tune about the same. "Mister," says the boss to me, "this rather beats my time. Do the people along this river mostly spend their nights fiddlin' and dancin'?" "Certain," says I; "that's their regular business." But now, I tell you, I was beginnin' to get bewildered and oneasy myself. So, pretty soon we passed another house, and another, and another, all dancin' and fiddlin' like blazes. The boss he set quiet, and didn't say a word for a while, but tuck a swig now and then. Next house we passed they were goin' it on Old Zip Coon with a will. Then the boss spoke up. "Pilot," says he, "there's one of two things—either we're drunk, or there's hell's doin's goin' on along this river tonight." "What time o' night is it?" says I. "About two o'clock in the mornin' by the stars," says he. "How many houses have we passed?" "I've counted nine," says he, and his voice began to shake a little. "Now," says he, "it might be that the hellish thing is a follerin' of us!" "Nine," says I, "is the devil's number," says I, pretty badly skeered; "if the thing appears agin, go call your wife, and if she can't see it, we're drunk, certain." "Listen!" says he; "don't you hear 'em? That's the lights! ten times! we're drunk, sure. Katy! Katy! sweetheart, wake up!"

This time I headed the flat a little in nearer shore, and we could hear 'em plain, cussin' and swearin'.

"Katy," says boss, "do you see or hear anything over there on shore?"

"I see lights," says she, "and hear a passel of drunken boatmen dancin' Old Zip Coon."

I wanted to put in, but boss says "No; but sure's I'm a man, if they're carryin' on at the next house we pass we'll tie up and make out the night with 'em!"

In about half an hour, as I expected, we come upon another spree.

"Head her in!" says he. So we tied up at the landing, and went in the house.

Now, stranger, how do you think it was? Why, this was old Jack Cogles' house, down thar fornense the Bilin' Pot, whar some fellers and some gals were dancin' all night; and we went bilin' around and around, passin' by the same place over and over agin! Now at fust it come to me like a sort of a dream; then it was all clare; and without waitin' to be cussed or laughed at, I streaked it. But it's all true, jist as I tell ye.

The keelboat was a homemade pioneer solution, owing something perhaps to European models, of the problem of navigating upstream. It was a long, narrow craft—7 to 9 feet wide, and 30 to 70 feet long—and in every way was much more like a real boat than the clumsy flatboat. It was built upon a keel, with a framework of ribs to which planking was attached. It was sharp at both ends, and might have graceful lines. Its cabin could be divided into compartments for passengers and freight.

When going upstream, the keelboat was propelled by manpower and muscle, aided by a crude application of the principle of the lever. Along the sides of the keelboat there was a cleated runway. The crew, evenly divided on the two sides, shoved the boat forward by setting their poles in the bed of the stream and by walking, or rather, almost crawling, toward the stern. As each man reached the limit of his push, he disengaged his pole, lifted it, and ran forward to take his place again in the cycle of pushing. The poles were metal-tipped. The crew were equipped with shoulder pads against which the butt of the pole was set. The steersman, who was generally the captain, sat or stood in an elevated spot on the cabin, governed the rudder, and directed the crew. If poling was not needed, the crew were put at the oars. There might be a sail to help out; and when rigged with a sail, the keelboat was sometimes called a "barge." The Great Seal of the State of Tennessee, using the transportation symbols of the times, carried a conventionalized representation of a keelboat equipped with sails.

When the river bottom was too deep or too soft for poling, the keelboat resorted to other methods of propulsion, which the steamboats were glad to copy when they had to buck a powerful current. "Cordelling" signified the use of a cordelle, or towline, carried ahead by the crew, who then pulled the boat along from the bank, fighting their way through brush and canebrake, swimming creek mouths, and scaling cliffs, all as a part of the day's work. "Warping" was the reverse of cordelling. It generally required two skiffs, each of which carried a towline. One skiff carried the towline upstream and fastened it to a tree or any other firm object, and the crew would then pull the boat up, hand over hand, or by a windlass if there was one on deck. Meanwhile, the other skiff carried its towline still farther upstream, and so on. "Bushwhacking" was used if the river was at flood stage, so that the boat could come near the line of trees on the submerged bank. The crew pulled the boat forward by seizing tree branches and walking aft, while polemen or oarsmen steadied the boat on the side toward the river.

The keelboat thus acquired maneuverability and motive power, but at great expense to human flesh. Quite evidently a keelboatman had to have powers of wind, muscle, and endurance beyond ordinary calculation. It may seem odd that the keelboatmen of the western waters never developed a "Pole, brothers, pole" chorus to parallel the Russian "Song of the Volga Boatmen." But they were frontiersmen and individualists, with no desire to sing in chorus, and therefore apparently did not indulge in chanteys.

For obvious reasons keelboats rarely, if ever, went up and down the entire length of the Tennessee. There are no memoirs of a round-trip voyage to New Orleans by Tennessee keelboat. The venturesome Ohio keelboats often brought immigrants and supplies up the Lower Tennessee. Newspapers of the 1820's note the arrivals and departures at Tuscumbia of such Ohio keelboats as *General Jackson, Bolivar, Choctaw, Eclipse, Maria Louisa, Mary, Phoenix, Pittsburgh, Harriet,* whose home ports were such places as Cincinnati or Trinity. These Ohio keels did not go above Muscle Shoals, but local keels did. They were indispensable in local traffic until steamboats arrived; and for a long time after steamboats came into use, keelboats served as auxiliaries and even gave steamboats direct competition.

On the Upper Tennessee, keelboats were apparently more reliable than the earliest steamboats. In 1836 and 1837, for example, the daybook of James King & Company, of Knoxville, shows that keels were more regular in back-and-forth traffic than such pioneer steamboats as the *Guide* and the *Knoxville.* In the twenty-one months from April, 1836, to December, 1837, the *Knoxville* carried shipments only twice, and the *Guide* ten times. During the same period five keelboats made a total of eighteen trips to various landings on the Upper Tennessee and its tributaries. The five keelboats used by James King & Company were the *East Tennessean, Swan, Jack Downing, Little River, French Broad.* Others known to have operated above Muscle Shoals were the *Hiwassee, Clinch, Cypress, Bonnie Bark,* and *Lucy Futter.*

The *East Tennessean,* which generally operated with Francis A. Chapman and A. T. Jones as masters, was apparently one of the most regular and serviceable of the Upper Tennessee keels. She is on record as plying between Knoxville and Decatur—a long and arduous trip for a keelboat. And she must have had a carrying capacity almost equal to that of the steamboats with which she competed. On July 9, 1836, the *East Tennessean* took on board more than two hundred "packages" from James King & Company: that is, barrels of sugar and salt, kegs of malaga wine and New England rum, bags of coffee, boxes of tumblers, glassware, carpenter's and painter's supplies, coils of manila rope, hides, brimstone, nails, bars of steel, kegs of alum and copperas, boxes of pepper, raisins, cinnamon, almonds, trunks, plaster, and other miscellaneous merchandise—all of which were billed to such points as Cleveland, Washington Landing, Lenoir's Ferry, Felicity Landing, Prestonville, Kelly's Ferry, Pond Creek, Athens, Kingston, Mouth of Chickamauga, "Chatenuga," Dallas, Ross's Ferry, Rossville, Shaw's Ferry, Philadelphia (Tennessee), Blair's Ferry, and so on. Her master for this particular trip was Marcus J. Parrott, who later became a well-known steamboat captain, as the masters of keels and flatboats frequently did.

A spectacular voyage was made in 1821 by the keelboat *Tennessee Patriot*. The master, a man named King, was evidently willing to test the theories held by some East Tennesseans, who argued that their transport difficulties could be solved by pushing up the farthest reaches of the Hiwassee, then portaging to the tributaries of the Coosa, and going down the Coosa and the Alabama to Montgomery and other ports. King and his crew actually accomplished this difficult feat. With a load of flour and whisky the intrepid keelboatmen poled their way up the Hiwassee to the Ocoee, then up the Ocoee to some point where they could beach their keel and load it on trucks. It was then hauled ten miles overland to the Conesauga, was again launched, and went down the Ustenaula, Coosa, and Alabama. The *Tennessee Patriot* was 50 feet long, with a beam of 6 feet, and a hull 6 feet deep. She could carry a load of 100 barrels.

The route opened by the *Patriot* was used often enough to cause the building of boathouses at the ends of the portage, on the Ocoee and the Conesauga. The possibilities of a canal to replace the portage were next contemplated. The canal was feasible, perhaps, though the physical difficulties were great. But there were other difficulties than the physical. The route ran through the Cherokee nation. The Cherokees did not view with pleasure the prospect of keelboats, which might stop and sell whisky in their country. They wanted no canal or even a survey for a canal. They resisted intrusion by resorting to the white man's shrewd methods of legal arrest, seizure, and fine.

In December, 1825, James Reid and Samuel M. Reid of McMinn County, Tennessee, encountered this new form of Indian resistance. They started for Alabama with a load of whisky, brandy, and flour. After portaging from the Hiwassee to the Conesauga, they were stopped by John Walker, an officer of the Cherokee nation, who arrested them and confiscated their liquor. Their affidavit, made later before a McMinn County magistrate, tells the story from their point of view:

> . . . [Walker] demanded all of our spirits, stating that he was bound to take the same, as an officer of the Cherokee Nation, and then violently took six hundred and fifty-three gallons of whiskey, and seventy-three gallons of peach brandy; and on the 23d of the same month, John Shepherd came to our boat, and stated that we must pay him one hundred dollars as a fine, for the same offense that they had taken the whiskey for: the breach alleged against us, was that of selling whiskey on the Conisauga river. We refused to pay said fine; and the said John Shepherd, with others, violently took from us, out of our boat, twenty barrels of flour. They took our loading, without adducing any proof that we even had sold whiskey on said river, or giving us any trial whatever. We then proceeded to go on to Alabama, with the balance of our loading, and sold the same. We believe we could have received for the whiskey, in Alabama, from seventy-five cents to one dollar per gallon; the flour was selling, at Cahawba, at twelve dollars a barrel.

Since it cost two or three thousand dollars, or more, to build a keelboat, only merchants like the Kings, of Knoxville and Kingsport, or others with capital to invest could

venture into the keelboat business. As soon as river improvements permitted steamboats to use the Upper Tennessee more
freely, and the first railroads were built to supplement steamboat lines, the keelboat was finished, except on the less navigable tributaries. But the flatboat, which had antedated the
keelboat, continued in use well into modern times, despite its
seeming anachronism.

It has been said, by people who ought to know, that
there were professional flatboatmen who made three or four
round trips a year between Tennessee ports and New Orleans.
It is a pity that some of these Sindbads of the wilderness did
not leave us at least a fragment of their personal memoirs. If
even a single one of them had decided, like Davy Crockett,
to run for public office and had found a talented ghost
writer to help him, we might have a better picture of what
it was like to go flatboating down the Tennessee in pioneer
times. As it stands, records are scanty, and the picture is in
part conjectural.

Professional flatboatmen were probably men like Malcolm Gilchrist, an Alabama pioneer of Scottish ancestry, who
settled near Melton's Bluff, at the head of Muscle Shoals. Gilchrist was a land broker who won the respect of the settlers
because—in contrast to many land speculators—he carefully
inspected the lands he bought at auction and resold. In addition, he ran a "line" of flatboats between the Great Bend and
New Orleans. Colonel James E. Saunders states that Gilchrist
employed the Indian, James Melton, for whom Melton's Bluff
is named, as a pilot to get his boats over Muscle Shoals. When
the last boat left his landing, Gilchrist himself got on board,
and while en route to New Orleans kept shrewdly in touch
with prices and business conditions. His freight charges were
one dollar per hundred pounds. For his "hands" he employed
the adventurous young men of the region, who were only too
eager to make the New Orleans trip and were satisfied with

low wages. Flatboating put money in Malcolm Gilchrist's pocket, and when he died he left a considerable inheritance.

A similar "line" of flatboats was run by Captain Thomas Rapier, one of the old settlers of Florence. His boats left from a regular wharf near warehouses built on the banks of the Tennessee. Simpson & Rapier's store, near by, was a convenient trade center of the frontier type, where Chickasaw Indians, including the members of the great Colbert family, mingled with the boatmen, the settlers, and the hopeful speculators.

Most often, probably, the flatboat owner was a farmer, who took his produce to New Orleans once a year on a boat that he himself had made. For his crew he no doubt had tall sons, but in any case there was no dearth of strong men who preferred a trip down the Tennessee to lying around home at a season when there was little to do. For flatboating offered them a fine, hearty outdoor life, with a spice of real danger. They slept on the deck where they worked, ate plain bread and meat with whisky to wash it down, and took time off for a dance and revel at the sparse settlements where they might tie up to wait for a rise or to load more cargo. In warm weather, they worked stripped to the waist and soon were fit to pass for Indians. They let their beards grow, and by the end of the long voyage probably resembled a gang of pirates. Alexander Wilson, the naturalist, who met groups of boatmen on the Natchez Trace, described them: "Dirty as Hottentots; their dress, a shirt and trousers of canvass, black, greasy, and sometimes in tatters; the skin burnt wherever exposed to the sun; each with a budget, wrapped up in an old blanket; their beards, eighteen days old, added to the singularity of their apearance, which was altogether savage."

Whoever he might be, the flatboatman waited for high water—in East Tennessee parlance, a "tide"—and then, with his load of whisky, salt, pork, cotton, or miscellaneous goods, cast off. Since high water came in winter or early spring, it was generally anything but a fine summer's day when he started the voyage.

If he came from the uppermost parts of the Tennessee, he had before him a trip down three rivers and a long journey back overland. In the early days, before the Great Bend was settled, a considerable part of his roundabout journey was through Indian country, and even as late as 1830, when Colonel S. L. Long made the first survey of the river, the Tennessee was anything but a well-inhabited stream. Once he had had his drink at Chisholm's tavern, at Knoxville, or at some "doggery," and passed Kingston and Hiwassee Garrison and Dallas, he was in Indian country. He might stop at Ross's Landing, the future site of Chattanooga, and trade and refresh himself at the store owned by the Cherokee chief, John Ross, by way of fortifying himself against the terrors of the Suck, just ahead, and Muscle Shoals, farther down. Before entering the Muscle Shoals stretch he might take on a pilot. There were regular "Muscle Shoals pilots" (the Indian, James Melton, was one) who dropped off at Colbert's Ferry, after seeing their charges through the Shoals, and then walked back to the head of the Shoals to make another trip.

Throughout the Great Bend—during the first decade of the nineteenth century—the flatboatman might see no white man's face, unless it would be some of the old "Indian countrymen" (white men who preferred the Indian life) like Old Man Ditto of Ditto's Landing or one of the Gunters of Gunter's Landing. At Colbert's Ferry, there might be company again, a mixed company of Chickasaws and white travelers waiting for the ferry, but below that was only the lonesome, uninhabited stretch of the Lower Tennessee. At the mouth of the Tennessee, where in the earliest years there lived only a small band of Indians whose chief was the amiable giant Paduke, he might note, as Christian Schultz did in 1807, that it was "a very fine site for the establishment of a town." But though the place—once owned by George Rogers

Clark—was early called Pekin, there was no town, no Paducah, until later days. And then he swung into the muddy Ohio, with some concern, perhaps, for the outlaws of Cave-in-Rock, and the state of water and weather on the Mississippi.

Such a trip, coming and going, was about equivalent to crossing the Atlantic, for after the flatboatman had reached New Orleans, disposed of cargo and flatboat, knocked around the city, and perhaps lost much cash to gamblers and women, he still had to face the wilderness and walk back home over many hundreds of miles. It was possible to make an ocean voyage from New Orleans to an Atlantic port, and walk back from the East, or even to hire out to a keelboat, and return part of the way by river. But nearly everybody walked home by way of the Natchez Trace. That was part of the adventure, and it was undoubtedly the worst part.

# CHAPTER XV

# Boatmen and Outlaws on the Natchez Trace

THE Natchez Trace was an Indian path. The archaeologist, using his own terms, says it was, in earlier times, the "Old Chickasaw Trail." It led from New Orleans to Natchez, and thence across Mississippi to Big Chickasaw town near Pontotoc, then through the Chickasaw country to the mouth of Bear Creek, which was the crossing place of the Tennessee in Indian times. From the Tennessee it led across the great oak barrens of the Highland Rim into Middle Tennessee, and so on to Nashville. It was still a primitive Indian path when the boatmen and other early travelers began to use it. After General Wilkinson's treaty with the Chickasaws · in 1801, the federal government began a series of meager improvements which were supposed to convert it into a wagon road. Except in the vicinity of Natchez and Nashville, however, it was never more than a stump-infested track for pedestrians and horseback riders. The numerous creeks and bayous that crossed it were not bridged, except occasionally by crude foot logs.

At the crossing of the Tennessee, however, there was a ferry, managed by the Chickasaw chief, Major George Colbert. The right to operate this ferry, as well as to run a tavern, or "stand," for benighted travelers was a concession exacted by the influential Colberts when the Chickasaw treaty was negotiated. At Major Colbert's suggestion, the crossing of the Tennessee was shifted a few miles upstream from Bear Creek. Levi Colbert "entertained" travelers also, at his large house at Buzzard Roost, some miles inland on the south side of the Tennessee.

There was frequent complaint against the Colberts for excessive ferry charges, and the federal government investigated the little monopoly when George Colbert made a good-sized claim for ferrying over the Tennessee volunteers in 1803 and 1804, during the Creek War. There was little doubt that Major Colbert profited considerably both on this occasion and in 1815, when he ferried Jackson's troops on their return from New Orleans. It was said that he made $20,000 from the later troop movement, but Jackson's account book showed a charge of only a few hundred dollars.

In his defense, Major Colbert admitted that his charges — fifty cents for foot passengers, a dollar for horse and rider —were high in comparison with those made in the settlements. But he pointed out that he was put to much expense to maintain his boats and crews at all seasons, and yet there was heavy travel only during the season when the boatmen were returning from New Orleans. The boatmen, too, were often enough objects of his charity, since by the time they reached his ferry many of them were sick and destitute. "In such cases," said Colbert, "I always give them provisions and carry them over the River ferriage free. No man goes away from my house hungry."

In truth, the Natchez Trace of the early days was not a healthy road for travelers of any kind. Although it skirted the Creek country and passed through the friendly Choctaw and Chickasaw nations, there was always the chance of Indian trouble. Until Andrew Jackson crushed the Red Sticks at Horseshoe Bend, there might be Creek war parties looking for scalps on the Trace, and even the friendly Indians were prone to steal horses. But the greatest danger was from the famous outlaws, or "land pirates," that haunted the Trace. Bold, and insolent in their boldness; rapacious and cruel beyond most of their kind; devilishly clever and capable even of large-scale conspiracy—these scoundrels were among the most inhuman highwaymen on record. They had none of the gallantry sometimes associated with bandits. They were not socially oppressed, and did not take the part of one element of society against another. They were against society, and for themselves alone. They liked boodle and blood. They were simply criminals.

The notorious Harpes—Big Harpe and Little Harpe—killed wantonly, as if to vent some wild spleen against humanity. They began their terrible career in the Knoxville country and ranged far and wide before they were hunted down, but most of their recorded murders were not done on the Trace.

When Big Harpe was caught and crudely beheaded, Little Harpe escaped, vanished, and finally reappeared, under the name of Setton, as a member of the band led by Samuel Mason.

Mason had made a good record in the Revolutionary War. In his old age he turned bad, and he and his gang became one of the great terrors of the Trace. In Spanish territory he passed as a respectable citizen, and shrewdly played off the Spanish against the American authorities in such a way as to evade punishment. On one occasion he was publicly flogged at Natchez, and was put in the pillory, but when released, he continued his savage depredations. Sometimes, after murdering a victim, he posted a sign on a near-by tree: "Done by Mason of the Woods." Finally he was betrayed by two of his own men, Setton (or Little Harpe) and Mays. They tomahawked him and brought his head to Natchez, rolled up in blue clay, expecting to obtain a handsome reward. But Setton was identified as Little Harpe by a man who had formerly known him. The two recreant bandits escaped justice momentarily, but were pursued, recaptured, and hanged. Then their heads were cut off and mounted on poles set near the Trace.

But while Mason lived, and gathered such men about him, he caused plenty of trouble on the Natchez Trace. In his *Old Times in Tennessee*, Judge Jo. C. Guild records in detail impressions of Mason that he had from John L. Swaney, who carried the mail between Nashville and Natchez. Swaney frequently talked with Mason, who was a vain man and wanted to find out from the mail carrier what the public was saying about him. Swaney himself was perfectly safe, the outlaw assured him, and "need not be afraid of him, as he had nothing but the mail."

According to Swaney, as reported by Judge Guild, Mason's gang sustained themselves from the plunder taken from boatmen and other travelers. They preferred the Trace to the river, since travelers on the Trace were likely to have money and valuables with them; on the river they would have only goods. The bandits knew every foot of the road. They lurked near the springs where travelers made camp, or ambushed them as they came down to some wooded ford.

In Guild's rendering of Swaney's narrative, we get sharp pictures, sometimes grim, sometimes comic in the "r'aring" backwoods manner, of what it was like to meet the Mason band on the Natchez Trace.

Among Mason's first robberies [reported Swaney] was a party of Kentucky boatmen returning from Natchez. They had camped at what was called Gum Springs, in the Choctaw Nation. They ate supper, and as a matter of precaution, were putting out pickets before retiring for the night. In going to their positions, one of the pickets stepped on one of Mason's men, who were hid in the cane and grass, awaiting an opportunity to pounce upon the boatmen. The robber thus carelessly trod upon, jumped up and gave a yell and fired off his gun, calling upon his comrades to shoot and kill every boatman. This was so unexpected to the Kentuckians, that they became panic stricken and ran off in the wildest confusion, leaving everything, some even their wearing apparel. Mason and his men went to the camp and carried away everything. The next morning, just at daylight, Mr. Swaney came along, and seeing the campfires burning rode out but could find no one. He was going toward Natchez, and having met no party that morning, he instinctively knew that something was wrong, and he began to blow his bugle. The boatmen recognized the familiar sound, and commenced coming to Mr. Swaney, one and two at a time, who asserted that they were the worst scared, worst looking set of men he ever saw, some of them having but little clothing on, and one big fellow had only a shirt. They immediately held a council of war, and it was unanimously agreed to follow the robbers and capture their property. It was an easy matter to follow their trail through the cane and grass. Their plan was, as they had no arms, to provide themselves with sticks and knives, and when they should overtake Mason and his men, attack them by a vigorous charge, knocking down right and left with their shillelahs, and if those in front fell at the fire of the robbers, those in the rear were to rush upon, overpower, and capture the robbers, under the lead of the big Kentuckian.

They had gone about a mile, when they began to find articles of clothing which had been thrown away by the robbers. The big Kentuckian found his pants, in the waistband of which he had sewed four gold doubloons, and to his great joy the robbers had not found them. After this it was noticed that the big Kentuckian's valor began to fail him, and soon he was found in the rear. The pursuit was kept up about two miles further, when they were suddenly halted by Mason and his men, who were hid behind trees, with their guns presented, and who ordered them to go back or they would kill the last one of them. This caused a greater stampede than that of the night before, and the big Kentuckian distanced the whole party in the race back to the camp. They abused the big Kentuckian at a round rate for his want of courage, but he only laughed at them, saying he had everything to run for. But to his credit be it said, he spent his last dollar in procuring supplies for his companions.

Joseph Thompson Hare was something of a dandy, who spent much of his swag on fine clothes and alternated spells of robbery on the Trace with periods of debauchery in the dives and brothels of New Orleans and Natchez. It was his practice to select his victims in those places—boatmen or merchants who boasted of their gains and flung their money around—and in due season to lie in wait for them. He operated in the wild region between Natchez and the Tennessee River, and he and his band had a hide-out in a "rock-house" concealed in a canebrake. "Our habitation," he wrote in his diary, "was in a cleft rock, where one rock jutted very much over another, and made a sort of cave." During one of his debauches, Hare's conscience began to trouble him, and he began to read his Bible and to keep a diary which he proposed to leave as a warning against a life of crime. As he rode on his plundering expeditions—which took him, in his own words, "from the Southwest Point to the Choctaw Nation"— he delivered pious lectures to his evil companions. One night he had a vision, just after he had robbed a drover and was riding from the Tennessee River toward Nashville. "As I was riding along very rapidly to get out of the reach of pursuit, I saw standing right across the road, a beautiful white horse, as white as snow; his ears stood straight forward and his figure was very beautiful. When I approached him, and got within six feet of him, he disappeared in an instant, which made me very uneasy, and made me stop and stay at a house near there, all night."

Later on, when he was waiting to be hanged, he wrote his interpretation of this vision: "I think this white horse was Christ and that he came to warn me of my sins, and to make me fear and repent."

Most dangerous of all the outlaws, because he had a genius for organization and a cold, pitiless heart, was the famous John A. Murrell—a man "of genteel manners," who wore a fine beaver hat and an elegant "Bolivar" coat, rode blooded horses, and carried a brace of silver-mounted pistols. Precocious in crime, Murrell learned to steal, from his own mother's teaching, almost as soon as he could walk. During the later stages of his career, Murrell owned a fine house at Denmark, Tennessee, a little west of the Tennessee River, and passed as a well-to-do, though somewhat mysterious planter. He had gone from ordinary murder, highway robbery, and casual Negro stealing to more ambitious schemes. In the terminology of those days, he was a "speculator"—the head of a large and well-organized band that engaged in Negro stealing and other forms of robbery on a wide scale. From his home at Denmark he directed the operations of this band, which he enlarged, by a subtle process of corruption and intimidation, to include not only ordinary slave stealers, bandits, and counterfeiters, but respectable citizens and officers of the law. Murrell's power was so great that he and his men laughed at sheriffs and courts. In West Tennessee and Mississippi, where his rule waxed strongest, men were afraid to inform against him or to testify in court. Murrell even worked with the abolitionists who came down from the North, and drew them, no doubt innocently on their part, into his schemes, for which they served as an excellent cloak. Sometimes Murrell disguised himself as a Methodist preacher and exhorted the great camp meetings of the backwoods. He used the opportunities afforded by such gatherings to pass out counterfeit money and steal farmers' wallets.

Murrell's arrangements for stealing Negroes and selling them over and over again were not unlike the "Underground Railway" of pre-Civil War times, with the difference, of course, that Murrell and his men always killed a Negro when they thought the game of stealing him, selling him, and stealing him again, had reached a point where suspicion might be attracted to them. The scheme lapsed temporarily when Murrell was caught for horse stealing in Williamson County, Tennessee, and was summarily flogged and branded with the letters "H.T." by the unintimidated officers of that county. He went forth, however, with a bitterer hate against society than ever, and with a still greater scheme. It was nothing less than a planned uprising of Negro slaves, which would be instigated and carried through by Murrell and his men. His organization would take advantage of the resulting confusion, and would loot and kill at pleasure. And they would secure power, or so he thought. This "Mystic Confederacy" would be a veritable kingdom of land piracy with Murrell at the head. The day of the uprising was to be Christmas Day, 1835.

But at this point Murrell met his nemesis in the person of Virgil Stewart. Stewart came to visit John Henning, a preacher living near Jackson, Tennessee, shortly after two slaves had been stolen from Henning's place. Henning told his visitor that he suspected his mysterious planter neighbor, John Murrell. Stewart then conceived the plan, which he proceeded to carry out, of working himself into Murrell's confidence by pretending to fall in with his schemes. Only in that way could evidence be secured which would bring the great land pirate to justice.

Murrell's vanity made him an easy prey. Bit by bit, he told Stewart everything. But when Stewart cast off his role of intimate and brought about Murrell's arrest, he found himself caught in his own devices. The only important witnes against Murrell was Stewart himself. Nobody else would appear. Murrell, accomplished in the ways of the law, used all his ingenuity and all the resources of his organization to blacken Stewart's character. Stewart's testimony was attacked by Murrell's attorney on the ground that he himself had taken the oath as a member of Murrell's "clan." Murrell was found guilty, but he got off with a prison sentence of ten years.

Now Stewart was under a cloud, and besides, he feared for his life. To explain his actions and justify his conduct he drew up and published a remarkable pamphlet, in which he told the entire story of his association with Murrell and of the revelations Murrell made to him. He accompanied his narrative with numerous affidavits from officers of the law and from friends and associates. The cloud was never quite removed; the men of the frontier distrusted Stewart because he betrayed a man—even if that man was John Murrell—who had confided in him. Yet eventually a kind of vindication came, when Vicksburg and other Mississippi towns found evidence of a planned Negro uprising. They formed committees of safety, hanged some suspicious characters, ran others out of town, and wiped out the notorious dives of Natchez-under-the-Hill.

How much is truth and how much is fiction or exaggeration in Stewart's narrative, it would be hard to say. Many people believe to this day that Stewart really was a member of Murrell's gang, who turned state's evidence to save his own neck and devised his ingenious story to camouflage his true relations with Murrell. It may well be that Stewart's account of how he secured Murrell's confidence is largely an imaginative concoction. But Stewart's pictures of Murrell's operations correspond with what is generally believed about the land pirates and their methods. We can be fairly sure that Murrell's own account, as told by Stewart, of how he killed a traveler on the Natchez Trace, is not altogether fiction:

We went a few hundred yards until we got out of sight of the trail. Then I hitched the horse and ordered the fellow to undress. He commenced to strip, and at length stood undressed to his shirt and drawers. Then I ordered him to turn his back to me.

He asked me if I was going to shoot him: he evidently had withheld the question before. I made no answer. He stretched his hands toward me, and begged for time to pray before he died. . . . He looked wistfully up and down, and at last he turned from me and dropped on his knees, and I shot him through the head. I felt sorry for him, but I could not help it. I had been obliged to travel on foot for the last four days.

As soon as he fell, I drew my knife and ripped open his belly and took out his guts. Then I scooped up a lot of sand, stuffed it in the vacant stomach and sunk the body in the creek.

Such were the perils of the Natchez Trace—aptly called, in early times, "the Bloody Path." Yet, as far as the boatmen were concerned, the tales of Judge Guild and others may represent the exceptional, not the ordinary, course of events. The boatmen were frontiersmen, skilled in rough-and-tumble fighting and handy with guns and knives. It is hard to conceive them as being very much awed by Mason, Murrell, and Hare.

Very likely, the wearisomeness of the trip impressed them more than its loneliness and danger. Boatmen generally traveled in company, for sociability and safety. If they had any money left after carousing in New Orleans, they put it in money belts or sewed it into their trouser bands, or stowed it in rawhide sacks which they mixed with other baggage and concealed in the bushes where they made camp. If they could afford an Indian pony, they used him for a pack horse, not for a saddle horse. A man could walk as fast on the Trace as he could ride. There were stories of famous walkers among the boatmen. "Walking Johnson" three times raced the mounted mail carrier, and three times won. Richard W. Anderson of Huntsville had the reputation of arriving always three or four days ahead of the boatmen of his neighborhood. One time, disgusted with the low price offered him at New Orleans for his boat cable, he coiled it about his shoulders, and thus laden, walked home as usual. He liked walking so well, it was said, that he often walked from Huntsville to Whitesburg and back—a matter of ten or twelve miles—to get up an appetite for breakfast. Probably the "walk" of such famous pedestrians was the Indian "dogtrot," easy and untiring. The boatmen carried the Indian ration, too: jerked meat, a little flour or meal, and a bag of parched corn.

Along the way, there were a few pleasant stretches. Entering the Indian country, at Grindstone Ford, on Bayou Pierre, the boatmen knew it was all of five hundred miles to Nashville. But some of the prairie country was not bad at all. And at the Chickasaw Agency, at Big Chickasaw town, they could stop and feast their eyes on beautiful Peggy Allen. Peggy was the daughter of Jim Allen, interpreter at the Agency, and of Susie Colbert, a chief's daughter whom Jim Allen courted and married in the Indian manner. Swaney, the mail carrier, called her "the prettiest woman he ever saw" and added that "it was almost incredible the number of travelers and boatmen who stopped at the Agency to see her." After staring at beautiful Peggy, and perhaps refreshing themselves from the peach trees that grew in the neighborhood of the Indian towns, or feasting on the wild strawberries that reddened the ground, the boatmen struck out on the forty miles between them and Colbert's Ferry.

At the ferry there was a tavern, and entertainment of a rough sort. After crossing the Tennessee, the boatmen had to scramble through the canebrakes and up the broken and eroded slopes of the plateau known as the Highland Rim. The cane grew to a height of twenty or thirty feet and made the bottoms seem, in Alexander Wilson's phrase, "the gloomiest and most desolate-looking places imaginable." On the plateau they were faced with a Hobson's choice. When the road followed the ridges, it was invariably rough; in the bottoms, it was a regular swamp road, where the Trace often vanished in what the peripatetic preacher, Lorenzo Dow, called "hell-holes." From the thickets of the swamps, mosquitoes and stinging gnats swarmed out to feast on the travelers.

But there were stretches of relatively level road among the great forests of scrub oak and white oak that give the region its enduring local name—the "Barrens." It is still one of the most lonely and backwoodsy spots of Tennessee. In the Barrens, even now, a traveler will feel oppressed—shut in and menaced by the unchanging ranks of scrub oaks that close about the journey and make every bend of the road seem like every other bend, for miles upon miles. There is a lurking threat in the untamable woods, a feeling of shapes that hide in the undergrowth and flicker half seen from tree to tree. In other days it was more than just a feeling. The boatmen kept scouts ahead. They watched the flicker in the shadows of the oak trees.

Local tradition deepens the shadows. In Wayne County, some twenty miles from the Trace and not far from the Tennessee River, is a place now called Natural Bridge, because of the enormous and peculiar tunnel that Buffalo River has cut through a wooded ridge. The winding passage is open at both ends, and above, on the ridgetop, is a depression. Outlaws used the cave as a hide-out, and kept their horses in the hollow above. Because some of the early meetings of the county court were held in the great principal chamber, the place used to be known as Rock Courthouse.

A little farther north, on the line of the Trace itself, was Griner's Stand, where Meriwether Lewis met his death on October 11, 1809. At this time Lewis was territorial governor of Louisiana, and he was traveling from St. Louis to Washington, taking with him vouchers and other documents by which he intended to vindicate himself against charges, real or imagined, brought in Washington against his official conduct. He had come by boat to Chickasaw Bluffs (Memphis). Learning there that war with England might break out at any moment, he abandoned his plan for an ocean voyage from New Orleans, purchased horses, and started across country, by way of the western branch of the "Old Chickasaw Trail," to reach the Natchez Trace and journey east. With him were Major Neely, Indian agent at Chickasaw Bluffs, and Lewis's two servants. On the way two of Lewis's pack horses, apparently those carrying his papers, strayed and were lost. While Neely stayed to look for the horses, Lewis pushed ahead, and at sunset came to Griner's Stand, where he asked for lodgings for himself and the two servants.

Griner was away, and Lewis was met by Mrs. Griner, who observed him to be in a state of considerable agitation. He could not eat, he muttered to himself, he walked nervously up and down. He refused the bed prepared for him and made his servant spread out bearskins and a buffalo robe on the floor of the small cabin. Mrs. Griner retired to the kitchen, and Lewis's servants went to the barn to sleep.

During the night Mrs. Griner heard Lewis walking back and forth and talking "like a lawyer." Then came a pistol shot, the noise of a heavy fall, and the cry "O Lord!" Then another pistol shot, and finally a voice groaning at the kitchen door, "O madam, give me some water and heal my wounds!" The woman was too much frightened to answer. Looking between the unchinked logs of the kitchen, she saw him fall against a stump in the clearing, then crawl to a tree and raise himself upright. She heard him scrape the gourd dipper against the bottom of the empty water bucket. But she did not offer to fill it for the dying man, nor did his servants hear and come to his aid. At daylight she sent her children to summon the Negroes. They found Lewis still conscious, but fatally wounded. A piece of his forehead was blown off, and the brain was exposed. He begged them to shoot him. "I am no coward," he said, "but I am so strong, so hard to die." As the sun rose above the treetops, he died.

Alexander Wilson, the famous ornithologist, visited the Griner cabin two years after Lewis's death and secured from Mrs. Griner the story here told. This story is completely at variance with the legend, circulated after Lewis's death, and persistently repeated today, that Lewis was murdered and robbed by Griner. Later investigations seem to support Wilson's view. In all likelihood, Lewis was in a semidemented state, and shot himself. His agitation was caused by fear that his precious papers were lost and that the demons of persecution had followed him on his journey. It was the reputation of the Natchez Trace, probably, that imputed Lewis's death to the treachery of Griner, for travelers who died on the Trace rarely ever shot themselves.

"I left this place," wrote Wilson, "in a very melancholy mood, which was not much allayed by the prospect of the gloomy and savage wilderness which I was just entering alone." But the boatmen, at this point, were putting that gloomy wilderness behind them. From Duck River Ford to Nashville was fifty miles. The boatmen descended from the melancholy Barrens into the infinitely varied hills and valley of the Middle Basin of Tennessee, heartened by the knowledge that a real settlement was not far ahead. It is claimed that they reached Nashville, generally, on about the fifteenth day after leaving Natchez. This would mean that they averaged 34 miles a day in traveling 500 miles—an incredible pace!

At Nashville, the parties broke up. If bound for the north, men went singly, or in twos and threes, into Kentucky. If they were bound for East Tennessee, they took the Walton Road across the Cumberlands and thus came back in a wide circle to touch the Tennessee again at Southwest Point. Boatmen who lived in the Great Bend of course turned off at Colbert's Ferry, or took some short cut home. But the East Tennesseans apparently went on to Nashville, for there were not as yet any traveled roads that ran eastward from the Great Bend all the way up the Tennessee Valley, nor was it possible for them to hitchhike home on the river itself until steamboats at last appeared.

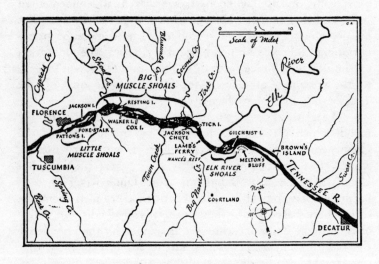

The map shows the Muscle Shoals region with labels including: Scale of Miles, BIG MUSCLE SHOALS, Second Cr., First Cr., Elk River, Blunzn Cr., Shoal Cr., Cypress Cr., JACKSON I., RESTING I., FLORENCE, WALKER I., TICK I., POKE-STALK I., COX I., JACKSON CHUTE, GILCHRIST I., PATTON'S I., LAMB'S FERRY, BROWN'S ISLAND, LITTLE MUSCLE SHOALS, NANCE'S REEF, MELTON'S BLUFF, TUSCUMBIA, ELK RIVER SHOALS, Town Creek, Big Nance Cr., TENNESSEE R., Swan Cr., Spring Cr., East Cr., COURTLAND, North compass, DECATUR

CHAPTER XVI

# Early Steamboat Days

THE real opening of the Muscle Shoals area to settlement came just at the time when Henry Shreve developed a steamboat that could navigate the western rivers. In 1815, Shreve's *Enterprise* became the first steamboat to go upstream from New Orleans to Pittsburgh. In 1818, seven million dollars' worth of land in the Great Bend was sold at Huntsville to eager migrants and speculators. There was no causal connection between the two events. Nevertheless, from that day to this, the price of land in the Muscle Shoals region has always been a sensitive barometer of the hopes of North Alabama. In that blessed country, any whisper of new possibilities—a canal, a railroad, a power dam—has never failed to start a cyclone of speculation. The throngs of people rushing into the Great Bend aimed to raise cotton on that rich new ground, ship it down the Tennessee, and sell it at New Orleans. The newcomers recked little of Muscle Shoals as yet. They expected great things of their land and of the Tennessee, and the fairly prompt appearance of steamboats on the Lower Tennessee did not diminish their already jocular hopes. Steamboats, indeed, were a part of the general jubilation; and it was at first assumed that the steamboats would conquer the river as the people were conquering the land.

The settlement of the Great Bend was not the slow, steady infiltration of the older pioneering. It was a stampede. From all directions except the Creek country to the south, the immigrants poured in. Some came down the Valley from East Tennessee and Virginia, some from the north by way of Nashville and the Natchez Trace, others from Georgia and the Carolinas by way of Augusta and Ross's Landing. Still others came, after 1812, by the "Georgia State Road" across Sand Mountain and then into the Great Bend by a road Andrew Jackson built during the Creek War, after he crossed the Tennessee at Fort Deposit and struck south. They came, no longer as roving individuals or in small groups walking guardedly with rifles ready, but in caravans and moving masses of families, clans, whole communities. The poor man came as best he could, on foot, leading a pack horse; or he crammed his goods into a hogshead fitted with shafts and drawn like a crude cart. If he lacked a horse, he put himself between the shafts. Rich planters came in cavalcades of wagons, carriages, riders, their lusty sons rollicking through the woods on fine horses, their Negro slaves driving the teams or riding the baggage or walking in long files.

Somewhere in the less settled part of Georgia, one of these cavalcades met a group of pretty girls, all galloping along on horseback. The sauciest of the group, casting her eye over the long train of wagons, spoke to one of the Negro drivers in a tone intended to carry a long way.

"Who's your master?"

"Marse Tom, right yonder—he de marster."

"Does everything here belong to him?"

"Yas'm."

"Is he married?"

"No'm, he ain't married yit."

"Well, tell your master to come and get me, any time!"

And in a gale of feminine laughter, with many inviting backward glances, the pert young women whipped up their horses and rode on.

The times were boisterous, and the settlement of the Great Bend was like a great frolicsome picnic. Nobody worried much, apparently, over the obvious fact that the burst of migration was in part due to the notorious Yazoo land frauds. The Tennessee Land Company, which was one of the Yazoo companies, bought from the state of Georgia, for one and one-half cents an acre, three and a half million acres of land in the Great Bend. The company defaulted in its payments, but proceeded to buy the same land again for two and one-fourth cents an acre. Ignoring both Indian claims and the interests of the federal government, the company surveyed these lands and sold them at a dollar an acre. Its transactions were finally declared fraudulent by the Georgia legislature, and the members of an earlier legislature who had connived in the deal were driven ignominiously from public life. Then, as an easement for innocent purchasers, scrip was issued, commonly known as "Mississippi stock," which these purchasers could use under certain prescribed conditions to buy the lands, now "public" lands, to which they thought they had got a title. Since plenty of this scrip was in circulation, and since the newly established banks were generous in extending credit, the stage was set for the first of the great booms in

which the highhearted people of the Great Bend have been
prone to indulge.

The land was there, and it was open to purchase. The
louder the clamor of fraud, the greater the volume of free
advertising. There was of course a great political and legal
mess, which involved federal government, state governments,
and the Indian nations in a noisome tangle. In a series of cessions extending over about thirty years, Indian titles were
gradually extinguished. The rest of the untangling was not so
easy. It went on interminably and provided many a lawyer
and many a surveyor with the beginnings of a career. Meanwhile, the settlers blithely came on.

In 1805, there was practically nobody in the Huntsville
area except John Hunt, who had planted himself strategically
by the Big Spring which even today furnishes Huntsville
with its water supply; and there was Old Man Ditto, some
miles to the south, at the landing which bore his name. Three
years later, there were five thousand people in that area, which
speedily became Madison County. By 1816, there were fourteen thousand people. Spilling rapidly westward, settlers were
building cabins at Athens by 1808, and within another decade Athens was a flourishing county seat. At the foot of
Muscle Shoals, Tuscumbia sprang up on the site of the Indian
town of Coldwater. In its neighborhood, four other towns
were projected: York's Bluff (long afterward, Sheffield),
South Port (old South Florence), Bainbridge, and Marion.
Meanwhile, just across the river, General John Coffee and
his associates of the Cypress Land Company raised up a city.
They employed an Italian engineer, Ferdinand Sannoner, to
lay out a sumptuous plan of streets and parks upon the un-
cleared wilderness. Sannoner performed so well that General
Coffee and his friends invited the Italian to name the dream
city, and he called it Florence after his native home. Downriver, Waterloo grew up, opposite the mouth of Bear Creek.
Courtland and other fine towns were built on the fertile plain

south of the Tennessee. Gunter's Ferry became Gunter's Landing, a hamlet with an Indian town at its back. But of the larger towns only Florence and Decatur were planted squarely on the riverbank.

The price of land jumped from a dollar an acre to almost anything. LeRoy Pope paid $23 an acre for the Big Spring tract at Huntsville—which he wanted to name Twickenham. John Coffee and associates paid $60 an acre for the land on which Athens was built. At a sale of lots held in Florence in 1818, eight of the best lots brought a total of $21,000. At Tuscumbia, bottom land sold for $100 an acre. At Triana, which hoped to become the port of Huntsville, a man paid $1,500 for a sixty-foot lot in a town which was little more than sketched.

Certain great men gave impetus to the speculation. General Andrew Jackson and his friends, especially John Coffee, got well acquainted with these lands when they crossed and recrossed the Tennessee during the Creek and Seminole wars. During the expedition to Florida, Jackson camped on York's Bluff, and tradition says that Old Hickory then and there dreamed of a metropolis which would someday rise at the foot of Muscle Shoals. He put money into his dream, and acquired, among other holdings, the plantation held by James Melton, the Indian pilot. The Melton's Bluff plantation was never a great satisfaction to the general. He had trouble with overseers and fugitive slaves and was a rather anxious absentee landlord. Coffee, on the other hand, came to live in the neighborhood of Florence, and waxed prosperous. President Madison was an investor in Florence land, and so was James Jackson, who was Andrew Jackson's business associate, and so were many other persons, prominent or famous.

In an incredibly short time, the wilderness of the Great Bend became a genially civilized region where, after the traditional southern pattern, the plantation, the farm, and the frontier merged to produce a life that was neither too rough nor too pretentiously elegant. North Alabama did not quite belong to the Deep South although it had vast cotton fields, chinaberry trees, high summer temperatures, and houses ornamented with iron grillwork as well as many orthodox pillared mansions. In fact, it was for a long time separated by lack of transportation facilities from the more southern parts of the state to which boundary lines allotted it. Politically and geographically, it had a more intimate connection with Middle Tennessee. Culturally, it was an amalgam of what had been brought to it from Virginia, the Carolinas, Georgia, and the newer lands of Tennessee and Kentucky. Whatever was brought—whether architecture, manners, politics, or song—lost nothing in being carried west, but seemed to have been awaiting this new acclimation to reveal its essence. When the log cabin grew, as it often did, into the "big house" of the plantation, the house that emerged had a form and grace which might have been predesigned. Houses that actually were predesigned were rarely built by professional architects, but by unknown or wandering carpenters with a genius for adapting Georgian and Greek Revival types to Alabama surroundings. Even when the houses were heavy and pretentious, they had an air about them; they belonged, in some homespun way, to North Alabama's wish to be both ambitious and comfortable. When James Jackson built his house, Forks of Cypress, in 1819, he wanted not only a porch but a colonnade around all four outer walls. The architect gave him twenty large Ionic columns, but they were not made of wood or stone. They were made of brick covered with a special plaster of sand mixed with molasses. The homemade mixture stuck; it was all right. And so it went. Furniture and chandeliers might have to be "brought on," but everything else came from the place where the house was built. The bricks were baked, the lime was burnt, the wood was cut, seasoned, and sawed on the land itself out of which such fine places as Belle Mina and Forks of Cypress, as it were, sprouted.

Mainly it was "quick cotton money" that did it, or the agricultural economy that was largely based on cotton. In that respect the people of the Great Bend were vastly pleased. But they were vexed to discover, as they became thoroughly settled and deeply committed, that they had made entirely too many fine assumptions about the Tennessee River. Only Tuscumbia and Florence lay below Muscle Shoals and could make regular use of the river. The other important towns were above the Shoals, and therefore were above the bottleneck. To make matters worse, such fine towns as Huntsville and Athens had been thoughtlessly pitched at some distance from the river. The transportation problem was complex and appalling. The more productive their lands the more irksome the problem became.

The cotton merchants of Huntsville, discontented with hauling ten miles to Ditto's Landing, turned their eyes to Indian Creek, which connected with their Big Spring and flowed into the Tennessee at Triana. In 1820, Thomas Fearn, LeRoy Pope, and other Huntsvillians set on foot a project for canalizing Indian Creek and making a navigable waterway from Huntsville to Triana. This canal, known as Fearn's Canal, was finally made usable in 1831, in which year two keelboats came all the way up to Huntsville from the Tennessee. The next step was to make the canal navigable for steamboats, but this brave project, though hopefully contemplated, came to nothing when it finally became apparent that Huntsville would have a railroad. The Fearn canal then fell into disuse.

Other people looked into the matter of improving the Flint and Paint Rock rivers. The Paint Rock seemed more promising, and the state of Alabama appropriated $10,000 to put it in order. Unfortunately, the contractors charged with improvements were possessed by the notion that the first step was to clear the riverbanks of all overhanging trees. They cut the great oaks and poplars and let them fall into the stream on the supposition that the winter floods would carry off the mass of debris. Instead, the trees sank into the bed of the river and stayed there, achieving a curious underwater immortality, and so, except during the flood season, the Paint Rock was the most unnavigable river in Alabama. A boy could hardly go swimming in it for fear of impaling his body on a snag.

Getting to the river was one part of the problem; getting over Muscle Shoals was the other and the greater part. Many of the people of the Great Bend were almost as badly off as the East Tennesseans, upriver: they could ship by river only two or three months out of the year, at the seasons when flatboats could go down. Or they could depend on keelboats, which could, it is true, navigate the Shoals both ways. But they had more stuff to haul, going and coming, than the keelboats could manage. As soon as steamboats became a real possibility, their hopes swelled. They had plenty of business for the steamboats. They had, or could get, the capital to promote steamboat service. They had experienced rivermen, skilled in the management of flatboats and keelboats, who could change over to the new thing. Could the steamboats conquer Muscle Shoals? Well, let them come and try.

When the steamboats came at last, they did not immediately attempt to go above Muscle Shoals. For the time being, it was trouble enough to navigate 250 miles of uncharted river and reach Tuscumbia Landing and Florence, at the foot of the great rapids.

The first steamboat to make this trip, according to the best information available, was the *Osage,* which brought a cargo to Florence in 1821, six years after Shreve's *Enterprise* made her pioneer journey up the Mississippi. Very likely the voyage of the *Osage* was promoted by the Alabama and East Tennessee Steamboat Company, which was organized at

Huntsville in 1819 and, like other navigation companies of
the period, represented the anxious joint enterprise of both
the Muscle Shoals region and East Tennessee.

There is an unverified tradition, however, that a boat
named the *Eagle* made an earlier attempt, and got as far as
the large island which stands in a bend of the river below
Clifton. She was wrecked on the head of this island, which
thenceforth was called Eagle's Nest Island. The year of this
luckless voyage and the details of the disaster are not known.

In 1822, William Keever brought up the *Rocket,* a light-
draft vessel of eighty tons burden, and began the first regular packet service on the Tennessee. A little later the *Courier*
and the *Velocipede* entered service on the Lower Tennessee,
and soon passengers and freight were moving with some regularity between Florence and points on the Ohio, Cumberland,
and Mississippi. These three boats, like others that came after
them in the early days, generally carried keelboats or flatboats
in tow. Until channel improvements finally made navigation
easier, keelboats furnished valuable assistance by acting as
lighters. If river conditions made it difficult for the steamboat
to get over Colbert Shoals, it could stop at Waterloo, and
send the passengers and freight on to Florence by the faithful
keels. Or if the steamboat grounded on a sand bar, the keels
came to the rescue by taking off part of the cargo.

For the time being, all goods and passengers destined
for points above Muscle Shoals were transferred at Florence
or Tuscumbia to keelboats that plied the region of the Great
Bend. The only alternative was an overland trip by wagon
or stagecoach. In reverse process, Florence and Tuscumbia became the great depots for whatever came downriver to await
steamboat transportation on the Lower Tennessee. Until Muscle Shoals could be conquered, Florence and Tuscumbia
marked the head of steamboat navigation on the Tennessee.

In 1826, the New Orleans and Tuscumbia Steamboat
Company announced that they were putting two "new and

fast-running steamboats" into service, on a regular schedule. These were the *Courtland* (Joseph Pierce, master) and the *Tuscumbia* (John Hall and William McKnight). The company announced that these boats would tow as many flatboats "as will not retard their progress." William H. Avery, clerk for the Tuscumbia company, used to wait until the *Courtland* or *Tuscumbia* had left the home landing, then go 320 miles overland by stagecoach, and arrive at Louisville, ready for business, some hours ahead of the boat.

Although no speed records were being made as yet, steamboats were multiplying. By 1830, more than twenty boats were plying the Lower Tennessee, and the Tuscumbia and Florence people could take their choice, within limits, of a locally owned packet or one of the Ohio and Mississippi boats, such as *Belle Creole, Emerald, Miami, Pittsburg, Plough-Boy, Rob Roy, Robert Burns, Scioto, Steubenville.* Furthermore, the Estells of Huntsville bought and put into service the *Nashville.*

Meanwhile, the Knoxville folks began to campaign for steamboat transportation above Muscle Shoals. If only some captain could be tempted to risk the dangerous passage, they could at least get local service on the Upper Tennessee. They offered a handsome purse to the first steamboat that would tie up at the Knoxville landing.

At first there were no takers. It was doubtful whether any steamboat then in existence could get over Muscle Shoals. High water, which was the prime condition for upward transit, necessarily created powerful eddies and currents which the weak engines then in use would find it hard to master. Nevertheless, in 1825, a small steamboat, name now unknown, actually did ascend the Shoals by making use of warps, and with great labor and anxiety reached Decatur. The captain of the boat then decided that he had had enough.

Two years later the momentous voyage was again attempted, with complete success. The intrepid *Atlas*, a small side-wheeler built at Cincinnati, became the first steamboat to navigate the Tennessee from Paducah to Knoxville. The master of the *Atlas*, Captain S. D. Conner, was joint owner of the steamboat with Messrs. Rider and Turner. The pilots who took her over the Shoals were Joseph Wyatt and Jack Clark.

As soon as it became known, in the winter of 1827-28, that the *Atlas* had left Cincinnati to try for the Knoxville prize money, her progress became an object of eager concern to all the newspapers of the Valley. She tied up at Florence to await favorable conditions for passage over the Shoals. On February 5 the *Southern Advocate* announced that the *Atlas* had reached Melton's Bluff; she had passed the worst stretch without any difficulty worth recording.

On February 15 the *Atlas* reached Triana, and the *Southern Advocate* gave a triumphant editorial whoop, while all Madison County flocked near to view the wonder and, if possible, to get a ride on the *Atlas*. "It cannot be denied," said the *Advocate*, "that many of the people here have always thought it as much impossible to bring a steamboat in full blast over these formidable Shoals as to navigate a 50-gun frigate into 'Symms' Hole.' But we are no longer in doubt—facts have proved all our sneers and predictions to be unfounded and fallacious; and now when the thing is done and the enterprise performed, we are ready to join in the cant phrase of 'I told you so,' although two weeks ago we did not believe a word of it."

After enjoying the hospitality of Alabama for a few days, Captain Conner turned the *Atlas* toward the perils of the Narrows and the unexplored channels of the Upper Tennessee. The voyage from Triana to Knoxville took two weeks and a day. The Narrows proved less formidable than had been anticipated. The *Atlas* passed up the Boiling Pot in fourteen minutes and came through the Suck in only nine minutes. She laid only one warp between Triana and Knoxville, and that one, for precaution rather than need, was at the Suck. The slow time of the voyage was not due to difficulties of navigation, but to the frequent stops for wood. As yet there were no woodyards for steamboats on the Upper Tennessee, and Captain Conner had to tie up every now and then and send his crew to chop wood from the forests along the bank.

As the *Atlas* puffed upstream, all who were forewarned crowded near to witness the miracle, and others, amazed at the sound of her cannon, bolted in haste to the nearest point of vantage. The *Atlas* had no whistle or bell. She mounted a small cannon which was used to signal landings. When she approached Washington Landing and delivered her warning blast, a crowd of waiting Negroes stampeded in terror.

Some of the more curious came long distances downriver to meet and inspect the great wonder, and then went back upriver to see it again. Among these admirers was a veteran flatboatman named Ross Neely, who had visited the *Atlas* and looked her over carefully at Ross's Landing. When the *Atlas* stopped at Little River Shoals, twelve miles below Knoxville, Neely was again in the crowd of visitors. As a riverman, he felt bound to explain the mysteries of steamboat operation to all those gathered. Suddenly the engineer opened the valve of the mud drum to blow out the mud. Steam filled the air; there was a terrific shrieking sound. Ross Neely thought he knew what was happening. "Save yourselves, people," he shouted. "She has busted her biler!" And he plunged into the river, while the crowd ran for safety. Coming to the surface, fifty feet away, he was crestfallen to see the *Atlas* intact. The joke was on him—for the rest of his life.

The *Atlas* arrived at Knoxville after dark on March 3, 1828, and on the next day made her official entry into port, to receive a ceremonial welcome from the mayor and aldermen and a jubilant unofficial greeting from the assembled throng. Captain Conner presented a flag to the city, and

Colonel Solomon D. Jacobs, speaking on behalf of Knoxville, hailed the captain as "the first navigator by steam of the Tennessee and Holston rivers." A new era of navigation was beginning, declared the colonel, and he said an oratorical good-bye to the days when there "re-echoed the splash of the oar, as the flatboat slowly drifted down the surface, or reverberated the firm, heavy tread of the bargeman, as with both hands he grasped the dripping cordel, which rested on his shoulder, and with his body almost bent to the planks on which he walked, he slowly and laboriously propelled his vessel against the current." There was a great public celebration, climaxed by a dinner at which thirteen regular toasts and thirty impromptu toasts were drunk to the bold navigators, to the propelling power of steam, to the steamboat *Atlas*, to Robert Fulton, to internal improvements, to the fair of Tennessee, and so on; and a purse of $640 was presented to Captain Conner.

To round out her trip, the *Atlas* steamed up to the mouth of the French Broad and tied up, by invitation, at Mecklenburg, the home of Dr. J. G. M. Ramsey, later the author of *The Annals of Tennessee*. It was like a visit of state. Dr. Ramsey gave a hospitable welcome to Captain Conner and the crowd of holidaymakers who came with him. But when called on for a speech, Dr. Ramsey upset the applecart.

Dr. Ramsey was a man of conviction, who truckled to nobody. He was disinclined to indulge in easy optimism. East Tennesseans might think their great problem solved. Not so Dr. Ramsey, who had thought long and hard about transportation. The arrival of one small valiant steamboat was not enough to convince him that regular packet service was about to be established between Knoxville and New Orleans. No, East Tennessee was "essentially an Atlantic country," and its hope was in improved forms of land transportation. He was for highways or railroads—so far as he was in favor of any kind of transportation. He was afraid, he said, that the proposed Coosa-Hiwassee canal and other plausible ventures would lead only to a quick exploitation of the resources of East Tennessee, and thus to its ultimate ruin. If they wanted connections with the outside world, let them seek connections with the Atlantic Coast, or else remain in isolation. Cotton was selling at a higher price in Charleston than in New Orleans, he reminded them. But what was cotton, that the need of hauling it should determine all their business? Even if the New Orleans trade were opened, it would only be to a limited extent, and any advantage would be "far overbalanced by the actual injury it will do to all the interests of East Tennessee."

The edge had been taken off the celebration. The Knoxville folks did not like such talk—besides, it was impolite. Dr. Ramsey afterward protested that his opinions had been misrepresented by the raging newspapers. He was not, in fact, opposed to improving the navigation of the Tennessee. Later, with his brother and other citizens, he invested money in the steamboat *Knoxville,* and he served (perhaps with his fingers crossed) on the Board of River Commissioners established by the Tennessee legislature.

Dr. Ramsey's pessimism, while inappropriate for the jolly occasion, was speedily justified in the fate of the *Atlas.* Captain J. M. Todd, one of the early rivermen, remembered what happened to her. "She was the first to make the trip, got the money, and never went there again. She was a financial failure, never made many trips, sank money, and finally sank herself on Bird Iron Shoals below Ditto's Landing . . . Eventually Solomon Bouldin, Charles Carlen, and myself . . . went in, bailed her out, and raised her. Captain Trotter, from East Tennessee, built a hull up the river, brought it down, put the *Atlas* machinery on it and called it the steamboat *Enterprise.* But she was as often called the *Polly Trotter* instead. She was also a failure, and steamboating on the Upper Tennessee was a slow go for the next several years."

A slow go it was, and yet the efforts of rivermen to es-

tablish regular service on the Upper Tennessee make a valorous chapter in the history of steamboating. In the 1830's
steamboats came above Muscle Shoals at the rate of about one
a year to enter the Upper Tennessee trade. These boats, in
the probable order of transit over Muscle Shoals, and the
daring captains who brought them up, were as follows: 1831,
*Knoxville* (Bearden); 1832 or 1834, *Reliance* (Coatney) and
*Guide* (Castleman); 1834, *Harkaway* (Nicholson); 1835,
*Holston* (French); 1836, *Huntsman* (Mahan); 1837, *Pickaway* (Bledsoe); 1838, *Samaratan* (Sneed); 1837 or 1838,
*Victoria.*

All these boats probably encountered much the same
difficulties in getting over Muscle Shoals. What the difficulties were we may guess from the brief remarks of an observer
who saw the *Reliance* struggling to make the ascent over the
Shoals in December, 1834. "The river at this point was three
miles wide," he said, "and presented a mass of waves and
rapid currents." The *Reliance* was "exerting all its power,"
yet was almost helpless against the current, and in a day's
time got only one mile upstream.

Of the eight boats that navigated the Upper Tennessee
during the 1830's, the *Knoxville* was the most important historically because, although she was a financial failure, she
was the first to attempt regular packet service between Knoxville and Decatur. The *Knoxville* was built at Cincinnati for
a company of Knox County men; Dr. J. G. M. Ramsey, his
brother W. B. A. Ramsey, William Swan, James Kennedy,
C. W. Crozier were among the stockholders.

The *Knoxville* ascended Muscle Shoals with much difficulty in April, 1831. When she approached the Narrows,
people came down from East Tennessee to watch the epic
combat between the power of steam and those ancient opponents of civilization, Boiling Pot and Suck. And there was a
reporter on hand to write, in a florid nineteenth century prose,
his eyewitness, round-by-round story of the fight, for the

East Tennessee newspapers. According to this eyewitness, the master of the boat at once saw it would be "unpardonable temerity" to fight the Boiling Pot with the power of steam alone. Therefore he laid warps, but even with this assistance spent most of Sunday in a vain struggle with the river. At daybreak of the next morning the struggle was renewed. Then—

About 12 o'clock, by the joint power of the steam and the capstan, the boat was seen in the middle of the stream, when the person whose business it was to unfasten the rope on shore, mistaking some cry on board for an order, cut the rope and left the boat to the stream and the current. For a moment she advanced—for another she hung trembling in a doubtful contest with the force of the water and began to—recede. "Let go that anchor," cried the captain. "Ay Ay Sir," responded the mate. " 'Tis done." For the anchor to be cast, for a plank to be shoved over the guards—for several men to spring on the end of it to make it fast,—for Barney Sedgewick, the mate, to leap from the end of it into the angry flood with a rope coiled around his neck and under his left arm—swim to the shore, make it fast, and for the boat to be secure from impending ruin [that is, collision with the jagged boulders of the narrow channel], was the work of a moment. But it was a moment to the spectators of indescribable excitement. . . . Barney Sedgewick's energies seemed now to be completely roused. For in a few minutes he was seen with another coil of rope wading and swimming ahead of the boat where it was made fast, and being attached to her, as soon as the anchor could be weighed, she was again under headway and safely over this formidable obstruction—the most formidable in the river at this stage of the water.

At the Suck, the *Knoxville* again had serious trouble, especially with the "sleek," as boatmen called the deceptively smooth part of the river where the current was strongest. There again she had to resort to warping. Nevertheless, she finally got through and was triumphantly welcomed at the city of Knoxville.

But the *Knoxville* proved to be too large and too expensive in upkeep for packet service on the Upper Tennessee. Once she got downstream, she could not be depended on to get upstream again, and was therefore often reduced to the necessity of serving the local trade between Decatur and the Suck until such time as the stage of the river would permit a return to Knoxville. This turned out to be a common experience for steamboats operating on the Upper Tennessee, and it soon enforced the keelboat-steamboat combination on the successors of the *Knoxville.*

When it became evident that the *Knoxville* was losing money for her owners, a stockholders' meeting was held to decide what to do. Each man in turn expressed his views. Finally it was the turn of old Mr. Shutterley, a prosperous farmer of German descent, who had risked his money in the venture. "Shentlemen," he said, "there is but one way to do to save ourselves from further losses. Every trip the d—d Boat makes brings us in debt—every voyage she goes costs more than it comes to, and my opinion is to run her up the river to the deep water at Dr. Ramsey's ferry, and to get some two-inch augers and bore holes through her bottom planks— let in the water—sink her and let her go to H—." The *Knoxville,* however, was sold to a Major Swan, who also lost money on her. Finally, after seven years of intermittent service, she was refitted and named *Indian Chief,* and then was used in the Cherokee Removal. Later, she reached the undignified end that seems to come to famous steamboats. Her boiler and engines were taken off and used in a sawmill; and her hull was converted into a wharfboat for use at Chattanooga.

But while she lasted, the *Knoxville* had the honors of a pioneer, and it is likely that a number of famous Tennessee rivermen had their first experience with steamboating in her pilothouse and on her decks. Captain John L. Doss, one of the greatest of the Tennessee captains, ran away from home to become a cabin boy on the *Knoxville.* Doubtless many another East Tennessee youngster wanted to do the same thing, for the *Knoxville* must have been to the boys of East Tennessee what the Mississippi steamboats were to young Mark Twain and his friends.

Probably it was that kind of attraction that gave the *Knoxville* a place not only in steamboat history but in American literature. Her master, for at least a part of her career, was George Washington Harris, the humorist, author of *Sut Lovingood's Yarns*. Undoubtedly Mark Twain in later years, like many another American humorist, learned much from the riotous and incorrigible Sut Lovingood, the greatest practical joker in all history and surely one of the keenest of all backwoods philosophers. More than one distinguished critic, in fact, is ready to argue that Tom Sawyer and Huck Finn might never have taken shape in Mark Twain's imagination if Harris had not earlier created his gangling, long-legged, fluently satirical yarnteller of the East Tennessee Knobs.

Rivermen still are prone to cast some doubt on the degree of Mark Twain's excellence as pilot. But there is no doubt about Harris's competence. He was master of the *Knoxville* at the age of twenty-three (or, some claim, at nineteen) and on at least one recorded occasion—in March, 1837 —took her from Knoxville to Decatur. A young man who could do that, in those days, was precocious in river knowledge. Possibly Harris's interest in the river took focus when the *Atlas* appeared at Knoxville in 1828. He was then fourteen years old, and soon after the event, constructed a model steamboat and let it be known that he would cause it to navigate the Flag Pond, in the center of Knoxville, at a certain date. The population turned out for the spectacle, and they were not disappointed. Harris's model steamboat paddled across the pond. Young Harris learned about machinery in the shop of his half brother, Sam Bell, a jeweler and metalworker who brought him from Allegheny City, Pennsylvania, to Knoxville, when Harris was a little fellow. But he could not have learned the river as an apprentice in a metal-worker's shop. It is altogether probable that, like other river-men, Harris served on flatboats and keelboats before he went on board the *Knoxville*.

The *Guide*, under Captain Chapman, was far more suc-cessful as a packet than the *Knoxville*. She was owned by James King & Company, merchants, of Knoxville, and ap-pears in their daybook entries as making ten trips from Knoxville to Decatur betwen April, 1836, and June, 1837. At times of low water she plied between the Suck and De-catur and used her keelboats to connect with Knoxville. The *Harkaway*, under Captain George Nicholson, was acclaimed in 1839 as "the leading boat in the Tennessee trade since she came above the Shoals." She was the first boat on the Upper Tennessee to substitute a steam whistle for the earlier cannon signal. "For speed, comfort, and safety," said a Knoxville paper, "she is surpassed by no boat of her class." But the *Harkaway* had to use keels, too—"FIVE KEELS of her own, manned by as good watermen as can be found in any coun-try." And like the *Guide* she spent much of her time plying between the Suck and Decatur. It is suggestive of the uncer-tainties of steamboat transportation in those times that the owners of the *Harkaway* described her as a "substantial, light-draught towboat" and promised the public that, although she was making regular trips between the Suck and Decatur, she would "take advantage of every rise in the water to come higher"; furthermore, with the help of the five keels, they were ready to guarantee delivery of goods and passengers any-where between Knoxville and Dacatur "without delay." "It is not our intention," they added, "where it can possibly be avoided, to have goods stored in warehouses on the river; but in every instance where the keels can be made to meet the boat, to have the freights shifted and 'pushed ahead' without detention."

The *Holston* was the first boat to attempt regular crossing of Muscle Shoals, but she had little success, and was finally renamed the *Kingston* and sold to a wealthy Cherokee, Joseph Vann. During the Cherokee Removal, Vann used the *Kingston* to transport his family and the family of John Ross to the west.

The first Muscle Shoals canal was built in the 1830's; but the sad tale of that canal and of other early attempts at river improvement makes a separate story. The gist of the first two decades of steamboat transportation on the Tennessee is simply this: below Muscle Shoals, from Florence to Paducah, steamboats flourished; above Muscle Shoals, from Decatur to Knoxville, steamboating was a bravely hopeful but risky endeavor; and in the hard middle stretch of the Muscle Shoals region (Decatur to Florence) was nothing but disappointment and doom where steamboats were concerned.

Florence and Tuscumbia, exulting in their favorable position, welcomed to their landings the fine Mississippi and Ohio packets and cotton boats. Of these the *Ben Sherrod* was in her day one of the best boats serving the Lower Tennessee. Much Tennessee freight went down with her when she was lost on the Mississippi near Natchez in one of the most ghastly steamboat disasters of the time. The *Ben Sherrod* was racing the *Prairie* upstream, and, as she was losing, the stokers added resin to get a hotter fire under the boilers. Cordwood stacked on the deck caught fire; the pilot burned to death at his wheel while trying to beach the *Sherrod;* and the boat was blown apart by explosions from the boilers and from the gunpowder and the barrels of whisky in her cargo. Two hundred persons were killed outright or drowned. But such accidents, it seems, did not happen on the Tennessee. And no disaster of this kind is recorded against other fine boats that called, regularly or intermittently, in the 1830's: the *Andrew Jackson, Asia, Brighton, Casket, Dover, Gladiator, Hero,*

*Mississippi, Mohawk, Mohican, Pennsylvanian, Walk-in-the-Water, Wheeling.*

The *Asia* (M. W. Irwin) was owned by William H. Reese & Company of Tuscumbia and Rhea & Ross of Decatur. She was announced in 1838 as a "new and substantial upper cabin steamboat of 350 tons burthen . . . with superior accommodation for passengers." But that all was not perfect, even below Muscle Shoals, was evident from the frequent promises made in steamboat advertisements "to prevent the delay at Waterloo, which had heretofore been the cause of so much complaint." In 1838, T. Limrick & Co., of Tuscumbia, supplemented their advertisement of the *Mohican* and other boats with the following hopeful plea: "We have in a state of forwardness, a splendid TOW BOAT, now on the stocks at Tuscumbia Landing, which will be ready in time for the transhipment of the cargoes of the large boats, which will enable us to give the utmost dispatch to goods reshipped at Waterloo. . . . We are aware of the numerous complaints in consequence of the delay of goods between this and Waterloo; but we have this consolation, that of having to compete with two opposition lines of keel boats during this much vexed delay."

The "splendid TOW BOAT" was probably the *Miner*, a smaller vessel that ran on a shuttle service between Tuscumbia and Waterloo. She towed eight or ten keels regularly. The *Warren*, which drew only twenty inches and carried ninety-five tons, later went into shuttle service.

Colbert Shoals was the chief cause of the embarrassing delay at Waterloo. At low water, big steamboats could not get over it. Nothing could be done about Colbert Shoals except to put keelboats and light-draft steamboats into the shuttle service between Waterloo and the foot of Muscle Shoals. The enterprising citizens of Tuscumbia, however, could do a little something toward circumventing Muscle

Shoals, and thus improving their connections with the Upper Tennessee.

They built a railroad. It was a "dinky" railroad, by modern standards, but it was a railroad—the first one west of the Appalachians. In 1832, they ran a line over the short distance between Tuscumbia and the river. In 1834, they carried it east to Decatur, a distance of forty miles. This, the Tuscumbia, Courtland, and Decatur Railroad, was a very primitive affair, built of "string pieces of wood scantlings on which flat bars of iron, a half an inch by two and a half inches, were laid." But it served a great need, since it provided an easy portage around Muscle Shoals, and it predicted more railroads and better railroads to come.

None of these great annoyances dimmed the spirits of lusty North Alabama, or East Tennessee, or aspiring West Tennessee and West Kentucky, which were beginning to be heard from. But the transportation arrangements of the Tennessee River in these years of unimprovement were a chain of makeshifts, an odd combination of all that was most primitive and all that was most advanced.

This is the way the traffic arrangements worked: If you started, say, from St. Louis or Cairo, intending to reach Knoxville by way of the Tennessee River, you might board a Mississippi steamboat and go upriver as far as Waterloo without undue delay. If there was high water, and if that steamboat had a clever captain and a good pilot, you *might* go all the way to Tuscumbia Landing or Florence without having to transfer. But if the Tennessee was at low stage, or was falling, the Mississippi boat stopped at Waterloo (or in later years at Eastport), and passengers and freight were transshipped to keelboats or to a light-draft steamboat, probably accompanied by keels, which took you to the foot of Muscle Shoals. Then, if you proceeded by river, you took a keelboat—of one of the keelboat "lines" operating in this region—and ascended Muscle Shoals to reach Decatur. If you went overland, you could go by stagecoach or by the Tuscumbia, Courtland, and Decatur Railroad to the same transfer point. At Decatur you waited, probably, for the packet to arrive from Knoxville or the Suck. You might wait a long while if river conditions were not favorable. If you were impatient, and gave up hope of seeing the Knoxville packet, you could go by stagecoach to Nashville, and thence overland to your destination.

When the Upper Tennessee packet at last arrived, it might take you as far as Knoxville, and it might not. If the river was low above Ross's Landing, you might have to transfer (at Suck Creek or Ross's Landing) to a keelboat for further passage. Or the Upper Tennessee packet might carry you upriver as far, say, as Kingston, where you could either transfer to a keelboat or take the stagecoach for Knoxville.

Coming downriver, you would go through a similar series of transfers and waits, although the waits, for downriver traffic, might not be quite as long as for the upriver journey. The Mississippi steamboats that called at Florence and Tuscumbia advertised handsomely in the Knoxville newspapers, and, if you started in good time, you could be fairly sure of making downstream connections. But much depended on the season. The Knoxville-Decatur packets kept their schedule fairly well for six months out of the year; the other six months were uncertain.

Probably it was not so fatiguing as it might seem to a modern. Nobody was in a great hurry, after all. The steamboat was worth waiting for. A cabin passage from Knoxville to Muscle Shoals, on the Steamboat *Knoxville*, cost $7; upstream, the same distance, $13. In later years, on the *Huntsman*, it was $10. But for that you got much more than transportation. You got excellent company, fine food, good entertainment, and a leisurely view of an extraordinary river, coursing unpredictably through a wild and beautiful mountain country. Yet, if you were a real American, you would be sure to wonder whether somebody could not do something about that river—something to make the river more manageable and the journey less intermittent.

That thought, exactly, was what many enterprising people in East Tennessee and North Alabama carried in their heads, day and night.

# CHAPTER XVII

# The Indians Go West

URING the eighteen-thirties flatboat, keelboat, and steamboat played a part in one of the great tragic occasions of American history. In these years the primeval inhabitants of the Tennessee Valley looked their last upon the forests and mountains to which their forefathers had wandered, untold centuries before. Chickasaw, Creek, and Cherokee journeyed beyond the Mississippi into the drier, less-wooded country of Arkansas and Oklahoma. In that country, new to them, strange tribes made room for them reluctantly, and they found themselves once more facing the walls of frontier forts, but as suppliants, not as attackers. They were moving back, a thousand miles or more, toward the fabulous "navel of the world" and "backbone of the earth" from which the dim, old traditions said their ancestors had come. But now there was no supernatural red stick to guide them, by leaning always in the direction the gods meant for them to take; no magical arrow to mark the camps and marches. The old gods were silent. The Christian God whom many of them had accepted offered them only the Christian virtues of forbearance and forgiveness with which to meet the violence and rapine vented upon them by the white men, also professing Christians, with whom their chiefs, sometimes acting in good faith, sometimes corrupted and bribed, had made vain treaty after vain treaty.

It was a forced migration. It was a removal. For the oracle of the gods, handed down through some revered chief, they were given a government order. For guides, they had superintendents, transportation contractors, and young lieutenants of the United States Army. For medicine men, they had civil doctors, who supplied pills, purges, blisters, and bleedings to mitigate the diseases that scourged them during the drouthy summers and relentless winters of their sorrowful journey. Robbed of property, cheated, made drunken, they were jammed into temporary cabins, then herded into flatboats, keelboats, and steamers, or else were marched across country in enormous ragged bands, with wagons carrying whatever meager goods had not been torn from them before departure. And as they went from dismal camp to dismal camp, they buried their dead and cursed the white man.

In all the history of the relations between white man and Indian, no episode is sadder or more inglorious than the removal of the southestern tribes. It is one of the scandals of American history. Nobody comes out of it with any credit, except the reluctant Indians, their few missionary friends, and an occasional individual like John Howard Payne, author of "Home, Sweet Home," who came to the Cherokee nation to write their story, only to be arrested and jailed by the Georgia militia and to see his manuscript confiscated and destroyed.

A doubtful mark, possibly a black mark, must go against the name of the Old Hero, Andrew Jackson. Although the final removal was carried out by troops sent by Martin Van Buren, his successor in the White House, it was through Jackson's imperious will that old treaties and assurances were flouted and the plan of forcible removal was initiated. It was Andrew Jackson who declined to intervene between the Indians and the governments of Georgia and Alabama, and who, by thus refusing, egged on the rapaciousness of speculators and thieves, until an intolerable situation arose that made voluntary emigration impossible and military action inevitable. Although James Mooney, in his history of the Cherokees, calls Jackson an "Indian-hater," it was probably not that simple. The situation had become too complex for any workable solution to be reached in the terms familiar to Jackson's age and Jackson's mind. After the long series of land cessions, the lands remaining to the Cherokees, Creeks, and Chickasaws still lay within the boundaries drawn for four states—Georgia, Tennessee, Alabama, and Mississippi. The white men could no longer argue that these lands were merely a "hunting ground." The Indians were established residents, firmly settled on acres belonging to them by inherited and undebatable right. But the clamorous citizens of the four states—and of Georgia especially—wanted those lands too, persisted in moving into them, and would not be denied. Furthermore, the network of railroads was already pushing inland and would inevitably demand passage; and besides railroads, there were highways to be built, and possibly canals.

To Jackson's blunt mind there was no solution except complete removal to lands provided by the federal government, west of the Mississippi. This he did, hurling back all protest. Let the Indians go west voluntarily if they would. If they would not, then remove them by force. To their pleadings, legal and oratorical, his answer was: theirs was a case of remedy, but not of right. But in the last analysis Jackson did not take much account even of remedy. He who had turned on Calhoun and the Nullifiers with stern rebukes and threats was supine and complacent when Georgia flouted the federal Union and the Supreme Court in the Cherokee case.

The Indians had known Jackson as a warrior. They respected Jackson the fighting man, and his name carried great weight when treaties were to be made. They trusted him, and then found themselves, according to their notions, basely betrayed. The Cherokees were exceedingly bitter, for their warriors had been Jackson's allies in the Creek Wars. At Emuckfau the Cherokees saved him from rout and disaster. At Horseshoe Bend they cut off the Creek retreat and made it possible for Jackson's men to destroy the last remains of Creek war power. One Cherokee warrior who took part in that battle—the chief Tsunu-lahunski (Junaluska)—spoke the sentiment of the nation: "If I had known that Jackson would drive us from our homes, I would have killed him that day at the Horseshoe."

After a long debate in Congress, an Indian Removal Bill was enacted in 1830 which, on the face of it, did not seem too severe since it made provision for an orderly exchange of eastern lands held by the Indians for other lands in the West. But when the treaty-making began, the same unfortunate sequence of events took place in each of the five tribes of the Southeast. First a treaty was made, or some agreement was signed, with chiefs who represented a faction of the tribe rather than the tribe as a whole. Returning home with the agreement, these chiefs found a storm of resentment brewing. Their fellow tribesmen were not willing to give up their lands. Often the treatymakers found themselves objects of intense scorn, and some of them, like Major Ridge and Elias Boudinot of the Cherokees, were sooner or later killed, or in Indian view, "executed," by members of their nation. Meanwhile, as soon as it was known that a removal was to take place, white settlers began to enter Indian lands and even to take possesion of Indian dwelling houses. Disorder and retaliation then began. The Indians fled to the woods and became guerrillas, held meetings and memorialized Congress and the legislatures, hoped against hope, and resisted by every means short of full-scale war. At the same time, the States aided confusion by sending in their militia or peace officers and by passing laws of pre-emption and seizure.

Only the Chickasaw removal was carried out in a reasonably orderly fashion. They were a small tribe, and the powerful influence of the Colberts kept them in hand, though it could not protect them against the encroachments of squatters. The attempt at Seminole removal was a failure; only a fragment of the tribe went west; and the United States fought a long, inconclusive war with the stubborn majority, deep in the swamps of Florida. The Choctaw removal followed the general pattern, except that there was no fighting.

In the Creek country, serious disorders occurred. Under the treaty of 1832, provision was made for the orderly purchase of the lands of those who would voluntarily remove according to the government's plan. Protection was promised. Unlawful intruders upon Creek lands were to be expelled. An appropriation of $100,000 was promised to liquidate tribal debts. But the solemn words were empty of meaning. Not only did the government fail to fulfill the treaty specifications, but in cynical negligence it permitted the very outrages that the treaty was designed to avoid. Swarms of white intruders multiplied into hordes, land frauds and dispossessions expanded shamelessly, pillaging and intimidation spread like an epidemic. Since most of the Indians did not know the value of their lands, or the legal process of buying and selling, or even the English language, it was easy for swindlers to cheat them, and to use some Indians as tools for cheating others. One scheme (as it was reported to Congress) was "to drill or coach an Indian who had sold his land or never owned any, to represent another who was the holder of a reservation; he learned his name and that of his tribe and town where he lived, the situation of his dwelling, and of the town-square and council-house, and such other circumstances as the agent would be likely to inquire into, with the view of identifying the reservee; and thus prepared, he was presented before the agent, and answering readily the usual questions, the officer was deceived, the contract certified, and

the proprietor of the land defrauded. The wages of this combined iniquity were generally $5 or $10."

Thus despoiled, hundreds of Creeks became belligerent.
Some fled into the Cherokee country of Alabama and Georgia.
There they came into collision with the Georgia militia, and
presently rumors of a new Creek war began to rise. Armed
bands of white men gathered for action. Finally troops, under General Winfield Scott, recalled from the fruitless Seminole campaign, took the field against the Creek chiefs and
their followers. Chief Eneah Emathla and one thousand of
his people were captured. The chiefs and warroirs were mana-
cled, and were marched off, with their women and children,
under military guard.

Other Creeks who had fled into North Alabama were
hunted out by soldiers. More than five hundred of these were
assembled, in a half-starved and destitute condition, at Gunter's Landing. Here they were crowded into nine flatboats and
taken to Waterloo, where they were transferred to the steamboat *Black Hawk* and its attendant keelboats and flatboats,
for the long voyage down the Tennessee, the Ohio, and the
Mississippi. Another group, removing voluntarily under the
auspices of an "emigrating company," marched from We-
tumpka to Tuscumbia. There they sent their ponies to be
driven overland to Memphis, and embarked on a small steamboat and two keelboats for Waterloo, where they were transferred to the steamboat *Alpha* and two large keelboats for
the voyage to Fort Gibson. The hardships of these relatively
small groups who went by river were much less severe than
the sufferings of the main body of the Creek nation, fourteen thousand or more, who trekked westward through
swamps and forests to the Mississippi, and then across Arkansas to their destination.

The fate of the Cherokees was the most tragic of all,
because it fell upon the one of the Five Civilized Tribes
which had gone farthest upon the White Path. At the time

of the removal, the Cherokees numbered between fifteen and sixteen thousand people. Since the time of Colonel Return Jonathan Meigs, the Revolutionary soldier from Connecticut who became Cherokee agent in 1801, they had had unusually good leadership. The agents, missionaries, and other white men who came to live with them had counseled well. The Brainerd Mission, near Chattanooga, had long been a center of education and advice. The Reverend S. A. Worcester of that mission, a Vermonter who became a Cherokee scholar and translator, was their steadfast friend in all their trials. Other missions, directed by Moravians, Baptists, and other sects, had greatly influenced them, and they had become in large measure a Christian people. Their native leaders were men of education and substance. John Ross, their principal chief from 1828 until his death in 1866, was one-eighth Cherokee and seven-eighths Scot. He was as much a Scotsman as his great opponent, Andrew Jackson, and fought as tenaciously. In 1820, under Ross's leadership, the Cherokees adopted for their nation a republican form of government, modeled upon the government of the United States. George Guess (or Gist), better known as Sequoyah, although he could not read English, had devised the Cherokee syllabary, or "alphabet." Once a Cherokee, whether adult or child, had learned the eighty-five characters of Sequoyah's syllabary, he could read anything written in Cherokee. A newspaper, the *Cherokee Phoenix* was established with educated Elias Boudinot as editor. The syllabary was used even by the nonprogressive elements of the tribe, the priests and conjurers, for recording ancient rituals and tribal secrets.

Above all, the Cherokees had changed their economy. They had long since ceased to be men of the Stone Age. They were agriculturists, who grew staple crops and raised cattle and hogs like their white neighbors. They were beginning to acquire mercantile establishments and manufactures. Quite conclusively, the were becoming American citizens in

all but constitutional right. In their inclinations and affiliations, too, as the Civil War would later prove, they were as "southern" as the Georgians and Alabamians.

In retrospect, there seems to have been little valid reason why the Cherokees could not have aspired to citizenship and advanced their "nation" to statehood. The difference of race was no mark of inferiority in their case, and carried no stigma. They had faced the white man as warriors, and few remembered the distant times when captive Cherokees might have been sold into slavery at Charleston or some Spanish fort. In this respect, their situation was in great contrast to the status of the Negro slave. There is queer irony in the historical fact that the federal government, which during the eighteen-thirties denied citizenship to the Cherokees, who deserved it and wanted it, would within a quarter of a century confer it as an unsolicited gift upon four million ignorant Negro slaves, who had not asked for citizenship and did not know what it was.

But Cherokee deserts were not recognized. Georgia, the most urgent of the states in its demands for Indian removal, rested its case principally upon a clause in the agreement of 1802, between the federal government and the state, in which Georgia ceded its western lands (the present Alabama and Mississippi) in consideration of the federal government's promise to extinguish Indian titles "as early as the same can be peaceably obtained on reasonable terms." The several treaties of cession following this agreement had whittled Cherokee lands to a small fraction of their original claims. The most sizable portion of this remainder covered the northwestern corner of what is now Georgia. The northwestern boundary was the Tennessee River, between Gunter's Landing and the Hiwassee. It extended as far south as Marietta, and it included some land in East Tennessee and North Carolina. It was nearly all mountain land, a forested and broken upland, with all its fertility concentrated in the narrow bottoms, and therefore not suitable for cotton growing. Today, particularly in North Georgia, the old Cherokee land is among the worst eroded and depleted parts of the South.

Nevertheless Georgia, standing on the treaty of 1802, led the other states in pressing for complete extinguishment of Indian titles.

In December, 1828, immediately after the election of Andrew Jackson, the Georgia legislature passed an act annexing the Cherokee lands within the state borders and declaring all tribal laws and customs null and void. The Cherokees were declared subject to state laws, but they were denied entrance to the courts. It was provided "that no Indian or descendant of an Indian residing within the Creek or Cherokee nations of Indians, shall be deemed a competent witness in any court of this state to which a white man shall be a party." The effect of this clause was to put the Cherokees at the mercy of the pillagers and land thieves.

To make matters worse, gold was discovered near the present Dahlonega in 1828, and a typical gold rush soon swelled the procession of exploiters. When Georgia surveyed the Cherokee lands, "land lots" of 160 acres and "gold lots" of 40 acres were offered to the citizens of Georgia under a public lottery scheme, under which every white citizen of the state received a ticket. Although Cherokee heads of families were supposed to be allowed reservations of 160 acres under the same law, no provision was made to safeguard their rights. Since Indians were held incompetent as witnesses in all cases involving white persons, the Cherokees were left helpless. By further enactment, the Cherokees were forbidden to defend their rights in court or to resist the seizure of their lands and dwelling houses, upon penalty of imprisonment. Still another law, directed at the missionary friends of the Cherokees, required all white residents of the Cherokee nation to take an oath of allegiance to the state of Georgia.

During the turbulent scenes that followed, the Cherokees stood their ground, always hoping that the threat of forcible removal might prove to be only a threat. The Georgia laws, of course, were calculated to bring about conditions so intolerable that they would consent to voluntary removal rather than continue the unequal struggle. But they chose to continue.

Turning for relief to the Supreme Court of the United States, they brought a suit of injunction against Georgia. The Supreme Court dismissed the suit on the ground, in an opinion given by Chief Justice Marshall, that the court did not have jurisdiction, because the Cherokee nation, although it was a tribe, was not a "foreign state" within the meaning of the Constitution. Justice Story and one other justice dissented from this opinion. Marshall, in his opinion, went so far as to say "that if courts were permitted to indulge their sympathies, a case better calculated to excite them could hardly be imagined." These and other expressions of the court led Cherokee leaders to hope that some way of obtaining legal relief might yet be found.

They were still further encouraged by the famous case of *Worcester* v. *Georgia,* which originated in Georgia and went speedily up to the Supreme Court. S. A. Worcester, with other missionaries, refused to take the required oath of allegiance to Georgia. He was arrested by Georgia officers, tried, and sentenced to four years of penal labor. When the case was appealed, the Supreme Court held, again in an opinion by Marshall, "that the acts of the state were unconstitutional and violated the rights of the petitioners and of the Cherokee Indians under the solemn treaty made with them by the United States." The conviction was reversed, and Georgia was ordered to release the imprisoned missionaries. Governor Gilmer of Georgia ignored the decision, but Worcester and Elizur Butler (the only other missionary who had held out with him) were finally released by Gilmer's successor, William Lumpkin. This is the case concerning which Andrew

Jackson is said to have made his famous remark: "John Marshall has made his decision; now let him enforce it."

Misled into optimism by the action of the court, the Cherokees held a national jubilee, and reinforced their opposition to the removal. A group of over six hundred Cherokees had been gathered on the Hiwassee River for a "voluntary removal" to be conducted by Agent Currey. When the Supreme Court decision was announced, enrollments ceased, and agitators came among the band who had already agreed to move west, with such subversive effects that the distracted agent had to post a ring of sentinels around the Hiwassee camp.

And now, although the Cherokees were more nearly united than they had ever been in primitive times, they showed their old capacity for internal schism. The national party, under John Ross, continued to oppose removal, but a party of conciliation at last came forward, under Major John Ridge, and the two groups competed for attention at Washington. Ridge's group made a treaty at Washington which looked toward removal. It provided, however, that it should not be made effective unless ratified by the Cherokee nation in full council. When presented to the council, it was rejected; and to the surprise of Commissioner Schermerhorn, even Ridge and some of his friends voted against it.

A little later, in December, 1835, Commissioner Schermerhorn managed to assemble a Rump Parliament of a few hundred Cherokees (counting men, women, and children) at New Echota, and pushed through a quasi treaty of removal. This treaty was signed by twenty Cherokees, among them Major Ridge and Elias Boudinot, but not by John Ross or any of his party. When this treaty was brought before the United States Senate, delegates of the national party, representing some sixteen thousand Cherokees, protested strongly. It was ratified, but by a majority of only one vote.

General John Ellis Wool, who was in command of the

United States troops that had been posted in the Cherokee country, transmitted to Washington resolutions of protest voted by the Cherokee councils. For his pains, General Wool was sternly rebuked by the president, and he was informed that the treaty would be carried out to the letter. A little later, in February, 1837, General Wool spoke frankly to the government about the situation. "It is," he said, " . . . vain to talk to a people almost universally opposed to the treaty and who maintain that they never made such a treaty. So determined are they in opposition that not one of all those who were present and voted at the council held but a day or two since, however poor and destitute, would receive either rations or clothing from the United States lest they compromise themselves in regard to the treaty. . . . Many have said they will die before they will leave the country."

Even Major Ridge, who, as one of the more conciliatory party, had signed the treaty of New Echota, protested against the conditions attending enforcement of the treaty.

"They have got our lands," Ridge wrote to the president, "and now they are preparing to fleece us of the money accruing from the treaty. We found our plantations taken either in whole or in part by the Georgians—suits instituted against us for back rents for our own farms. These suits are commenced in the inferior courts, with the evident design that, when we are ready to move, to arrest our people, and on these vile claims to induce us to compromise for our own release, to travel with our families. Thus our funds will be filched from our people, and we shall be compelled to leave our country as beggars and in want.

"Even the Georgia laws, which deny us our oaths, are flung aside, and notwithstanding the cries of our people, and protestation of our innocence and peace, the lowest classes of the white people are flogging the Cherokees with cowhides, hickories, and clubs. We are not safe in our houses—our people are assailed by day and night by the rabble. Even justices of the peace and constables are concerned in this business. This barbarous treatment is not confined to men, but the women are stripped also and whipped without law or mercy."

Not even the highest chiefs, in fact, escaped molestation. John Ross's Georgia estate was seized by Georgia authorities under the lottery law, and the holder of the ticket for Ross's lands took possession of his farm, his house, and his ferry at the head of Coosa River. Mrs. Ross, who was in bad health, was allowed to remain in a room on the ground floor, but Ross had to seek refuge in Tennessee. Joseph Vann, who had a fine plantation of eight hundred acres and a brick house worth $10,000, was even more grossly mistreated. His property was seized by the Georgia militia, on a trumped-up charge. But there were rival claimants to his property. A man named Spencer Riley took possession of the upper part of the house, armed to defend his claim. When W. N. Bishop, commander of the Georgia guard, entered the lower part, the two groups of white men staged a battle in the house while Vann and his family sought to escape the flying bullets. Riley, though wounded, would not give up. Thereupon Bishop set fire to the house, smoked him out, and obtained possession. Vann and his family fled through the snow to seek refuge in a log cabin across the Tennessee line.

To the last, the Cherokees kept hoping that the removal might be prevented. All but a few clung to their homes, despite the abuse visited upon them, or, when ousted, fled to isolated cabins or to the open woods. A minority yielded to the persuasions of removal agents, and at various times assembled at the encampments to receive them, on the Hiwassee River and elsewhere. While crowded into these temporary shelters, they were cheated and debauched by the trading boats, or "floating doggeries," that came down the Tennessee, the Holston, and the Clinch. Lieutenant Joseph H. Harris, a young West Pointer, who was in charge of one of the parties gathered at the Hiwassee camp, wrote that the doggeries, "with their loads of cakes and pies and fruit and cider and apple jack and whiskey *shark* it here for the annuity arrearages of the poor Indians, or the hard-earned and illicit gains of the worthless white men; and become the nurseries and receptacles of idleness, drunkenness, and vice." An epidemic of measles broke out in this group, and an epidemic of cholera was threatened in the regions through which they must pass.

Harris's group embarked on the flatboats *John Cox, Sliger,* and *Blue Buck,* passed through the Suck and over Muscle Shoals, and arrived at Waterloo in March, 1834, only again to meet the corruptions of doggeries and brothels. With increments received from Gunter's Landing, the party numbered 457. At Waterloo they were transferred to the steamboat *Thomas Yeatman,* which carried three keelboats in tow. By the time they arrived at their western destination, eighty-one Cherokees had died, mostly from cholera. By the end of the year, more than half of these emigrants were dead. Many of the dead were young children.

Another group of voluntary emigrants, numbering several hundred, assembled at Ross's Landing and embarked on flatboats for Gunter's Landing. Here the steamboat *Knoxville* took the flatboats in tow. At Decatur they disembarked and were carried in open cars, over the Tuscumbia, Courtland, and Decatur Railroad, to an ill-provided camp at Tuscumbia, suffering greatly all the while from cold and exposure. At Tuscumbia, after a long wait, the *Newark* and her attendant keels finally took them on board, already greatly weakened by cold weather and disease. Dr. C. Lillybridge, the physician who accompanied this party, found them suffering from colds, wounds, influenza, diarrhea, fevers, toothache, gonorrhea. Extracts from Dr. Lillybridge's diary tell a great deal about the troubles both of the Indians and of the doctor:

Henry Clay better than last night, got him a comfortable situation near the chimney of the Steamboat and a breakfast of

Coffee and Sea Bread, which appeared to afford him much satisfaction considering his case, consumption. Daughter of Young Squirrel sick with headache and fever; gave cathartis. . . . Applied Blister to the chest of Henry Clay. Stand Watie has been in quite a feeble state of health since I first saw him at New Echota. . . . His cough very troublesome. . . . James Williams taken very suddenly with inflammation of the Spleen. Bled him and applied Blister. . . .

Sally Raincrow has been slightly indisposed for some days. She is a doctress and a Conjuress herself. She refuses the aid of the *Doctor*, except when her case becomes alarming. She has acquired the art of Cupping with the Horn of a Yearling, which exhausts the air by sucking. She has a servant also whom she has taught the practice. Sally has great faith in Cupping and within the last three days has had the operation performed on almost every part of her body. The poor negress is kept almost constantly tugging away with her fat lips. The practice being so free from objection I have humored her caprice. . . . Found Henry Clay about 4 o'clock P.M. laboring under much inflammation of the chest and difficulty of respiration. Ordered him to the Steam Boat, where he could be near the fire. Got Sally Rain Crow's woman to cup him; directed her to cup him as many times as she could place the Horn on his breast.

Such more or less voluntary removals as these did not much diminish the Cherokee nation, and therefore, in 1838, the forcible removal finally began. Protests continued to arise in the North, the missionaries kept on pleading, and even in the South itself, where the better element became aroused at the disgusting spectacle, there was a stir of complaint. Nothing did any good. Even General Wool's efforts to protect the Indians against swarming intruders brought down more wrath upon his head. He was usurping the powers of civil government, state officials declared, and "trampling on the rights of citizens."

General Wool's softheartedness finally brought about his relief from command, and General Winfield Scott was sent to take charge of the swelling contingents of United States troops and militia who were to carry out the removal. Apparently considerable sentiment in support of the Cherokees' cause finally arose in Tennessee. Some of the East Tennessee counties made formal protests against the cruelties that were being enacted. General Dunlap, who commanded some Tennessee militia sent to forestall a supposed threat of a new Cherokee war, withdrew his soldiers and declared "that he would never dishonor the Tennessee arms by aiding to carry into execution at the point of the bayonet a treaty made by a lean minority against the will and authority of the Cherokee people."

Perhaps this turn of sentiment was communicated along the river itself. At any rate, there is a story of how sharply the author of *Sut Lovingood's Yarns* dealt with General Winfield Scott himself. Harris was captain of the *Knoxville* once more, it seems (though she had been renamed *Indian Chief*), and was taking on some contingents of Cherokees for the downriver trip. For some unknown reason General Scott countermanded Harris's orders. Harris, who was small of stature, walked up to General Scott, who was six feet four, and looked him in the eye.

"Did you countermand my orders?" asked Harris.

"Yes," replied the general.

"General," said the determined young Tennessean, "I am captain of this boat; my orders are going to be obeyed, and if you, in any way, attempt to interfere, my next order will be to place you ashore."

No more of Harris's orders were countermanded.

John Ross made one last effort for his people. Two months before the time set for removal, he presented to Congress a memorial of protest signed by more than fifteen thousand Cherokees. But the Senate only laid the memorial on the table. President Van Buren knuckled under to Georgia and ordered the removal to proceed.

From his headquarters at New Echota, General Winfield Scott issued a proclamation which said, in part:

My troops already occupy many positions . . . and thousands and thousands are approaching from every quarter to render resistance and escape alike hopeless. . . . Will you, then, by resistance compel us to resort to arms . . . or will you by flight seek to hide yourself in mountains and forests and thus oblige us to hunt you down?

Many had to be "hunted down," but the majority came peaceably, if reluctantly. Some fled into the deep forests of the highest mountains and could not be "hunted down."

Stockades were built near Calhoun, Tennessee, on the Hiwassee, and at Ross's Landing and Gunter's Landing on the Tennessee. To these stockades, during the spring and early summer of 1838, most of the fifteen thousand Cherokees were marched under military guard and there detained until river transport could be provided or arrangements made for a westward march overland. The eleoquent words of James Mooney best describe this vast man hunt:

The history of the Cherokee removal of 1838, as gleaned by the author from the lips of actors in the tragedy, may well exceed in grief and pathos any other passage in American history. Even the much-sung exile of the Acadians falls far behind it in its sum of death and misery. Under Scott's orders the troops were disposed at various points in the Cherokee country, where stockade forts were erected . . . From these, squads of troops were sent to search out with rifle and bayonet every small cabin hidden away in the coves or by mountain streams, to seize and bring in as prisoners all the occupants, however or wherever they might be found. Families at dinner were startled by the sudden gleam of bayonets in the doorway and rose up to be driven with blows and oaths along the weary miles of trail that led to the stockade. Men were seized in their fields or going along the road, women were taken from their wheels and children from their play. In many cases, on turning for one last look as they crossed the ridge, they saw their homes in flames, fired by the lawless rabble that followed on the heels of the soldiers to loot and pillage. So keen were these outlaws on the scent that in some instances they were driving off the cattle and other stock of the Indians almost before the soldiers had fairly started the owners in the other direction. Systematic hunts were made by the same men for Indian graves, to rob them of the silver pendants and other valuables deposited with the dead. A Georgia volunteer, afterward a colonel in the Confederate service, said: "I fought through the Civil War and have seen men shot to pieces and slaughtered by thousands, but the Cherokee removal was the cruelest work I ever knew."

To prevent escape the soldiers had been ordered to approach and surround each house, so far as possible, so as to come upon the occupants without warning. One old patriarch, when thus surprised, calmly called his children and grandchildren around him, and, kneeling down, bid them pray with him in their own language, while the astonished soldiers looked on in silence. Then rising he led the way into exile. A woman, on finding the house surrounded, went to the door and called up the chickens to be fed for the last time, after which, taking her infant on her back and her two other children by the hand, she followed her husband with the soldiers.

Not all the Cherokees were so resigned. The relatively small parties that went down the Tennessee were not always well guarded, and escapes were therefore frequent. At Ross's Landing, in June, 1838, a party of eight hundred were marched on board a steamboat and six flatboats. The Cherokees were so resentful and turbulent that Lieutenant Edward Deas, who was in command, did not try to check his muster roll until they were moving down the river. The steamboat captain lashed three flats on each side of his boat and proceeded, but when he came to the narrow entrance of the Suck he decided to break his tow and take the flatboats through in pairs. Even with this precaution, one flatboat ran aground and was damaged. At Decatur, the party took the train, but it was so overcrowded that the lieutenant had to leave behind a large part of his military escort. With the guard absent, the whisky sellers had their chance. At Tuscumbia, there was a drunken commotion, during which more than one hundred Cherokees escaped to the woods. The party was more or less reassembled at Waterloo, but when Lieutenant Deas at last checked his muster roll and counted his Indians, on arriving at Paducah, he had only 489 left. Another party of over a thousand were marched overland to Waterloo. The summer was hot and drouthy, and they suffered greatly. At Belle-fonte, they heard a rumor that General Scott had ordered removals to be suspended until cooler weather arrived. But the superintendent, General Nat Smith, ordered this particular party to go ahead, whereupon three hundred Cherokees "broke for the woods" and refused to load their baggage for the march. The Alabama militia had to be called in to help, but out of the thousand who started, only 722 reached their destination. Some died en route, but many others escaped. Still another group of seven hundred, however, which was drawn largely from the Ridge party, proceeded overland separately, and, receiving rather favorable treatment from the government, traveled in relative comfort.

The main body, firmly loyal to John Ross, held their last council on their native lands at Rattlesnake Springs, near Charleston, Tennessee, and voted that, upon arrival in the West, they would retain and continue the constitution and laws they had already devised. Then they marched by the long overland route, unescorted, under their own chiefs, with their own organization.

They moved northwest, after crossing the Tennessee at Tucker's Ferry, a little above the great island at the mouth of the Hiwassee, where Sam Houston once lived with Chief John Jolly. The march led across the Cumberland plateau and the Middle Basin of Tennessee to Nashville, then on across Kentucky to the Ohio River. The Cherokees moved in "regiments" of about one thousand. "It was like the march of an army," said an eyewitness, "regiment after regiment, the wagons in the center, the officers along the line, and the horsemen on the flanks and at the rear." The sick, the aged, the infirm had to go along, regardless of their condition. The venerable chief, White Path, was carried on the march, although he was at the point of death. White Path died during the march, near Hopkinsville, Kentucky, and was buried on the spot. It was the day of tollroads and tollgates, and so the white man levied tribute on the moving column. At one point on the Cumberland plateau, the charge was 73 cents a wagon, 12½ cents a horse. The head of the column, which left the Cherokee country in October, encountered good marching weather, but the parties in the rear, who did not get under way until November, met the fall rains. The roads, cut by hundreds of wheels and thousands of hoofs, became ravines of bottomless mud. The advancing winter found the greater part of the Cherokee nation still on the road, with their sufferings increasing. In bitter privation and hardship, they crossed the Mississippi at Cape Girardeau, the river filled with ice, hundreds of the sick and dying penned in wagons or stretched upon the ground. Thence they moved through Missouri toward the Indian Territory, hungry and ill fed because the parties who came first had killed off all the game.

About four thousand of the Cherokees never reached the western lands. In other words, nearly one fourth of the nation died along the way, or in the stockades before the march began, were killed by soldiers, or else escaped.

A thousand or more of those who escaped, most of them mountain Cherokees, and full-bloods, found a refuge in North Carolina, at the head of Oconaluftee River, among the great peaks on the eastern flank of the Great Smoky Mountains. Under the leadership of Utsala (the Lichen) they held out, defying capture. They were deep in the laurel and rhododendron, hidden in inaccessible ravines and coves. General Scott and his soldiers found it difficult to get at them. And yet he might have rounded them up, in the end, if it had not been for the sacrificial heroism of an old Cherokee named Tsali—known as "Charley" to the whites.

Tsali rebelled against the brutality of the soldiers who captured him and his family. Among other indignities, they prodded his wife with the bayonet to make her hurry. As they went along the path, Tsali called out a few words in Cherokee to his brother and two sons. They turned suddenly upon the soldiers, wrenched away the guns, killed one soldier, and put the rest to flight. Tsali with his family then escaped to the mountains.

General Scott could not capture Tsali, who was now charged with murder; neither could he very easily root out Utsala's band. He decided to use a stratagem which would save his face to some extent and yet enable him to punish Tsali for "murder."

There was a trader, William H. Thomas, who knew how to communicate with Utsala. Thomas had lived among the eastern Cherokees since childhood, and he was the adopted son of their peace chieftain, Yonaguska (Drowning Bear). Using Thomas as an emissary, Scott sent word to Utsala that, if Tsali, the "murderer," were surrendered for punishment, he would withdraw his troops and leave Utsala's band unmolested. But if Tsali were not delivered, he would summon his seven thousand troops and hunt down Utsala's band, to the last man.

After much debate, Utsala consented that Tsali be surrendered. Thomas took upon himself the task of communicating with Tsali. It was his plan to persuade Tsali to surrender himself and his sons voluntarily—to make them a sacrifice for his people. Then, says Mooney, "declining Scott's offer of an escort, he went alone to the cave, and getting between the Indians and their guns, as they were sitting around the fire, he walked up to Charley and announced his message. The old man listened in silence and then said simply, 'I will come in. I don't want to be shot down by my own people.' " The brother and the sons also consented to surrender.

Joining a group of Utsala's warriors, who came on behalf of the chief, the four Cherokees went to Scott's headquarters and surrendered. Scott ordered that Tsali, his brother, and the eldest son be shot; that the execution be carried out at the point where the "murder" had been committed; and that the Cherokee warriors of Utsala's band act as the firing squad. So, with Scott's soldiers at their backs, and Tsali and the others facing them, Utsala's warriors fired.

Scott kept his word. Utsala's band were not disturbed. William H. Thomas, who had helped to bring about Tsali's sacrifice, became the great leader and friend of the eastern band of the Cherokees. By persistent effort, Thomas obtained permission for them to remain in their mountain home and to receive a share of the annuities due the Cherokee nation. And there, on the Qualla Reservation, they dwell to this day.

And there are tales among the Cherokees of a different kind of intervention, by which other Cherokees found refuge from General Scott. Just before the removal, the story goes, people living in the Hiwassee Valley heard strange voices calling in the air. Hearkening, they understood these voices to be warning them and urging them to gather in their townhouses and fast in religious silence for seven days in order that they might be transported to the home of their old supernatural visitants, the Nunnehi, with whom they could dwell forever. One townhouse, where the people obeyed the voices and religiously fasted, was carried off bodily by the Nunnehi, and it can be seen today, changed into a great rock, on a certain mountaintop. But not all of it was carried away. When the waiting people felt the townhouse move in the grip of the Nunnehi, one woman cried out in fright. The Nunnehi, startled, dropped one corner of the building. It remains on its old site, an earthen mound. The Nunnehi transported the people of another town to a place underneath the waters of the Hiwassee, where they live on forever. It is a place where fishers' nets always hang, as if caught on rocks. But it is not rocks, it is the hands of the people of the lost Cherokee town that clutch the nets and remind the fishermen that they are still there in the deep underwater home of the immortals.

CHAPTER XVIII

# The First Attack on Muscle Shoals
# and the Suck

THERE WAS an old story that the Indians had a lead mine somewhere at the head of Muscle Shoals. A Courtland blacksmith, named Newton Smith, was fishing with a gig one night between Watkins Island and Periwinkle Bar. He threw his gig at a fish and missed. In the torchlight he saw that the gig had plowed a groove in a vein of pure lead. Afterward he looked for the place by daylight. He was never able to find it, but Newt Smith's fish-and-lead story went the rounds.

But it was time to stop talking about phantom lead mines and discover what Muscle Shoals and other great obstacles to navigation were like, in the practical sense, so that measures might be taken to overcome them. What was Muscle Shoals? Well, certainly not a lead mine! What was the Boiling Pot? A dangerous place, but not one that could be rendered safe for navigators as long as men sat around repeating old Indian tales about a fabulous gambler who waylaid travelers there.

So, at last, sixty-nine years after Lieutenant Timberlake first "took the courses" of the Tennessee, and made a map which was lost, the calculating eyes of a military man, an engineer, came to look at the troublesome and beautiful river creature that was at once the hope and despair of all who tried to master it. The Tennessee must be surveyed and mapped. The work began on the upper part in 1830.

Colonel Stephen H. Long, who made this first extended survey, was loaned to the state of Tennessee by the Topographical Bureau of the federal government. His party consisted of three army lieutenants and two civil engineers, and of course the necessary chain carriers and helpers. For pilots and guides, he had two good rivermen, Captain Pleasant Cresey and Captain George Wells. Dr. William E. Cocke and Mr. David A. Deaderick, of the Board of Internal Improvement for East Tennessee, also went along, at least were officially present.

Of the difficulties of his work, Colonel Long had little to say. That it was not without peril and hardship we can be certain. The river took toll. On the evening of June 6, 1830, when the party was nearing the end of its survey, Philip R. Van Wyck, one of the civil engineers, attempted to swim the Boiling Pot—whether as a feat of strength or in line of duty, the colonel does not say in his report. At any rate, Untsaiyi was not to be trifled with and drew in the bold swimmer. Van Wyck was caught in the whirl and drowned. They found his body a day later, a mile and a half below the Pot, buried him on the right bank of the river, and erected a cairn of stones over his lonely grave.

A "formidable pass" was Colonel Long's phrase for the Suck. The river as a whole, though, merited a different description. The Tennessee, in Colonel Long's technical account, was a series of long pools, slanting and winding down the slope of its mountain valleys, like some vast, crudely shaped stairway of giants. The pools themselves were navigable; but at the upper and lower extremities of every pool or basin there were invariably shoals that made navigation difficult. The shoals were caused by reefs of rocks, upon which sand and gravel accumulated, and they extended across the width of the river. At one point the narrow ridge of the reef might emerge from the water and form what rivermen called a "hogback." But always, too, there was some place where the water had cut a narrow channel through the rocks. At such a point boats could get through, if the river was not too low; and there, accordingly, channel improvements were practi-

cable. An entirely different kind of obstacle, however, might sometimes be in the way. Log drifts might accumulate in the deep water, just at the points where boats would seek to approach the reef; or there might be overhanging trees whose boughs swept close to the surface of the only available channel.

Colonel Long's simple and inexpensive improvements were aimed at removing such obstacles. The overhanging trees could be cut away. The log drifts could be removed. The openings in the reefs could be widened and deepened by blasting and digging, and boulders could be dragged out of the channel or demolished. For keeping the channels open at

critical points, Colonel Long planned wing dams. He drew
designs for simple, easily constructible wing dams which
could be made out of logs and stones obtainable on the spot.

But for stretches where the current was swift, and the
channel was narrowed by projecting rocky points, as at the
Suck, an entirely different kind of treatment was necessary.
At the Suck, he observed, the usable channel narrowed to a
mere 150 feet, and the rocks jutting into the bed of the river
partially dammed it up, and increased the force of the current from an average velocity of 7 miles an hour in this general area to 13 miles per hour. At high water, however, the
difficulty lessened to some extent, because the Boiling Pot
backed up the river into the Suck proper, and thus deepened
the channel and diminished the force of the current. The
Suck was therefore most difficult of navigation at low water,
but in the Boiling Pot the opposite condition prevailed: it
was easiest at low water, and exceedingly dangerous at high
water. How deep the Pot was, the colonel did not undertake
to say. Very deep—a "formidable pass." And below, at the
Skillet and the Pan, there were similar conditions: the same
protruding rocky points, the same effect of damming the
river partially and backing it up at high water. And also,
above the Suck, there was the Tumbling Shoals, an entirely
different kind of effect: a stretch of deep water, with a swift
current, and huge boulders strewn irregularly right where the
water was deepest.

Since Colonel Long could not remove mountains or
change the course of the Tennessee, he could do but little to
improve the river itself in the region of the Suck. Some boulders could be taken out. Some excavation and widening of
rock ledges could be achieved. Beyond this, there was nothing
to do but to make provision for helping steamboats through
the channel by means of warps. The fixtures for warping
were to be set on the left side of the channel at the Suck, the
Pot, and the Skillet, and on the right side at the Pan. Capstans

were to be set up, to which steamboats could attach their lines. They were so located as to be useful at both high water and low water. In some instances, however, Colonel Long proposed to set ring bolts into the rocks jutting close to the channel, or to rig booms projecting over the water; in other instances he wished to provide chains with ring bolts or hooks attached.

Colonel Long's survey extended from Kingsport to the Alabama line. Below that point, the problem was quite different.

Also, the problem lay in a different state of the Union, and therefore the topographical engineers who performed the early surveys were loaned, by the curious arrangements prevailing in the days of Andrew Jackson, to the state of Alabama. A survey of the Muscle Shoals region was made in 1828 by Captain William Tell Poussin, but some of the preliminary work was done by Ferdinand Sannoner, the city planner of Florence, who was in the employment of Alabama. A second survey was made in 1830 by Lieutenant Colonel James Kearney.

The great, the famous obstructions were really four groups of obstructions: Elk River Shoals, Big Muscle Shoals, Little Muscle Shoals, and Colbert Shoals. The first three, taken together, formed an almost continuous chain of difficulties, a steamboatman's hell of agony and danger, that impeded navigation for about 37 miles, from Brown's Ferry to Florence. Below Florence, it was not so bad, but Colbert Shoals, to say nothing of Bee Tree Shoals, could hardly be ignored.

For a boat going downriver, Elk River Shoals, with its wide shallows, was the beginning of the trouble. And then, if he got through, Muscle Shoals was just ahead—Big Muscle Shoals. Fifteen miles of tumbling water, flung about in irregular cascades. A fall of 85 feet in those 15 miles. A narrow, twisting channel, where there was a channel. The most unhealthy single stretch on all the great inland rivers.

The cause of the phenomenon, said the engineers, was the belt of flinty rocks that overlay or was mixed with the softer rocks and came squarely athwart the bed of the Tennessee. Elsewhere, the rock beds of the Tennessee were prevailingly limestone (though there was sandstone at the Suck). Limestone and other soft stones of the river would dissolve, rub off, in short, erode, from the action of running water. But the flinty rocks, the damnably hard flinty rocks, would not yield, did not dissolve, could not be carved and grooved into deep channels. In a valley where all else eroded with disconcerting ease at the touch of water, where the slightest wash might turn into a gully and then into a ravine, where even stone could be ditched and worn by water, these flinty rocks alone would not erode. And, as fate would have it, they were situated precisely where nobody wanted them, at mid-point in the course of the land's mightiest river. Anywhere else they would not have mattered. Where they were, they were of no earthly benefit, except to the mussels that loved these shallow waters, that clung to the rocky ledges and crowded the pools.

Because the Tennessee could not dig a channel through the flinty rocks, it had attacked its banks in ages past, spread out enormously, and become for many miles a shallow, westward-sloping basin, sown with numerous islands large and small, crowded with tumbling rapids and foaming cascades. Among the rapids and cascades was many a hidden reef, many a rock waiting with jagged tooth. There was no regularity, no rule of configuration. The softer stone, mingled with the hard flint, had worn away, and left grim, uncouth protrusions, an irregular wilderness, a chaos of rock and water.

The engineers found that the Muscle Shoals basin had a width varying from a half mile to one and a half miles. They counted the islands among which the narrow and dangerous channel twisted. There were sixty islands of considerable size, and there were about as many islets, or towheads. At low water, there was no channel worth the name—not more than twelve inches of water. In a drouthy season, when the river was really low, a man might walk across Muscle Shoals without wetting his feet. Even at high water, the dangers remained; and the river was so wide that a rise of 50 feet at Chattanooga—a big flood—would produce a rise of only 5 feet at Muscle Shoals.

The river place names that came down from early flatboat days told the tale more vividly than the reports of the engineers. Not far above Bluewater Creek was a notable rapids to which the boatmen had given the name Gallop Water. And between Gallop Water and Campbell's Ferry was an obstacle known as the Big Jump, a ledge of rocks that stretched from shore to shore and caused a fall of four feet. The only way to get over the Big Jump, when coming downstream, was to make for a thirty-foot gap in it, where the water went through with a great rush. If you were coming upstream—well, you didn't come upstream, except at high water, when the Big Jump was less pronounced, but the current still swifter.

Between Big Muscle Shoals and Little Muscle Shoals there was a stretch of three miles where navigation was easy because there were no flinty rocks. Then the flinty rocks resumed their interference. There were more islands, including two or three very large ones, and for three miles more, until Florence came in sight, Little Muscle Shoals offered about the same kind of difficulties as Big Muscle Shoals.

There was, it seemed, no possible solution to the difficulties of Muscle Shoals, except by building a lateral canal around the great series of obstructions. The question was, who would build it—or rather, who would pay for it?

Not the federal government, of course. Not by any means. Those were the days of state rights, and American political leaders were generally of the firm opinion that the federal government lacked constitutional authority to make direct appropriations for the improvement of rivers. The federal government was interested, however. It loaned engineers for the survey, and John C. Calhoun, then secretary of war, had reported in 1824 that solution of the Muscle Shoals problem was a matter of national and not purely local interest. Furthermore, in 1827, the Congress, holding its breath at its temerity, actually made an appropriation toward the expenses of a survey: the sum was $200, the first federal money allocated to the Tennessee River.

But building the canal, and defraying the expenses thereof, was strictly Alabama's business. Maybe it was only North Alabama's business, for current opinion held that local improvements ought to be paid for by those who immediately benefited from them. The improvement of Muscle Shoals was a local improvement. But where would Alabama, or North Alabama, raise the money estimated by the engineers as necessary for building a suitable canal: $1,388,102.54 for a canal sixty feet wide, or $1,434,523.37 if it was made seventy feet wide?

A solution was reached in terms that fitted handsomely the spirit of the times. Andrew Jackson was in the White House, and he was as iron against the notion of spending from the general treasury for local benefits; in fact, he was against spending; he even supposed that it was the bounden duty of the government to pay up its borrowings, to the last penny. But there were public lands in Alabama, to which the federal government held title. It was finally agreed that the federal government would "relinquish" four hundred thousand acres of these lands to Alabama, provided that the moneys received from the sale of these lands should be devoted to the building of the Muscle Shoals Canal—or the Tennessee Canal, as it was then called; and provided further that the canal should be built according to plans approved by the federal government and that Alabama should charge no tolls for passage through the canal.

This roundabout way of giving federal support was at once approved. Everybody appreciated the perfect legitimacy of selling public lands. In North Alabama, in particular, such things were extremely well understood.

The plan of the engineers—an ambitious one for those days—in its original form called for a lateral canal following the north bank of the Tennessee all the way from Brown's Ferry to Florence. It involved building two dams across the river, one below the mouth of Elk River, another at Campbell's Ferry. Creeks entering the canal zone would be properly dammed to prevent their clogging the trunk of the canal; Shoal Creek, however, would be crossed by an aqueduct. Furthermore, the engineers estimated that for an additional expenditure of about $50,000 enough channel improvements might be made between Florence and Waterloo to give large steamboats regular access to the canal. To all of this, Andrew Jackson gave his approval.

Construction work began early in 1831. Unfortunately, for reasons that even yet seem a little mysterious, the sale of the public lands did not bring anything like the sum needed for building the complete canal. The Alabama commissioners then asked Congress to alter the plans. Instead of beginning at the lowest point of obstruction (which was, really, Colbert Shoals, but which might be taken to be Little Muscle Shoals), as the plan approved by the government required, the commissioners begged permission, for the present, merely to build a canal around Big Muscle Shoals. The plea was allowed, and this stretch was therefore canalized, at a cost of $644,594.71. When the canal was opened, in 1836, Alabama further asked permission of Congress, and was granted it, to charge tolls, with a view to using the money for completing the canal as originally planned.

But the shorter canal, around Big Muscle Shoals only,

turned out to be almost useless. At low water, boats could not enter it through Elk River Shoals and Little Muscle Shoals. At high water, they did not need it and did not always use it. The aqueduct over Shoal Creek was not built, and the creeks were not properly dammed. Within a year, the canal was an evident failure, and Alabama's enterprising project was wasted. In 1838, Thomas Williams, chief engineer for the canal, reported that seventy flatboats loaded with cotton had passed through the canal, only to discover that they must tie up at Campbell's Ferry and wait for a rise to take them over Little Muscle Shoals. And meanwhile the *Holston,* which wanted to go to Knoxville, had stopped at the upper end because she could not get over Elk River Shoals.

In 1837 and again in 1838, Alabama asked Congress to appropriate money for finishing the canal. The House Committee on Roads and Canals finally recommended an appropriation of $56,769.33, but the appropriation was never made. Previous to this appeal, the canal commissioners had made a plea to the Alabama legislature, but without success. In their memorial they charged the state, in effect, with diverting for other purposes money which ought to have gone toward completing the canal. Their argument was that the canal project was entitled to receive not only the sums acquired from the sale of lands, but also the interest on those sums, which interest, accruing while the money was on deposit in state banks, had been used for general revenue.

Nothing more happened. The canal was neglected and soon fell into disuse and disrepair. Possibly the hard times prevalent during the Jackson administration had something to do with the failure to procure sufficient funds. But the rising interest in railroads may also have caused a certain lukewarmness toward the canal project.

The Tuscumbia, Courtland, and Decatur Railroad, in fact, was in direct competition with the Muscle Shoals Canal. Although it was inefficient by modern standards, the little railroad could do its hauling regardless of whether the river was up or down. The untying of the knot of Muscle Shoals could be achieved, it was apparent, by building railroads to go where steamboats could not go.

So the railroads, which were afterwards to prove the great rivals and enemies of river transport, entered the scene, but, at this stage, as friendly assistants and complements of the steamboat lines. Steamboat advertisements proudly began to tell how conveniently their schedules connected with railroad schedules. The owners of the *News*, for example, boasted that passengers taking their boat at Decatur would reach Charleston in only seventy-two hours. To a considerable degree, indeed, the early railroad lines were projected to deal with a transport problem that had its origin in disappointments encountered on the Tennessee River. In the thinking of the people, the Tennessee remained a principal artery of commerce and travel. But it was strangulated, and railroads came in to relieve the strangulation.

Although there were many conventions, schemes, and projects, none of the major railroads of the Tennessee Valley was actually completed until the last decade before the Civil War—just in time to be of service in that war. In 1851, after fifteen years of planning, the state of Georgia completed the Western and Atlantic, between the brand-new town, Atlanta, and the not much older one, Chattanooga. Georgia retains the ownership of the Western and Atlantic to this day; under a lease arrangement, it forms a part of the Nashville, Chattanooga, and St. Louis Railroad. In 1855, the East Tennessee and Georgia Railroad, paralleling the Tennessee River, was completed between Chattanooga and Knoxville, and East Tennessee was no longer isolated. The Memphis and Charleston Railroad, when finally completed in 1858, filled in the east-and-west gaps. It joined in one trunk line the Memphis and La Grange Railroad, which had started east from Memphis in 1835; the old Tuscumbia, Courtland, and Decatur road; and the new-built link crossing the river at Decatur and running through Huntsville to connect with the N., C. & St.L., which brought its line to Bridgeport, Alabama, in 1853. A little later the N., C. & St.L. carried its road into Chattanooga by a route on the south side of the Tennessee. This last link furnished a kind of portage around the Narrows as the Tuscumbia, Courtland, and Decatur Railroad had earlier furnished one around Muscle Shoals.

With the coming of the railroads, the scene changed rapidly. By a singular paradox, the towns that had been built on the Tennessee River became railroad towns rather than river towns. Chattanooga in particular, now that the Cherokee Removal had opened the south side of the river to settlement, became a railroad center. Inevitably, when industrial development began, Chattanooga would become a real city; mineral wealth and ready transport would make it that. And while Chattanooga, Decatur, Tuscumbia, and Huntsville were becoming railroad towns, old Triana, Whitesburg, Bainbridge, and other small places that had staked their hopes on the river could only curse Muscle Shoals and dwindle away. And all the canal projects dwindled away too: the Hiwassee-Coosa scheme, the French Broad-Savannah scheme; and the rather frantic and foolish plans which impetuous citizens on the Lower Tennessee had drawn up for making water connections with the Mississippi, by way of the Big Hatchie and other small tributaries of the Mississippi that rise in West Tennessee. But the project of joining Bear Creek, in the Great Bend, with the Tombigbee River, and so with the Gulf, lived on vigorously into the twentieth century.

All the while steamboats never ceased to wrestle with the perils of the Tennessee. The flinty rocks of Muscle Shoals and the windings of the Narrows, to say nothing of lesser troubles, made it impossible for the Golden Era of steamboating on the Ohio and Mississippi to extend its full glory to the Tennessee. There was comparatively little boat-

building anywhere on the Tennessee, even when steamboating
was at its height; and first-class facilities for repairs were not
available except at Paducah, whose excellent "Marine Ways"
were built by Elijah Murray in 1853. Still, the gallant captains were faithful to their river, as a lover to a moody
mistress.

On the Lower Tennessee, luxurious packets came regularly. Most of these were owned outside the Valley. The *Pennsylvania,* a fine boat of the railroad line, brought the mail,
along with passengers and freight, to Florence and Tuscumbia
in the late forties. The *North Alabama,* a large, fast boat,
built at Pittsburgh for the New Orleans trade, appeared on
the Lower Tennessee in the fifties. By way of special promo-
tion, her owners announced that their excellent new boat
would start from Louisville at the hour when the Paducah
packet (name now lost) left Paducah. With this handicap,
she would race the Paducah packet to Tuscumbia Landing. A
large holiday crowd gathered to witness the finish of the race
and to take advantage of the free excursion to Florence advertised by the promoters. The Paducah boat arrived first,
but only an hour ahead of the *North Alabama.* Next day the
*North Alabama* left for Florence, her decks crowded with
excursionists. At Florence she loaded a thousand bales of cotton. On the way back, the holidaymakers were startled by
the cry of "Fire!" The fire was among the cotton bales, some
of which were flung, sizzling and smoking, into the river.
When the scattered bales had been laboriously pursued and
recovered, the *North Alabama* tied up and loaded four thousand more bales. This load of five thousand bales, if correctly
reported, might constitute a record on the Tennessee. But in
1856, certainly, Alabama and Tennessee newspapers were announcing boats of large capacity. The *Cherokee* could carry
3,000 bales; the *Eastport,* which would soon figure in the
Civil War, could carry 4,000; and the *Choctaw,* 5,000—if
advertisements are to be believed. Other Lower Tennessee

boats of this period were: *Decatur, Excel, Fawn* (a low-water packet), *Hard Times, Huntsville, John Tompkins, Mazeppa, Mogul, Muscle, O.K., R. M. Patton, Wave.*

In the 1840's and later, new boats came steadily into service on the Upper Tennessee. Most of them were built in the North. But at last steamboat building began on the Upper Tennessee. The *Frankland,* built at Knoxville, about 1844, was, it is claimed, the first steamboat to be built in East Tennessee. The *Joe Jaques,* a small boat of thirty-one tons burden, was built at Loudoun in 1855. Her master was J. H. Johnston, and she was in the Knoxville-Chattanooga trade.

The *Cassandra* (Captain Boyd) was the first steamboat to enter Sullivan County. In 1847 she ventured the ticklish journey up the Holston. She had come within a few miles of Kingsport when engine trouble developed, and she had to return to Knoxville. Later, probably in 1850, the *Cassandra* and the *Mary McKinney* actually reached Kingsport, and the jubilant citizens immediately claimed for their town the distinction of "the head of navigation." Their rejoicing was premature. The Holston promptly fell and left the two steamboats grounded on a sand bar. They got off only after a long wait, and did not go to Kingsport again.

On February 5, 1850, in one of the few major accidents recorded on the Upper Tennessee during this period, the *Cassandra* collided with the *Ellen White* opposite Kingston and suffered considerable damage. The rivalry between the boats is reflected in the charge subsequently made, but probably unjust, that the captain of the *Ellen White* deliberately brought about the collision in order to injure a competitor. The *Ellen White,* described as "a beautiful, fast boat," came into the Upper Tennessee trade in 1849 after seeing previous service under the name *Tennessee.*

Other boats on the Upper Tennessee in the 1840's were: the *George Nicholson* (Captain Doss); the *Huntsman* (Captain Mahan), which, when renamed the *News,* became the first boat to carry the mail on the Upper Tennessee; the *Huntsville* (Captain J. H. Wilson); the *Jim Jackson* (Captain Mahan); the *Pickaway* (Captain Merrill), so called from her ability to pick her way among shoals and bars; the *Sam Martin* (Captain Rogers), a small boat owned by Chattanooga interests and used for engineering operations between Knoxville and Decatur, with the object of proving the navigability of the Tennessee and so influencing the builders of the Western and Atlantic Railroad to fix their northern terminal at Chattanooga.

In the fifties the number of steamboats on the Upper Tennessee continued to increase. The river improvements of the thirties and forties, meager and unsatisfactory though they were, made the river more accessible to light-draft steamboats. Keelboats were no longer needed, and they disappeared from the main river. Chattanooga, with its web of rail-and-river connections, was rising to the place of importance that it later assumed. The segmentation of the upper river had become a definite feature of steamboat traffic. There was little "through traffic" from Knoxville to Decatur. Chattanooga was the great transfer point. Some boats operated between Chattanooga and Knoxville, others between Chattanooga and Decatur, and regular schedules were maintained.

Among the notable boats of this period were the *Chattanooga* (Captain Mahan), a fine passenger boat; the *Lincoln* (Captain Doss), advertised as equipped with a "doctor" for supplying water to the boilers; the *Lookout*, which her proud captain, J. M. Todd, called "the boss of all boats"; and the *Mollie Garth*. The *Mollie Garth* deserves a special place in history if only for the fact that the money for her purchase was raised by the farmers of the Valley; and furthermore, she made a profit for her owners. The *Lookout*, built at Pittsburgh in 1852, stayed in continuous service until 1860, when she was rebuilt and chartered by the Confederate government. She was finally captured by the Federals, and was sunk at Ross Towhead in 1865.

There were a few unlucky boats. The *Elkton* (Captain Cliff) caught fire while she was tied up at the Suck, and was lost, along with 168 bales of cotton. The *James Williams*, which was owned by Captain J. L. Doss and associates, lost money for her owners. She also had the misfortune to be frozen up near the mouth of Pond Creek in Roane County during one of the rare spells when there was ice on the Tennessee, and her passengers had to walk cross-country to Kingston and Loudoun. Later she sank on Little River Shoals and was abandoned. The *Lincoln,* in 1851, ran on a rock and sank in four feet of water just below the Suck.

But such accidents as these were the exception on the Upper Tennessee. There were few wrecks, despite the many obstacles to navigation. And there were none of the fearsome boiler explosions that brought tragedy to many a fine packet on the Mississippi in those days.

As navigation of the main river became easier, steamboats began to push up the tributaries, and some boats apparently were constructed for this special service. The *Holston II* (Captain Jaques), built for the Knoxille Coal Company, carried salt down from Knoxville and up the Clinch to Clinton —a haul of 192 miles by steamboat, as compared with only twenty miles overland, but the steamboat haul was cheaper. The *Jefferson* (Captain Nicholson) was built to run between Dandridge on the French Broad River and Decatur, but she proved to be too large to navigate regularly the shoals of the French Broad and was sold to North Alabama interests. The *Lady of Augusta,* however, showed what could be done: she went up the French Broad and above Dandridge to the mouth of the Nolichucky. The *Union* (Captains Spiller and Shields) hauled ore from the Ducktown copper mines to Charleston, Tennessee, and possibly was the first boat to operate regularly on the Hiwassee.

And what was it like, from a traveler's viewpoint, to journey along the Upper Tennessee on one of these boats, in those days? For that question, one rather professional traveler had an answer. David Hunter Strother ("Porte Crayon") took a trip on the *James Williams* in the late fifties, from Knoxville to Chattanooga.

The scenery on the river [he reported in *Harper's Magazine*] is bold and pleasing without ever rising to sublimity. But the weather was delightful, the stream was full, and the stern wheelboat made good speed, and as she frequently landed to put off or take on freight, the artists had opportunities of sketching characteristic scenes on shore. At night the young folks had the privilege of the promenade deck by the light of a glorious moon while the elders stupefied themselves with cards and dominoes in the cabin.

The first night on a Western steamboat is not usually an agreeable one. The thundering explosions from the escape-pipes, the rush of the wheels through the water, the frequent signals from the bell, the shouts of command, all confused and half understood, are little calculated to soothe the nerves of those unaccustomed to such sounds, especially if the imagination has been properly stimulated beforehand by newspaper accounts of fires, snags, and bursted boilers. One who has been well brought up, is apt on such an occasion to say his "Now I lay me down to sleep" with especial fervor and emphasis, and to welcome the coming dawn with uncommon thankfulness. It is not, therefore, to be wondered at that some of our friends looked a little haggard and sleepy, when they appeared at the breakfast-table next morning; nor is it strange that they laid all the blame upon the narrow uncomfortable beds which they occupied. All travelers do the same thing. But people soon become accustomed to anything. The imaginary dangers disappear, the real are forgotten, and in less than twenty-four hours after embarkation the most timid traveler sinks to sleep as free from apprehension as if he were in a church or on shore. . . .

Porte Crayon, then, found the Upper Tennessee all right —if not quite "sublime." But of course he never tried Muscle Shoals.

# CHAPTER XIX

# How It Was in the Old Days

By 1850 it almost seemed that the mighty days were over in the Tennessee Valley and that folks could sit back and enjoy life for the next two or three hundred years. What if the thunderous quarrel over slavery did shake the nation's politics! Let it shake! Tennessee had sent Andrew Jackson and James K. Polk to the White House; it had been mother state to the new Southwest; its sons, led by Sam Houston, had helped win independence for Texas; then, when Polk added Texas to the galaxy of states, had streamed forth to help win the Mexican War and so to extend the boundaries of the United States to the Pacific Coast. Who could ask for more?

Tennessee and Kentucky were not for secession or nullification. They were not antislavery, either. They were moderate, for a change. Since Jackson's time the Whigs had been dominant in state politics, and Tennessee Whigs, though proslavery at home, had no burning desire to see slavery extended into the new West. As for the Democrats, a large number of them were good Jackson men and therefore good Union men. It was no time to get excited.

The borders of Tennessee had been rounded out. It now had three Grand Divisions: East, Middle, and West Tennessee. The terms had more than mere geographical meaning. The Supreme Court met in the three divisions in turn, and they were otherwise officially recognized. They had certain regional differences that made Tennessee almost three states in one.

East Tennessee, reaching from the divide of the Great Smokies approximately to the meridian of Chattanooga, included the river valleys of the Upper Tennessee system, the high mountains of the east, and some of the Cumberland plateau. Oldest of the divisions, seat of the oldest towns and of the first capital, it inherited the tradition of the Lost State of Franklin. Retarded by its isolation and its lack of reliable transportation, it was more old-fashioned than the other two divisions. Its terrain forbade any great development of the plantation system, and it therefore had fewer Negro slaves than the other divisions: 11,000 in 1854, as compared with Middle Tennessee's 62,000 and West Tennessee's 44,000. Mildly antislavery in spots, it had sheltered Elihu Embree's *Intelligencer* and his *Emancipator*, the first abolitionist periodicals in the nation. Nevertheless, it was more pro-Union than antislavery, and its mountain folks, no matter what their politics, disliked Negroes.

Middle Tennessee extended from its irregular eastern boundary to the Tennessee River on the west, and included the mountainous Cumberland plateau, the oak barrens of the Highland Rim, and the rich bluegrass basin which was the chief seat of its diversified and highly prosperous agriculture. On the north it had easy commercial access to Louisville and Cincinnati; on the south it linked with North Alabama, and, through the gateway of Chattanooga, with Georgia and the Deep South. In Middle Tennessee were more plantations, and yet not many large plantations. The small farmer flourished along with the planter. Like the Bluegrass of Kentucky, the region represented a westward extension of the Virginia tradition, in which the planter set the tone of society and was willing to live up to his responsibilities. Yet he did not make any too absurd pretensions to aristocracy. The rough-and-tumble tradition of Old Hickory and the negligible distance between planter and farmer forbade that. Middle Tennessee was decidedly proslavery, and had some secessionist tendencies, but it liked the Whig program too.

Between the Tennessee and the Mississippi, there was West Tennessee, won for the state by the Chickasaw Treaty of 1818, and so the youngest of the three divisions. The narrowness of the Tennessee Valley west of the river put all of West Tennessee except a narrow strip in the Mississippi Valley proper, and its economic affiliations were with New Orleans, Natchez, and the Delta country. It was a great land for cotton, a land of big plantations with many slaves. Nevertheless, in its swampy and hilly parts, and especially in certain counties bordering the Tennessee, it was as defiantly backwoodsy as the wildest regions of the state.

The differences of these three divisions were real and would persist, and yet the people were in very important respects one people, just emerging from the great experience of pioneering and deeply marked by it. Because that experience was not fully understood, the people, then and later, were very often not understood. By 1850 they were being confronted with the stereotypes that the too articulate visitor unjustly fixed upon them.

Already the North, gulled by journalist, politician, and crusading clergyman, was quite wrongly dividing all the people of the South, and with it the people of the Tennessee country, into three tight classes: planter aristocrat, poor white, Negro slave. There were plenty of Negro slaves, in truth, as well as some Negro freedmen, but the presence of slavery had not stratified the Tennessee country into three absurdly simple divisions.

Actually, as the historical studies of Frank L. Owsley have clearly proved, the ownership of land was widely distributed. A heavy majority of all agriculturists owned their land. The most numerous and influential "class"—if there was such a thing as "class"—was the large group of "yeoman farmers": those who tilled holdings of about two hundred acres, or even less. These farmers, who might be either slave-holders or nonslaveholders, were close neighbors of the big planter. Next to the plantation of a thousand acres, on which the owner had put up a fine brick house with "Greek Revival" columns, would be a farmer who had only lately weather-

boarded over a pioneer cabin of hewn logs—loopholes and bullet marks still in it—and added an ell and a detached kitchen. Not far off would be a still smaller farmer who had done nothing more to his log cabin than improve the win-dows, doors, and furniture.

As for the "poor whites," the term was a misnomer for all save a very small unfortunate group. The so-called "poor whites" were for the most part simply frontiersmen who out of strong preference continued, with varying degrees of suc-cess, the frontier occupations of hunting and cattle herding, and who did little farming. These people had often been

among the first settlers. They used the valleys as long as the
valleys offered an open range for their herds, but when farmers invaded the valley land and thus narrowed the range,
the cattle herders, clinging to their preferred life, moved into
the uplands that farmers did not want. Even in the 1850's
there was still plenty of open range, especially in the Cumberlands and on the Highland Rim. The greater part of the
Tennessee country was still wilderness. In its forests the
cattle, roaming the glades and woods, fattening in cane
bottoms and brushy pastures of wild grass, succeeded to the
old domain of buffalo and deer; and hogs found rich pro-
vender in the nuts and mast.

These old-fashioned frontiersmen of the uplands, in truth,
were the predecessors of the cowboys of the trans-Mississippi
range. They "rounded up" their cattle, used recognized
brands, and drove both cattle and hogs to market over long
distances. (David Crockett, in his famous autobiography,
tells how, as a boy, he drove a herd of cattle from East
Tennessee far up into the Valley of Virginia.) Although they
did not have "corrals," they had "cowpens"—the same thing
under an English name. They used the "lasso," though they
did not call it that; and they could "cut out" a steer from a
herd as skillfully as any cowboy—though, unlike the cowboy,
they used dogs to help in the herding. They were likely to
ride wiry Indian ponies—the Chickasaw breed was long preferred on the frontier.

The journalistic traveler of the fifties saw only the dwellings and small clearings of these people; he could not see their
cattle and hogs, which were ranging the forest. Misled by ap-
pearances, he often mistook them for shiftless farmers. After
a while, when the new West began to produce cattle, the
backwoodsmen lost their markets, were driven into farming
on land unsuited to agriculture, and so became "poor." Or
else, disliking agriculture and loving independence, they clung
to hunting as a mainstay, and on the side made whisky, did

a little flatboating or rafting, or, if and when it suited them, burned charcoal for the iron forges, or did other casual labor —not too much of it, for men who ride horses are never addicted to working with their hands.

The inquiring visitor, his head full of stereotypes, might misunderstand or underrate these people. The Tennessee country itself did not. Of course the fashionable society of the growing cities, which were importing theatricals, concerts, lyceum lectures, and, presently, hoopskirts, might be privately supercilious about "rednecks" and "crackers." But not so in public. Not only planter and farmer, but lawyer, preacher, politician, merchant took them into account, and often acknowledged their own community of interest with the backwoods by cultivating, in one way or another, a studied backwoodsiness of manner.

Frontier tradition, in fact, exerted far more influence upon civilization than civilization was able to exert on the frontier tradition. The uniform of the Tennessee militia symbolized the fact. In the Mexican War, and almost to the outbreak of the Civil War, the Tennessee volunteers wore the hunting shirt of other days. The planter with broad-brimmed hat and polished boots, riding his well-curried thoroughbred, and attended by some faithful black Achates, might put up a more elegant appearance than the man of the farm or the woods, but they agreed on fundamentals, and so did their families. The planter could quote from Vergil or Blackstone, and he—or his daughter or wife—was reading *Ivanhoe* or *Pickwick Papers*. But like his homespun neighbors he said "ain't," "git," and "pore" for "are not," "get," and "poor." He, too, pronounced "touch" as "tetch" and "were" as "wair." He swore the same oaths and told the same jokes.

The planter's house might have a wide gallery and high-ceilinged rooms to guard him from summer heat. But he, like his less wealthy neighbors, was overrun with dogs. His careless Negroes left things lying around, so that he lived in genial disorder. On his back porch, as in the cabin home, was the traditional wooden bucket, gourd dipper, and wash-pan —he would have no bathroom as yet. Guns, saddles, mowing blades, samples of seed, all the loose impedimenta of outdoor life, cluttered his porch or hall, as the log cabin dogtrot was cluttered. And though, after returning from a hot ride, he might drink a julep brought to him on a silver tray by Uncle Remus, he sat in his shirt sleeves and sock feet as he drank, and opened his collar like any countryman.

In the code of the duel the planter would be more ritualistic and punctilious—though on occasion he simply brawled, as Old Hickory did with the Bentons. But a fine sense of honor was not limited to dwellings fronted by pillars, approached by boxwood-bordered paths. Mountain man and farmer also cherished their honor and resented, as a life-and-death issue, any breach of the chivalric code, any raw intrusion upon the sacred individual. Their manners, while not always polished, had true decorum. They, too, would turn away no stranger unprovided. They, too, taught children to say "sir" and "ma'am" to their elders. And they practiced the genial arts of hospitality and conversation with a relish as marked as the most courtly planter could exhibit.

People were deeply, universally religious, but aristocratic Anglicanism and learned Presbyterianism did not thrive except in the aspiring but as yet undominant cities. Baptist and Methodist and the new sect promulgated by Alexander Campbell waxed mightily. The first two, in particular, were the great churches of the frontier, which had come to associate a ceremonious church with an oppressive government and regarded a too-unctuous theology as likely to be the cloak of overweening self-righteousness. The frontier prized spontaneity and cherished the miraculous. It wanted to feel the grace of God flooding the contrite heart. There were shouting Methodists and footwashing Baptists in plenty.

As for formal education, nobody denied that it was a

very good thing, least of all the people who did not have it. There were many of the latter class, perhaps more, relatively, than in the 1770's. Almost one-fourth of the adult population were illiterate. Folks had been too busy clearing land to bother with schools. There was really no disesteem for learning. But it was generally assumed that schooling was a private rather than a public business—at most an affair of church, certainly not an affair of state except for unfortunate persons, like orphans, who might be taught at public expense. And so, although there were flourishing academies and colleges for those who could afford them, the common schools were hardly above the level of the "old field schools" of pioneer times.

In 1854, Andrew Johnson became governor, and under his sturdy prompting the state for the first time in its history levied a tax for the support of common schools. The holocaust of Civil War soon wrecked that beginning. But up to Andrew Johnson's administration it was hard for people to grasp the notion of *public* education. The mere fact that a person existed did not, it was then felt, entitle him to education at public expense. That any really determined person could get a book education, if he wanted it earnestly, was proved by the case of Andrew Johnson himself. He could make as good a classical oration as, say, Gustavus Henry, the "Eagle Orator of Tennessee," who was a university graduate. Yet this same Andy Johnson—the "bound boy of Raleigh," the "mechanics' governor," the tailor by trade—had never been to school a day in his life! His wife, it was said, helped him with his book learning while he snipped and stitched in his tailor's shop at Greeneville.

Although the Tennessee country might be short on book learning, it did not lack education of the sort it needed for the affairs of life. The family, the community, the church, the fields, the woods, the shops, the river supplied through traditional means the knowledge and craft which surely no school system of those days or later could have provided. The home was a school. Farm and cabin households, though bookless save for the Family Bible and *The Sacred Harp*, taught the girls to spin, weave, quilt, cook, sew, and mind their manners; the boys to wield gun, ax, hammer and saw, to ride, plow, sow and reap, and to be men. The social arts that went with frontier life were highly developed. Barbecues, church services, camp meetings, political debates, logrollings, housewarmings, weddings and infares, funerals, all-day singings— these were schools in which no lesson, once learned, was ever forgotten. Besides, the capacious folk memory supplied an infinite store of tales and songs, continually refreshed by new creations. Nobody need ever be bored. Amusement did not have to be bought. In all that enriched the immediate experience of life itself the Tennessee country was amply provided. It did not have to hire a schoolmaster or schoolma'am to tell it or its children what to think or how to live.

It was in fact a sound traditional society, ready to take a fresh start. Some might think it backward, but it was also possible that civilization was lagging behind it rather than the contrary. Would you, after all, tinker with the culture of a strong country boy by teaching him Mr. Longfellow's imitation ballad "Excelsior" when he could already sing, if not read, the original "Lord Randal" or "Sir Patrick Spens"—and in addition could tame a horse, split rails, run a flatboat, play a fiddle, and keep the family table provided with game and fish? To this very question, in principle, Sut Lovingood answered with a ribald "No." G. W. Harris, in one of the "Yarns," made Sut speak out in pointed condemnation of Mr. Longfellow's "Excelsior," which he compared unfavorably with a saucy bit of native folk song.

The country was self-reliant, and, conscious of its strength, it obliged its leaders to watch their step. No use for lawyer, legislator, or preacher to parade borrowed finery. A boiled shirt and a Ciceronian rhetoric would be accepted only if the crowd knew that the speaker also commanded, for the right moments, a proper frontier waggishness. In the newspapers Harris's political satires, put into the mouth of Sut Lovingood, keyed the mood of the fifties. "Hit am an orful thing," said Sut, commenting on his greatest asset, his long legs, "tu be a natural born durn'd fool. Yu'se never 'sperienced hit pussonally, hev yu? . . . I orter bust my head open agin a bluff ove rocks, an' jis' wud du hit, ef I warnt a cussed coward. All my yeathly 'pendence is in these yere laigs —d'ye see 'em? Ef they don't fail, I may turn human sum day, that is sorter human, enuf tu be a Squire, ur school cummisiner. Ef I wer jis' es smart es I am mean, an' ornary, I'd be President ove a Wild Cat Bank in less nor a week."

Such humor, with its exaggerations and its gibes at pompous folk, was a safeguard and solace in a country where life was still perilous, and full of amazing ups and downs. If you could not laugh, if you could not be reasonably unserious in the face of trouble, you had better look out. Fate would take you down a peg; or Sut and his pals would. The whole country laughed and spun magnificently impossible yarns about victories and rebuffs.

There was Colonel Nicholas Johnson, one of the richest men in all the Great Bend, who came from Georgia with seventy-five slaves and settled, out of preference, on poor land because, he said, he wanted to raise stock and get rich off the cotton planters by selling them what they ought themselves to be raising. A visitor found him living in a plain but large log house and dressed, as he came in from the fields, in a straw hat, cotton shirt and pants, and coarse shoes without any socks. All around him were signs of prosperity: Arabian horses, bountiful orchards, fat hogs and cattle. When asked to explain his system, the colonel complied, and, to point up his explanation, asked the visitor if he would like to see a $4,000 mirror. The guest, full of curiosity, was led to another room in which was hanging a small mirror in a frame of veneered mahogany. When the visitor confessed himself perplexed, the colonel then enumerated the articles he had possessed when he married and told how tremendously his estate had increased in value. And if that cheap mirror, he said, had increased in value at the same ratio, it *must* be worth $4,000.

There were always barbecues, and there were tales of feats of gourmandry. A certain newspaper editor sat down at an outdoor feast with the hindquarter of a pig on his right, half a buffalo fish on his left, and a bottle of whisky in front of him. With gusto he proceeded to the attack, and when he began to waver, his joking friends rigged a lever on the tree above him, attached a cord, passed a noose beneath his arms, and raised and lowered him with a jerk at strategic moments, "to settle his victuals." The same editor once remarked that "a turkey was of a very inconvenient size, since it was rather too much for one man, and not quite enough for two."

From the companies of loungers who whittled and spat beneath the shade trees of the square, the rollicking satirical humor jostled upward into the courtroom and nudged its way into the proceedings of legislatures. No matter how great man's dignity, he could not always be standing on dignity alone. If you could not take a joke, you must not expect people to take you seriously. The people made laws, but what could be funnier than laws and lawmaking? The people were religious, but what was more ridiculous than doctrinal disputes? The famous burlesque sermon, "The Harp of a Thousand Strings," was endlessly repeated. In the traditional rendering, the sermon is delivered by a Hard-Shell Baptist preacher, who is also captain of a flatboat with a cargo of whisky, ready for sale. The points of doctrine become creatures of a humorous fable, in which the Episcopalian is likened unto a turkey buzzard and the Methodist to a squirrel that runs up a tree "from one degree of grace to another" until at last he "falls from grace." As for the Baptists, they "hev been likened unto a 'possum on a 'simmon tree, and the thunders may roll, and the earth may quake, but that 'possum clings thar still, ah! And you may shake one foot loose, and the other's thar; and you may shake all feet loose, and he laps his tail aroun' the lim', and he clings fur-ever!"

More often, the humor was not fable, but shrewd wit or sharply pointed anecdote. A man who heard a well-known preacher deliver a sermon on hell-fire was asked how he liked the preaching. "I would not have abused a dog as Mr. S— abused the devil," he answered. "He seemed to have a special spite against him." When emigrants drifted into the hot, tree-less regions of the Great Plains, there were many jokes about Texas. For instance, there was the comment of a Tennessean who went to Texas and saw there, deep in the heart of a strange and, to him, an unpleasant country, a bird he did not recognize. He asked what it was. "Bird of paradise," he was told. "Then it's a damned long way from home!" he said.

Turned loose in politics, the frontier humor brought un-expected upsets. It overthrew locally the regime of Andrew Jackson at a time when the Old Hero was most powerful nationally. The coonskin philosopher, Davy Crockett, was wafted into Congress on a gale of laughter. The Whigs liter-ally laughed the Jacksonians out of office in Jackson's own state.

To retrieve the situation, the Jacksonians brought out James K. Polk to run for governor. Polk was artful and able, a great stump speaker, without a peer in public debate. Against the unbeatable Polk the Whigs put up a curious fig-ure, James C. Jones—commonly known as "Lean Jimmy" Jones. Polk was small of stature, dapper, and elegant. Jones was six feet two and weighed only 125 pounds. He had an enormous nose, a wide slit of a mouth, and the deceptively solemn countenance of the backwoods humorist. The audience began to roar as soon as he stalked to the front of the platform. To Polk's elaborate argument, made in the classic style, Jones attempted no direct reply, but ran his bony fingers gently over a coonskin that he displayed to the audience and said, "Did you ever see such fine fur?" Jones was elected.

All this did not mean that life was a joke. The creed of those days has been well set forth by the Mississippian, Reuben Davis, who spent his boyhood and youth in Tennessee and North Alabama. "Their creed," he wrote, "was generally simple. A man ought to fear God and mind his business. He should be respectful and courteous to all women; he should love his friends and hate his enemies. He should eat when he was hungry, drink when he was thirsty, dance when he was merry, vote for the candidate he liked best, and knock down any man who questioned his right to those privileges." To this Davis added a more general observation: "The world has of necessity grown colder and more selfish as those primitive days recede into the dim past, and in grasping all things, men let happiness slip out of their hands."

Devotedly religious, devotedly political, the people never neglected the pursuit of happiness. It never occurred to them that happiness might be purchased, like some piece of brought-on goods. They contrived it out of homemade materials.

They were passionately fond of hunting, and there was still plenty of big game to hunt. Long remembered in North Alabama was the hunt for the "big buck," the elusive beast whose antlers every hunter craved but nobody had got. One morning word came to Matthew Clay that the big buck had been seen in his cornfield. He passed the word to his friends, and, as soon as he was ready, took down his old hunting horn, went to the front porch, and blew a long blast. Other horns answered from far and near, and Matthew Clay went riding forth. His Negro boy, Horace, mounted on "Long Hungry," was "driver" and led the hounds. Horace carried a ram's horn whose notes everybody in that country knew.

Presently they raised the big buck from cover, and the chase began, with Horace's horn telling every movement of the deer and the hounds, as the riders drew to him from every quarter, and pack began to answer pack. The advancing hounds turned the deer away from the woods, and he began to run straight north for the Tennessee River. The galloping hunters closed in. The buck, racing for a low bank that would have given him entrance to the river, was turned back by a wild shot from an excited huntsman. He reversed his course and then, finding himself hemmed in on all sides but one, dashed straight down the one narrow street of the settlement at Melton's Bluff, and toward the bluff itself. Clay fired but missed. The buck leaped over the bluff, and three of Clay's best hounds leaped after him. They found the deer and hounds dead on the rocks below, and Clay took the great crumped antlers to hang with his trophies.

It was all informal. Hunt clubs, pink coats, and great pretensions were unknown. Folks hunted deer, bear, coon, possum, turkey, fox, quail because they wanted to, not because society said they ought to. Horse racing might stand a little apart, as a special province of the highfalutin set, since only the wealthy could carry the expense of fine race horses. Hunting belonged to everybody, and might be either social or solitary.

Where civilization was weak, the folk culture was strong. It was the invisible part of the baggage carried across the mountains, along with the Bible and Shakespeare. Most of it was far older than the century in which it found new opportunity to bourgeon. It was as if the seventeenth and eighteenth century culture of Briton and Scot had been transplanted almost intact, to continue in a new environment, undisturbed by the later European influences that touched the eastern seaboard. Sut Lovingood's language might have seemed barbarous or quaint to Henry Wadsworth Longfellow, who had already turned to the later Europe, but it would not have seemed so to Walter Raleigh, who "spake broad Devonshire to his dying day." Sut's language was Devonshire, or southwest England, with some mixture of Scots and brand-new American. In later times the ignorant would foolishly call it "negroid" or "illiterate," but it was not. The very old and very new were blending.

The countryman of the Tennessee Valley had great store of traditional ballads and also a capacity for finding new outlaw heroes and tragic maidens to put into new ballads. Often he Americanized the old ballads. To the delight of children, the ancient English song about the strange wedding of the frog and the mouse became a merry and singable tale called "Frog Went A-Courtin'," which pictured Little Mousie as unwilling to marry even the president without Uncle Rat's consent and staged a wedding supper of homely American grub 'way down yonder in a hollow beech tree. Fiddle music underwent a similar transformation. Traditional airs like "Soldier's Joy" were at every good fiddler's command, but unknown geniuses of the backwoods made new adaptations and creations like "Money Musk," "Leather Breeches," "Old Joe Clark," "Sally Good'n." For the religious, to whom the fiddle had become the devil's instrument, the play-party offered an evasion. Young people at a play-party sang a kind of game song, or pairing-off song, which might or might not turn into a "kissing game." Boys and girls "stepped out" these songs to what were really dance tunes, and acted out the implied love drama, but could always say they had not sinned by dancing to a fiddle.

In one such song, the "leading couple" step forth and sing to one of the boys—

## Mister Boatlander

Mis-ter Boat - land - er, 'tis    time we were march-in':

March-in' a - round   for    true    love___ s'ar-chin'.

Call your   true      love,   call  her now or    nev - er.

Call her by her   name  and Tell her how you  love her.

So "Mister Boatlander," who has been studying the girls
out of the corner of his eye, calls out "Mary Lou." And Mary
Lou steps out to meet her partner as the gay crowd sing:

> Miss Mary Lou, this child says he loves you:
> Nothin' in the world he loves like he loves you.
> His heart you've gained, his hand he'll give you.
> One sweet kiss, and sorry for to leave you.

And so it would go until all were paired off. Then it
would be time to sing another song, like "Hog Drovers," or
perhaps "Weevily Wheat," with its echoes of the Highland
Scot's "Charley Over the Water."

The boatman whose delight it was, according to the
song, to dance all night and go home with the girls in the
morning, also sang or fiddled, or hearkened to singing and
fiddling while his craft went with the river. The Negro
roustabouts, wagon drivers, field hands, needed no teaching
to catch the theme. Their rare gifts for melody and rhythm

took hold and added a sonorous new flavor. Any task that could be sung to—and most tasks could—was done with more dispatch and joy when a song could be "h'isted." As the walls of Thebes rose to the music of the harp, so boats were loaded and unloaded, cotton bales rolled, weights lifted to chorales of African voices, leader chanting and improvising, the crowd surging with muscle and tune while the work song made work easy. Presently the mixed pattern of Celtic air, western words and rhythm, and Negro addition was captured for the stage by the purveyors and adapters of the blackface minstrel shows. Finally there came a genius to explore and use the mode. And so, while Boston and New York turned operatic and Barnum exploited the genius of Jenny Lind, Stephen Foster made, from the idiom of folk tradition —current in the Tennessee country and widely prevalent elsewhere—the only songs that all Americans have fully accepted.

For solemn moments another kind of song prevailed throughout the South and was abundantly known in the Tennessee country. This was the type of sacred song known in the old days as "spiritual song" and today as "spirituals."

The spirituals were genuine part songs of a very antique type, perhaps related to Elizabethan musical tradition. In the scholarly account of their past given by George Pullen Jackson, they are viewed as having originated, probably, in the "Deep North"—rural New England, upper New York— where certain methods of vocal instruction were used in the eighteenth century singing school. As the civilization of the Boston Brahmins advanced, the singing-school masters fled west and south, and found their offerings most welcome. In the South the tradition flowered anew. Native singing teachers arose and began to compile songbooks and make new tunes, for which they borrowed freely from secular folk music. In the singing school the master taught the "rudiments" according to the "fa-so-la," or "four-note," method.

As an aid to sight reading, the notes in the books were "shaped" rather than uniformly round, so that they might be recognized from their shape as well as from their position. The earliest books arranged the songs in only three parts—treble, tenor, bass. The musical treatment was polyphonic, as in a motet or madrigal, not harmonic, as in the orthodox church hymn. The singing groups that practiced these songs became community choral groups adhering to the particular songbook out of which they had learned. William Walker's *Southern Harmony* and B. F. White's *The Sacred Harp* were among the most popular; indeed, the latter has survived in common use in the twentieth century. East Tennessee contributed *Harp of Columbia*, by W. H. and M. L. Swan of Knoxville, and *Knoxville Harmony*, by John B. Jackson of Madisonville.

The songbook compilers were also composers and adapters, who worked on the principle that the devil must not be allowed exclusive use of the catchy tunes. Therefore they boldly seized and arranged for their books, to sacred or at least edifying words, any "worldly" tune that caught their fancy. So the "Harps" and "Harmonies" contained few hymn tunes but a great many secular tunes, appropriated from the tradition of English-Scottish-Irish folk song and fitted with words selected from Watts, Cowper, or the Wesleys as well as from the nameless poets of the folk. Ancient carols and almost medieval religious ballads were incorporated into the miscellany. They produced elaborate "fuguing songs" of the anthem type, but they also caught up, probably from the camp meetings, simpler and more enthusiastic songs, like "Great Day," "Heavenly Port," "The Old Ship of Zion."

Whatever the song was, it found—if it was good—a ready group of promulgators and rememberers. The tradition swept the country before the Civil War and dominated the field of religious song. It was in all its aspects majestic and remarkable, and not the least important of its results was that the white spirituals, like the white secular songs, were taken up by the Negroes, who in their turn developed the Negro spiritual.

Few local references crept into the spirituals, and in that respect they were very different from ballads and other secular songs. They were Biblical and otherworldly. They spoke of the joys of the Redeemed; of the "wondrous love" of Christ for man's soul. They sang consolation to men about to be wrapped in the "evening shade" of death. They poured out "holy manna" for those gathered to worship in song. They portrayed the awful splendors of the Judgment Day, when the "morning trumpet" would sound and the "poor wayfaring stranger" would pass over the river to join father, mother, and all who had gone before.

Yet sometimes the tune names suggest definite local attachments. After all, the people who sang the tunes had themselves been pilgrims and strangers marching through an actual wilderness, where there were valleys of death, many rivers to cross, and mountain heights beyond which the promised land beckoned. "Singing Billy" Walker, who struck his famous tuning fork all over the South, put into his *Southern Harmony* a fine, austere tune that he called "French Broad." "This song," he said, "was composed by the author in the fall of 1831, while traveling over the mountains, on French Broad River, in North Carolina and Tennessee."

Another tune, surely among the greatest of southern and American folk melodies, appeared in 1848 in William Hauser's *Hesperian Harp*, and was there given the name "Tennessee." How it got that name we shall never know. But in its later associations and transformations it became associated with a rolling river; and that river can be either the Jordan or the Tennessee, or it can be both. The tune itself is very old. It was first printed by Jeremy Ingalls of New England in 1805, but it was already ancient then. Stephen

Foster encountered it somewhere, gave it a dancing humorous lilt, and the result was, in two variants, "Oh, Susanna" and "The Camptown Races." In the camp meetings it took a different twist and became "Roll, Jordan," a song which added, to Charles Wesley's grave words about the coming day of judgment, a rousing popular chorus of shouts and hallelujahs. In its "Tennessee" variant, it is a religious ballad, which moralizes about the prodigal son—then breaks into a contrasting jovial movement reminiscent of Merrie England, yet not far off from the fiddle tunes to which Sut Lovingood's friends cut the pigeonwing:

## Tennessee

Af - flic-tions though they seem se-vere, In mer-cy oft are sent. They stopp'd the pro-di-gal's ca-reer, And caused him to re - pent. Al-though he no re - lent-ing felt Till he had spent his store; His stub-born heart be-gan to melt, When fam-ine pinched him sore.

In its simpler form it retains the old melody, then breaks suddenly into the cadence of the shouting camp meeting, the rollicking backwoods, the surge of the mighty river. In this form it passed into the hands of both white and Negro and became one of the great exultant musical patterns in which frontier America, and the memory of frontier America, continues to find expression:

## Roll, Jordan

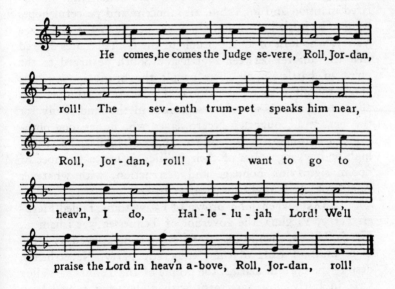

He comes, he comes the Judge se-vere, Roll, Jor-dan,

roll! The sev-enth trum-pet speaks him near,

Roll, Jor-dan, roll! I want to go to

heav'n, I do, Hal-le-lu-jah Lord! We'll

praise the Lord in heav'n a-bove, Roll, Jor-dan, roll!

# CHAPTER XX

# Secession

B UT now the golden years were done. Alike in pillared mansion and log cabin, all innocent and peaceful hopes were to be hurled into ruin. Upon the people of the Tennessee Valley, who least of all the people of the United States desired that the quarrel between North and South be urged to the point of battle—upon these people the brunt of war was about to fall with terrible force. The seventh trumpet was about to peal, was already resounding in the land. Only for the inert and thoughtless Negro slaves, who understood nothing of the issues, would it be a trumpet of jubilee. To others, high or low, regardless of their politics, it was a trumpet of doom, signifying bondage and destruction, with whatever residue of glory might linger after battle.

In 1859, when John Brown of Osawatomie raided Harpers Ferry, Virginia, the governor of Tennessee was Isham G. Harris. Harris, then in his second term, sympathized with the more militant wing of the Democratic party. Nevertheless, despite the current alarms, the people of the Tennessee Valley were in fairly close agreement with such views as had been earlier enunciated by Aaron V. Brown of Middle Tennessee. "The Union is my property—my inherited property—which I regard as of great value," Brown had said. "I never mean to permit the North to take it from me, nor to induce me by its aggressions to throw it away." Harris knew that this was the opinion of a heavy majority of the people of Tennessee.

318

But the progress of events was inexorable. When the Democrats split three ways in the election of 1860, Tennessee, with Virginia and Kentucky, gave its electoral vote to its able native son, John Bell, who as candidate of the Constitutional Unionist segment of the Democratic party at last revived the Jacksonian tradition. Yet Bell was an old Whig leader, and it was the relics of the Whig party, in combination with East Tennessee Democrats and other antisecession elements, which gave Bell the electoral vote of Tennessee. Lincoln got no support in Tennessee or elsewhere in the South. But Lincoln was elected.

In December, 1860, South Carolina seceded from the Union and was soon followed by the states of the Deep South. The secession of Alabama put the Muscle Shoals region of the Tennessee Valley into the Confederacy.

In January, 1861, the Tennessee legislature, called into special session by Governor Harris, met "to consider the present crisis and to take such steps as may be necessary." The legislature, conscious of a growing division of opinion in Tennessee, resolved to ask the people to vote on the question of whether or not a convention should be called to consider the grave issue of secession. The election was held, and the convention was defeated, the vote being 57,798 for a convention and 69,675 against it. But pro-Union sentiment at this time was stronger than these figures revealed. In the same election, citizens voted for delegates to a convention, if one should be held. The vote for delegates favoring allegiance to the Union was 88,803.

Then in April, 1861, after Lincoln ordered the garrison of Fort Sumter to be provisioned, Beauregard's artillery opened fire, and a state of war existed, at least in South Carolina. Even yet many a patriot hoped that war might be averted. But Lincoln called for seventy-five thousand troops to compel the southern states to return to the Union.

In Kentucky, where a Unionist group held the balance of power, a dubious policy of "neutrality" was announced. But it was immediately evident that the majority of Tennesseans, like their neighbors of Virginia, would not be parties to Lincoln's program of compulsion. Lincoln's request for troops brought angry solidarity where there had been indecision and reluctance. Popular sentiment, which had been slow to adopt Governor Harris's secessionist views, now swung strongly in his favor. The legislature, again in special session, authorized the governor to enter into a military league with the Confederacy. Then, after a few days of debate, it passed an Ordinance of Secession, but voted that it be submitted to a referendum of the people.

Already, in North and South, armies were assembling. In northern Virginia, not far from Washington, a Federal army under McDowell was facing a Confederate army under Joseph E. Johnston and Beauregard. The Battle of Bull Run was imminent.

On June 8, 1861, the people of Tennessee held their referendum. By a vote of 104,913 to 47,238 they ratified the Ordinance of Secession. Harris proclaimed it in effect, and Tennessee became a Confederate state.

It was the last of the Confederate states to secede. Its citizens were unwilling to separate from the old Union until war was actually unavoidable. When it became a question of either standing with the South or fighting against the South, Tennessee stood with the South. Never, never, and least of all upon order of Abraham Lincoln, would Tennessee as a state take up arms against Virginia, North Carolina, and South Carolina, from whom it had derived its being, or against Georgia, Florida, Alabama, Mississippi, Louisiana, Texas, Arkansas, to whom it was blood kin.

But though the majority favoring secession was now overwhelming—more than two to one—the referendum of 1861 revealed a complex alignment. Middle Tennessee and

West Tennessee favored secession heavily, but three of the counties lying on the Lower Tennessee River—Decatur, Hardin, Wayne, all backwoods counties—voted against it, and so became one of the doubtful spots of the Confederacy. In East Tennessee, on the other hand, which had voted against secession by a majority of twenty thousand, old Sullivan County and six other Tennessee Valley counties voted to go with the South. Furthermore, all but one of the counties of the Cumberland plateau in Middle Tennessee—backwoodsy, nonslaveholding counties—voted to go with their richer slaveholding neighbors and stand with the South. They answered the old call of clan and blood. They hearkened to the leaders to whom they felt their loyalty belonged.

In East Tennessee, where the tradition of the state of Franklin persisted and the idea of union was cherished despite much local dissent, the possibility of seceding from the seceders was promptly advanced. Twenty years before, in 1841, Andrew Johnson's bill to create a state of Frankland out of East Tennessee passed the upper house of the legislature and was accepted in an amended form by the lower house. It failed only when the legislature adjourned without Senate action on the amended bill. Now Andrew Johnson, supported by fiery Parson William G. Brownlow and others, headed a new separatist movement. Twenty-nine East Tennessee counties sent delegates to a convention held in Knoxville in May, 1861. This convention adopted resolutions protesting the action of the legislature in passing an Ordinance of Secession and urged the people to vote against it. On June 24 they met again, issued a Declaration of Grievances, and took steps to establish an independent state. The ill luck of the old state of Franklin pursued them. Before the new government could be formed, Confederate troops took control of East Tennessee. Union sympathizers had to yield or flee the country. Many began to join the Union army.

Thus brother was set against brother. For the "Provisional Army of Tennessee," which was soon turned over to Confederate authority, more than a hundred regiments of all arms had been recruited. Surreptitiously or openly, other units were being recruited for the Union side in East Tennessee. The resources of the state, hastily mobilized, were straining to meet the aggressive blows likely to come soon from the North. Confederate generals were taking charge. Confederate armies were moving in. If the South should be successfully invaded west of the Alleghenies, the route of invasion was bound to fall across Kentucky and Tennessee soil. But where, just where? By its disposition of troops the Confederate government seemed to be guessing that the blow would come through central Kentucky and incline toward the Unionist region of East Tennessee. The earliest moves of the Federal army seemed to confirm that view.

But it was a bad guess.

The real attack would be straight up the line of the Tennessee River. There, there, at Paducah, Fort Henry, and at Fort Donelson on the Cumberland, and soon, too, at Shiloh, the trumpet would sound, the bugles of two great armies would begin to call.

Because the story of the Tennessee River is long, complicated, and has never been told in its entirety, THE TENNESSEE is being published in two volumes. Volume II, by the same author, will be published in 1947. It will cover the history of the river during the Civil War, the Reconstruction period, the commercial, industrial and agricultural growth of the valley through the last decades of the nineteenth century, and will contain the momentous story of the TVA, bringing the development of the region up to date.

# Acknowledgments

To various institutions and persons who have been so kind as to aid me in the course of this work, I gratefully acknowledge my debt, and I take this occasion to express my sincere thanks for their trouble and care.

My daughter, Mrs. Eric Bell, Jr., gave invaluable assistance in research and in preparation of the manuscript.

Miss Martha Ellison made available to me valuable material from the McClung Collection of the Lawson McGhee Library, Knoxville. I owe very special thanks to Dr. A. F. Kuhlman, Director, Mrs. Frances Cheney, Reference Librarian, and the staff of the Joint University Libraries, Nashville, as also to Mrs. John Trotwood Moore, State Library of Tennessee, and Robert T. Quarles, Jr., Tennessee Historical Society. The Carnegie Library of Nashville and the Alabama State Library gave generous access to their excellent collections of newspapers.

Edward McGehee of Montgomery, who checked certain old North Alabama newspapers, and Bernard Breyer of Nashville, who did the same for Nashville and Knoxville papers, assisted me most materially in closing certain gaps in river information, and I am deeply grateful to them.

Among my colleagues of Vanderbilt University, I wish to thank Dr. L. C. Glenn, Professor Emeritus of Geology, who gave me access to the collection of maps owned by the Department of Geology, and also gave me instruction and guidance; Dr. George R. Mayfield, Professor of German and member of the Tennessee Conservation Commission, who checked local references in my manuscript; Frank L. Owsley, Professor of History, to whose researches in ante-bellum southern society I am obviously indebted; Professor Richmond C. Beatty of the Department of English, who read my manuscript; Dr. George Pullen Jackson, Emeritus Professor of German, whose pioneer studies in religious folk song afforded me solace and help.

Stanley F. Horn of Nashville kindly permitted me to use documentary material in his possession and counseled me on certain difficult questions.

Gilbert Govan, Librarian, University of Chattanooga, gave me suggestions about the local history of the Chattanooga area. Professor James W. Livingood, Department of Economics and Commerce, University of Chattanooga, graciously sent me information collected by him regarding steamboat activities.

To Fred Neuman, of the Paducah *Sun-Democrat*, I owe interesting and helpful suggestions concerning Paducah history. Miss Mary U. Rothrock of Knoxville, Miss Nina Leftwich of Tuscumbia, Professor Walter Blair of the University of Chicago, Colonel Frank Scott of Mentor, Ohio, gave me assistance on various specific problems.

Miss Mildred Haun, of Franklin, Tennessee, aided me materially in research.

For information about the Tennessee River and its steamboats that would not have been readily available from other sources I owe many thanks to Captain Donald T. Wright, editor of the *Waterways Journal*.

W. L. Sturdevant, Director of Information, Tennessee Valley Authority, was most generous and considerate in assisting my inquiries and in assembling data of various kinds, as were other members of the staff of the Tennessee Valley Authority.

The quotations in Chapter XIV from the diaries of Lieutenant Harris and Dr. Lillybridge are from material quoted in *Indian Removal*, by Grant Foreman, copyright 1932, University of Oklahoma Press, Norman, Oklahoma, and are used by permission of Mr. Foreman and the University of Oklahoma Press. I owe thanks to Mr. Grant Foreman also for his kindness in lending me certain valuable material and in commenting on it, and in general am indebted to him for the guidance and help afforded by his authoritative and distinguished works, especially *Indian Removal*.

I wish to thank Mrs. Flora L. McDowell, Smithville, Tennessee, for her permission to reprint "Shoot the Buffalo" and "Mr. Boatlander," from the volume *Folk Dances of Tennessee*, by herself and the late L. L. McDowell.

Finally I should record here my general indebtedness to Judge Samuel Cole Williams of Tennessee, to whom this book is dedicated. His scrupulous historical works, which are listed in the bibliography, were my indispensable guides in the study of early Tennessee history, as indeed they must be to all who would explore the period. *Old Frontiers*, by John P. Brown of Chattanooga, was most helpful in its unique presentation of the long struggle between Cherokees and pioneers, and I have accepted Mr. Brown's authority, rather than that of earlier historians, in noting the location of certain of the Five Lower Towns. I wish to pay tribute also to the late T. J. Campbell, whose little book, *The Upper Tennessee*, was the first to deal specifically with the navigation history of the upper river.

Other acknowledgments will more properly appear in Volume II of this work. (*See Note, page 323.*)

# A Selected Bibliography

**BOOKS**

ABERNETHY, THOMAS P., *From Frontier to Plantation in Tennessee: A Study in Frontier Democracy*. Chapel Hill, 1932.

ADAIR, JAMES, *The History of the American Indians* (London, 1775). Edited by Samuel Cole Williams. Johnson City, 1930.

*Alabama, a Guide to the Deep South*. Work Projects Administration of the State of Alabama. New York, 1941.

ALDEN, JOHN RICHARD, *John Stuart and the Southern Colonial Frontier*. Ann Arbor, 1944.

ARMSTRONG, ZELLA, *The History of Hamilton County and Chattanooga, Tennessee*. Chattanooga, 1931.

BALDWIN, LELAND D., *The Keelboat Age on Western Waters*. University of Pittsburgh Press, 1941.

BARTRAM, WILLIAM, *Travels through North and South Carolina, Georgia, East and West Florida, the Cherokee Country, etc.* Dublin, 1793.

BETTS, EDWARD CHAMBERS, *Early History of Huntsville, Alabama, 1804-1870*. Montgomery, 1916.

BOURNE, EDWARD GAYLORD, ed., *Narratives of the Career of Hernando de Soto in the Conquest of Florida* (The Knight of Elvas, De Biedma, Ranjel). New York, 1904.

BROWN, JOHN P., *Old Frontiers. The Story of the Cherokee Indians from Earliest Times to the Date of Their Removal to the West*. Kingsport, 1938.

CAMPBELL, T. J., *The Upper Tennessee*. Chattanooga, 1932.

COATES, ROBERT M., *The Outlaw Years: the History of the Land Pirates of the Natchez Trace*. New York, 1930.

CRANE, VERNER W., *The Southern Frontier, 1670-1732.* Durham, 1929.

DAVIS, REUBEN, *Recollections of Mississippi and Mississippians.* Boston and New York, 1891.

DRIVER, CARL S., *John Sevier, Pioneer of the Old Southwest.* Chapel Hill, 1932.

*Early Travels in the Tennessee Country, 1540-1800.* Edited by Samuel Cole Williams. Johnson City, 1928.

FOREMAN, GRANT, *Indian Removal. The Emigration of the Five Civilized Tribes of Indians.* Norman, Okla., 1932.

———, *Sequoyah.* Norman, 1938.

GARRETT, WILLIAM R., and GOODPASTURE, ALBERT V., *History of Tennessee.* Nashville, 1900.

GILMORE, JAMES R., *John Sevier as a Commonwealth Builder.* New York, 1898.

GUILD, Jo. C., *Old Times in Tennessee.* Nashville, 1878.

HARRIS, GEORGE W., *Sut Lovingood. Yarns Spun by a Nat'ral Born Durn'd Fool. Warped and Wove for Public Wear.* New York, 1867.

HENDERSON, ARCHIBALD, *The Conquest of the Old Southwest.* New York, 1920.

HOWARD, H. R., comp., *The History of Virgil A. Stewart, and His Adventure in Capturing and Exposing the Great "Western Land Pirate" and His Gang.* New York, 1836.

JACKSON, GEORGE PULLEN, *White Spirituals of the Southern Uplands.* Chapel Hill, 1933.

———, *Spiritual Folk-Songs of Early America.* New York, 1937.

JAMES, MARQUIS, *Andrew Jackson: Portrait of a President.* Indianapolis and New York, 1937.

LEFTWICH, NINA, *Two Hundred Years at Muscle Shoals. Being an Authentic History of Colbert County, 1700-1900.* Tuscumbia, 1935.

LEWIS, T. M. N., and KNEBERG, MADELINE, *The Prehistory of the Chickamauga Basin in Tennessee* (Mimeographed). Knoxville, 1941.

McDOWELL, LUCIEN L., and McDOWELL, FLORA LASSITER, *Folk Dances of Tennessee.* Ann Arbor, 1938.

McGUFFEY, CHARLES D., *Standard History of Chattanooga, Tennessee*. Knoxville, 1911.

NEUMAN, FRED S., *The Story of Paducah*. Paducah, 1927.

*Original Sacred Harp* (Denson Rev.). Haleyville, Ala., 1936.

PHELAN, JAMES, *History of Tennessee*. Boston, 1889.

PUTNAM, A. W., *History of Middle Tennessee*. Nashville, 1859.

RAMSEY, J. G. M., *The Annals of Tennessee to the End of the Eighteenth Century*. Charleston, 1853.

ROTHERT, OTTO A., *The Outlaws of Cave-In-Rock*. Cleveland, 1924.

RULE, WILLIAM, *Standard History of Knoxville, Tennessee*. Chicago, 1900.

SAUNDERS, JAMES EDMONDS, *Early Settlers of Alabama*. New Orleans, 1899.

SCOTT, WINFIELD, *Memoirs of Lieut.-General Scott, LL.D. Written by Himself* (2 vols.). New York, 1864.

SKINNER, CONSTANCE LINDSAY, *Pioneers of the Old Southwest*. New Haven, 1919.

SUMMERS, THOMAS O., D. D. (ed.), *Joseph Brown, or The Young Tennessean Whose Life Was Saved by the Power of Prayer*. Nashville, 1860.

TAYLOR, OLIVER, *Historic Sullivan*. Bristol, 1909.

*Tennessee, a Guide to the State*, Work Projects Administration of the State of Tennessee. New York, 1939.

TIMBERLAKE, LIEUT. HENRY, *Memoirs* (London, 1765). Edited with Introduction and Annotations by Samuel Cole Williams. Johnson City, 1927.

WHITAKER, ARTHUR PRESTON, *The Spanish-American Frontier, 1783-1795*. Boston, 1927.

WHITE, ROBERT H., *Development of the Tennessee State Educational Organization, 1796-1929*. Kingsport, 1929.

WILLIAMS, SAMUEL COLE, *Beginnings of West Tennessee in the Land of the Chickasaws, 1541-1841*. Johnson City, 1930.

———, *Dawn of Tennessee Valley and Tennessee History*. Johnson City, 1937.

———, *History of the Lost State of Franklin*. Johnson City, 1924.

———, *Tennessee During the Revolutionary War*, Tennessee Historical Commission. Nashville, 1944.

OFFICIAL DOCUMENTS, MANUSCRIPTS, REPORTS, AND
GOVERNMENT PUBLICATIONS

*American State Papers, Indian Affairs,* Vol. 1; *Miscellaneous,* Vol.
21.
*Autobiography of J. G. M. Ramsey* (Typescript). McClung Collection, Lawson McGhee Library, Knoxville.
*Calendar of Virginia State Papers.*
*Canal Around the Muscle Shoals of the River Tennessee.* Report of
Committee on Roads and Canals, 1838. 25th Cong., 2nd Sess.,
House Rep. 985.
*Colonial Records of North Carolina.* W. L. Saunders, ed.
*Colonial Records of the State of Georgia.* A. D. Candler, ed.
*Daybook of James King & Co., 1836-1837.*
*Diary of Drury P. Armstrong, 1846-1849* (Typescript). McClung
Collection, Lawson McGhee Library, Knoxville.
*Final Report of the United States De Soto Expedition Commission.*
76th Cong., 1st Sess., H. Doc. 71. Washington, 1939.
GAUDING, H. H., *Water Transportation in East Tennessee Prior to
the Civil War* (Unpublished thesis). University of Tennessee,
1933.
HEFLIN, JOHN J., *George Washington Harris ("Sut Lovingood").
A Biographical and Critical Study* (Unpublished thesis). Vanderbilt University, 1934.
MOONEY, JAMES, *Myths of the Cherokee.* 19th Annual Report,
Bureau of American Ethnology. Washington, 1900.
MYER, WILLIAM E., *Indian Trails of the Southeast.* 42d Annual Report, Bureau of American Ethnology.
*Natchez Trace Parkway Survey.* 76th Cong., 3rd Sess., Sen. Doc.
148.
ROYCE, C. C., *The Cherokee Nation of Indians.* 5th Annual Report,
Bureau of American Ethnology.
*South Carolina Indian Affairs.* Vols. V and VI (Typescript). McClung Collection, Lawson McGhee Library, Knoxville.
[*Survey of the Holston and Tennessee Rivers*] *Report of Examinations and Surveys with a View of Improving the Navigation
of the Holston and Tennessee Rivers.* Brevet Lt. Col. S. H.

Long, 1830. 29th Cong., 2nd Sess., H. Doc. 167. Reprinted with maps in 43rd Cong., 1st Sess., H. Doc. 167.

[*Survey of Muscle Shoals, 1828*] 20th Cong., 1st Sess., H. Doc. 284.

[*Survey of the Tennessee River, Brown's Ferry to Waterloo*] *Report on the Improvement Projected in the River Tennessee, from Brown's Ferry to Waterloo.* Lt. Col. James Kearney, Major William Tell Poussin, and others. 29th Cong., 1st Sess., H. Doc. 167.

SWANTON, JOHN R., *Early History of the Creek Indians and Their Neighbors.* Bulletin 73, Bureau of American Ethnology. Washington, 1888.

TENNESSEE VALLEY AUTHORITY. *A History of Navigation on the Tennessee River System.* 75th Cong., 1st Sess., H. Doc. 254. Washington, 1937.

WEBB, WILLIAM S., *An Archaeological Survey of the Norris Basin.* Bulletin 118, Bureau of American Ethnology. Washington, 1938.

——, *An Archaeological Survey of Wheeler Basin.* Bulletin 122, Bureau of American Ethnology. Washington, 1939.

WEBB, WILLIAM S., and DE JARNETTE, D. L., *An Archaeological Survey of Pickwick Basin.* Bulletin 129, Bureau of American Ethnology. Washington, 1942.

PERIODICAL LITERATURE

ADAMS, GEORGE I., "The Course of the Tennessee River and Physiography of the Southern Appalachian Region," *Journal of Geology,* XXXVI.

COOKE, THOMAS H., "The Fort Loudoun Massacre," *Tennessee Historical Magazine,* VII.

CRANE, VERNER W., "The Tennessee River As the Road to Carolina," *Mississippi Valley Historical Review,* III (June, 1916).

DAY, DONALD, "The Humorous Works of George W. Harris," *American Literature,* XIV (January, 1943).

GOODPASTURE, A. V., "Indian Wars and Warriors of the Old Southwest" (Published serially), *Tennessee Historical Magazine,* IV.

HAMER, PHILIP, "Fort Loudoun in the Cherokee War, 1758-1761," *North Carolina Historical Review,* II.

HAYES, C. WILLARD, and MANN, R. CAMPBELL, "Geomorphology of the Southern Appalachians," *National Geographic Magazine*, VI.

"Historical Relation of Facts, Delivered by Ludovick Grant, Indian Trader, to his Excellency the Governor of South Carolina," *South Carolina Historical and Genealogical Magazine*, X.

LOWELL, JAMES RUSSELL, "A Virginian in New England Thirty-five Years Ago," *Atlantic Monthly*, XXVI.

MOORE, J. H., "The Death of Meriwether Lewis," *American Historical Magazine*, IX (July, 1904).

OWSLEY, FRANK L., "The Pattern of Migration and Settlement on the Southern Frontier," *Journal of Southern History*, XI (May, 1945).

OWSLEY, FRANK L., and OWSLEY, HARRIET C., "The Economic Basis of Society in the Late Ante-Bellum South," *Journal of Southern History*, VI (February, 1940).

———, "The Economic Structure of Rural Tennessee, 1850-1860," *Journal of Southern History*, VIII (May, 1942).

REDD, JOHN, "Reminiscences of Western Virginia," *Virginia Magazine of History*, VI (April, 1899), VII (July, 1899, June, 1900).

ROTHROCK, MARY U., "Carolina Traders Among the Overhill Cherokees, 1690-1760," *East Tennessee Historical Society's Publications*, No. 1, 1929.

STORM, COLTON, ed. "Up the Tennessee in 1790: The Report of Major John Doughty to the Secretary of War." *East Tennessee Historical Society's Publications*, No. 17, 1945.

STROTHER, DAVID HUNTER ("PORTE CRAYON"), "A Winter in the South," *Harper's Magazine*, XVII (August, 1858).

SWARTZ, GEORGE W., "First Boat Trip Over Muscle Shoals, 1828," *Alabama Historical Quarterly*, I (Fall, 1930).

TAYLOR, THOMAS JONES, "Early History of Madison County and Incidentally of North Alabama" (Published serially), *Alabama Historical Quarterly*, I, II.

*Waterways Journal, The.* St. Louis, Mo.

## NEWSPAPERS

*Alabama Republican* (Huntsville)
*Brownlow's Knoxville Whig*
Florence *Gazette*
*Franklin Enquirer*
Huntsville *Democrat*
Knoxville *Argus and Commercial Herald*
Knoxville *Inquirer*
Knoxville *Register*
Knoxville *Sentinel*
Nashville *Union and American*
*North Alabamian*
Paducah *Sun-Democrat*
*Tuscumbian*
*Southern Advocate* (Huntsville)

# Index